# PRAISE FOR KEN HOLLINGS

"Ken Hollings has placed his critical focus at the precise point where the high technologies of information control and social manipulation intersect the passionate search for scientific ways to probe the human mind. *Welcome to Mars* is a searingly accurate and deeply disturbing exposé of the fantasies of American modernism that have inspired the many nightmares and the few hopeful visions of our new Millennium." —Dr. Jacques Vallée, computer scientist and astronomer; author of *Messengers of Deception*

"Ken Hollings has been described as both a genius and an alien. He is the kind of writer who looks up at a million points of light in the sky and starts to connect the dots." —Toby Amies, BBC Radio 4

"There aren't that many people prepared to exist in their own space the way Ken does." —Kathy Acker, novelist and poet

"Ken is truly one of the most thought-provoking, out-there thinkers on technology and the human condition I have ever come across. He makes Clay Shirky look like a broken automaton." —Becky Hogge, journalist, author of *Barefoot into Cyberspace*

"… an exemplary exercise in cross-specialism history … a rollercoaster ride through the dreamtime of post-war American esoteric, technological and mass culture with a wealth of often amazing and sometimes shocking information on every page." —Furtherfield

"Ken Hollings is brilliant as always." —Aleksandra Mir, artist

"Ken Hollings's *Destroy All Monsters* is a hallucinogenic spiral into future nightmare." —Lydia Lunch, singer and author

"*[Destroy All Monsters]* is a mighty slab of trippy, cult, out-there fiction, mind-bending reading." —*The Scotsman*

# WELCOME TO MARS

## POLITICS, POP CULTURE, AND WEIRD SCIENCE IN 1950S AMERICA

### KEN HOLLINGS

North Atlantic Books
Berkeley, California

Published by
North Atlantic Books
P.O. Box 12327
Berkeley, California 94712

Cover design by Jasmine Hromjak
Cover illustration © iStockphoto.com/HultonArchive
Cover illustration © iStockphoto.com/Redemption

Book design by Mark Pilkington

Printed in the United States of America

*Welcome to Mars: Politics, Pop Culture, and Weird Science in 1950s America* is sponsored by the Society for the Study of Native Arts and Sciences, a nonprofit educational corporation whose goals are to develop an educational and cross-cultural perspective linking various scientific, social, and artistic fields; to nurture a holistic view of arts, sciences, humanities, and healing; and to publish and distribute literature on the relationship of mind, body, and nature.

North Atlantic Books' publications are available through most bookstores. For further information, visit our website at www.northatlanticbooks.com or call 800-733-3000.

Library of Congress Cataloging-in-Publication Data

Hollings, Ken, author.
Welcome to Mars : politics, pop culture, and weird science in 1950s America / Ken Hollings.
pages cm
Reprint of: London : Strange Attractor, 2008.
Summary: "Drawing on newspaper articles, ad campaigns, declassified government archives, and old movies, Ken Hollings shows the culture of postwar America and its dream of limitless technological and human development" -- Provided by publisher.
Includes bibliographical references and index.
ISBN 978-1-58394-761-6 (pbk.)
1. Science–Social aspects–United States–History–20th century. 2. Nineteen fifties. 3. Popular culture–United States–History–20th century. I. Title.
Q175.5.H635 2014
303.48'3097309045–dc23
                                                    2013035279

1 2 3 4 5 6 7 8 9 UNITED 19 18 17 16 15 14

The main effect of so-called modern literature is that it prevents us from being truly modern.

    –Louis Pauwels and Jacques Bergier, *The Morning of the Magicians*

You are interested in the unknown, the mysterious, the unexplainable. That is why you are here.

    –Criswell, *Plan 9 from Outer Space*

# CONTENTS

# FOREWORD
# BY ERIK DAVIS

*1945 was a crossroads year,* one of those rare junctures in the flow of history where everything seems to change. The world before Hiroshima is a distant, black-and-white place, a gone world whose artifacts have the ghostly air of Victrolas or the faded photographs of distant relatives. On the other hand, the decade or so that follows the war, which is the subject of the hallucinatory history you now hold, is an altogether more recognizable environment. Even from today's perspective, which follows the sixties, the fall of the Berlin Wall, and 9/11, the immediate postwar era—the politics, the culture, and, perhaps most of all, the gadgetry of the late 1940s and '50s—are all somehow familiar, sometimes uncannily so. The era's artifacts are less like the photographs of departed relatives than hazy magnetic recordings of our own earliest memories—partly fantasized, partly opaque, a feedback loop of dream and trauma.

The end of World War II unleashed powerful and genuinely new forces onto the world stage, as concepts and technologies developed in the heat of wartime leaked into and transformed secular society. The war had destroyed enough older structures and traditions to make plenty of room for this new phase of global culture, just as the rubble of bombed-out Rotterdam made space for all that city's odd and marvelous New Building experiments to fill. But of course, Europe was not to be the birthplace of this new phase—that honor goes to America, which would dominate the last half of the twentieth century with its pop culture, its machines, its ideologies. Though we are now far from bobby sox and *The Lone Ranger,* postwar America laid the foundations of our world: our mindscape, our media, our technological myths.

It is no accident that Thomas Pynchon set *Gravity's Rainbow,* perhaps the most prophetic American novel of the last fifty years, in the immediate aftermath of World War II. Pynchon used the phrase "the Zone" to describe the fluid and borderless space of occupied Germany following VE day, but the term also could be said to describe the fluid and unmapped postwar world that is the deeper subject of the novel. Early on, Pynchon offers us a key to navigating this larger Zone. During a séance, the directors of the German cartel IG Farben contact a departed spirit named Walter Rathenau, who tells them how to read the signs that will enable them to understand the new world system:

> *These signs are real. They are also symptoms of a process ... to apprehend it you will follow the signs. All talk of cause and effect is secular history, and secular history is a diversionary tactic ... If you want the truth—I know I presume—you must look into the technology of these matters. Even into the hearts of certain molecules ... You must ask two questions. First, what is the real nature of synthesis? And then: what is the real nature of control?*

*Welcome to Mars* is a map of the postwar Zone, a nonfiction *Gravity's Rainbow* that follows the arc of Germany's V2 rocket to the end of the rainbow—in other words, to America. To tell his tale, Hollings takes Rathenau's prophetic suggestions to heart. To begin with, Hollings has collected together a mass of real signs and symptoms drawn from a myriad of fields: suburban architecture, psychology, Hollywood B-movies, military history, cybernetics, flying-saucer lore. At first these items may seem disjointed, almost scatter-shot, but the networks they form together reflect the profoundly interconnected process that characterizes the Zone, a place where televisions deliver electroshock therapy and UFOs pop out of microwave ovens. Applying a dream logic to real events, treating pulp fictions as history, and history as myth, Hollings ignores the conventional logic of cause and effect that you find in most nonfiction books about the past. Instead, he coaxes us into the process by drawing us into an associational network of facts and figures that both mirrors and manifests the deeper labyrinth.

Hollings has looked into the technology of these matters as well, and not just the gadgetry and synthetic molecules that transform domestic space and media culture in the 1940s and '50s. He has also looked deeply at the UFO, an apparatus whose very status as a technology is both dream-like and deeply mediated through Hollywood and pulp magazines. He groks that postwar technology is not just about the machines but about the assemblage—the system—that connects reason to the unconscious, human beings to devices, and how those connections increasingly constitute society. The cybernetic cycles unleashed by this emerging system of relay links and feedback loops are perhaps the key expression of Herr Rathenau's "process," and it directly foregrounds today's network society. As Hollings plays connect-the-dots between monster movies, nuclear submarines, and LSD, between Sputnik, brainwashing, and TV dinners, he is tracing the wires of our own unconscious, and filtering the electronic ether that we breathe.

As you move through this 3D funhouse of facts and figures, I strongly suggest that you keep Herr Rathenau's two questions in mind. What is the real nature of synthesis? And what is the real nature of control?

The nonlinear leaps and patterns in this text are a way of probing the first question. What are the deep patterns that connect Thorazine and magnetic tape, *Forbidden Planet* and Scientology? To answer the question, you must let go of the cause and effect links that keep us chained to the diversionary tactic of secular history, and plunge into the process. And don't try to hold onto all these amazing human characters as you move forward, because just as Pynchon evaporates his main character halfway through his book, Hollings invites us to follow the webs between human beings more than the beings themselves (who may of course be brainwashed robots, or pod people).

But even more important is Rathenau's second question, because it cuts to the heart of our present "posthuman" predicament. The cybernetic loops that characterize the Zone are all about control, but who controls the controller? When we decide that our minds are like magnetic tape, that they can be erased and reprogrammed, who makes the decision, who presses rewind? And when we put all our eggs in the expanding basket of cybernetic control systems, what do we do with the paradox that the system itself is out of control? Perhaps the atomic tests of 1945—or even the discovery of Nag Hammadi's great Gnostic library, as Philip K. Dick believed—set off a chain reaction in reality itself, and LSD and Dianetics and Robby the Robot are all telling us the same thing, a message we still haven't really processed:

Welcome to Mars.

# INTRODUCTION:
# SCENES FROM A HISTORY AS YET UNWRITTEN

*The future started a long time ago*, and we have been trapped in it ever since. "We are, alas, imprisoned in a cell with three walls," Jean Cocteau wrote in 1956, toward the end of his preface to Aimé Michel's *The Truth about Flying Saucers.* "It is on the impalpable fourth wall that the great minds I respect write their loves and their dreams." Scratched indelibly into that wall is a story of weird science, strange events, and even stranger beliefs. It is set in an age when the possibilities for human development seemed limitless. Between 1947 and 1959, the future was written about, discussed, and analyzed with such confidence that it took on a tangible presence, especially in the United States, where an unprecedented economic boom, coupled with a growing sense of importance on the international stage, prompted Henry R. Luce, the founding father of Time-Life Inc., to speak with renewed vigor of the "American Century."

This was manifest destiny writ large at a time when the United States not only remained the sole nation to possess an atomic arsenal but also maintained strict copyright control over the A-Bomb footage shot at Hiroshima and Nagasaki. Reaching far beyond any Cold War statement of political intent, Luce's bold declaration also reflected a precise linking of material progress with human evolution in which they came to be held as one and the same thing. Out of this strange discrepancy came the notion of science as fantasy and of human history as some kind of grand cosmological adventure. "Why should we make a five-year plan," the *Partisan Review* was wondering aloud by the middle of the 1950s, "when God seems to have had a thousand-year plan ready-made for us?" How many consumer goods and technological innovations were summed up in the formula "ready-made"? How many indicators of prosperity and aids to gracious living? The future was no longer some vague and distant prospect. It was happening right in front of people's eyes.

"Progress is our most important product," future president Ronald Reagan announced in a black-and-white television pitch for General

Electric as the company's profits reached an all-time high. "If you're sitting back at General Electric, you're probably falling behind."

It seemed as if some radical change in the way humanity perceived both itself and its place in the universe was about to take place. Greater and more adventurous minds believed that an evolutionary shift of gigantic proportions might be only a few years away. Predictions about the future were made with the utmost confidence, whether in terms of the blindest optimism or the most crushing pessimism. While one group of experts described utopian visions of automated suburban living, flying cars, and robot servants, another foresaw nothing but a bleak nuclear wasteland overrun by communists, giant ants, and juvenile delinquents. Either view was more than capable of embracing Mars in its vision of the future: either as a holiday destination, as a distant site for far-flung colonies, or as a warlike invader, an angry red planet presiding over alien conquest.

Whatever the outcome, some mysterious evolutionary leap looked set to take place sometime during the course of the 1950s, the full implications of which would prove bafflingly difficult to ascertain. The average family of the period could never be certain where progress would be taking them by decade's end. Who really knew for sure? They might find themselves driving down one of the new multi-lane parkways in their atomic-powered sedan or cowering in some suburban bomb shelter listening to the sirens' last mournful wailings. No wonder the psychiatric fraternity enjoyed a newfound prestige during this period, and the pharmaceutical companies happily made a fortune selling tranquilizers to an increasingly troubled populace. Thanks to the mathematicians and electrical engineers at Princeton, MIT, and the Josiah Macy Foundation, the human mind would become a complex piece of machinery that might someday be rewired and reprogrammed for greater efficiency.

The future, however, was not the sole property of Big Business or the Backroom Boys in Research and Development. It had to be shared with the Chemical Division of the CIA, the rocket scientists at White Sands and Huntsville, Alabama, along with the determined ranks of the newly formed Atomic Energy Commission. The war-gamers in the Pentagon and the global strategists at the RAND Corporation would also demand their say. Such people were just as confident about the future, even if they never seemed to be particularly cheerful about it. The dangers of nuclear annihilation, radiation poisoning, and the effects of atomic fallout were becoming manifestly apparent even to those who had flunked out of science in high school. A trip to the drive-in could teach you an awful lot in those days.

When hard science impacted on soft bodies the authorities usually kept the results a closely guarded secret—and not without good reason. What few facts were available would quickly become the subject of fantasy and speculation. This, however, was also the age of the freelance investigative reporter, the exploitation moviemaker, the comic-book artist, and the pulp magazine publisher. They helped fill in the blanks, becoming in the process the true ideologues of progress at a time when Big Science seemed to be making the future up as it went along. The long shadows cast by supposition and make-believe became as much a part of the big picture as the tiny pieces of information deemed fit for public consumption by the experts in Washington.

Then there were the ones who had the future bagged and tagged before it even left the ground: the fanatics, the fantasists, and the dreamers. They came in all shapes and sizes during the 1950s, from the amateur astronomer to the television psychic, the retired airman, the basement inventor, and the alien contactee. Every secret door that remained locked against humanity could, according to their take on things, be pried open with a little imagination and ingenuity. To say that such individuals thrived on the turbulent paranoia of an age in which the heady mysteries of LSD, the "truth" about flying saucers, and the hard facts of atomic science were kept safely from the masses would be to put it mildly. Thanks to them, the future would never be the same again. Under their exuberant influence, anything was possible because everything they said, did, or believed was true. Or, at least, it was no less true than anything else you might have been told at the time. When those few brief years had passed, however, the excitement and exhilaration offered by the future appeared to have passed with them. An opportunity for change had presented itself and then disappeared again, perhaps forever.

It has always seemed to me that a historian's main function is not so much to prevent the past from being forgotten as to stop it from becoming a commonplace. To that end, my novel *Destroy All Monsters* was concerned with presenting history as fantasy, in the hope that its readers might be reminded of just how much the world had been transformed in the fallout from Operation Desert Storm. The fact that this particular campaign is now referred to as "Iraq I" says everything about the tragic consequences of such an unacknowledged shift in awareness. As it was, *Destroy All Monsters* came out just days before the attacks on the World Trade Center and the Pentagon, prompting comments on how the novel's "hallucinogenic spiral into future nightmare" had "time-slipped onto the front pages."

In many ways *Welcome to Mars* is about the opposite process: trying to locate a specific fantasy as precisely as possible in time and space. You will consequently find nothing original here, and for that I make no apology. The bibliography appended to this text is more than a set of mere references or lines of future inquiry for any prospective reader: it is a sign of my fond indebtedness to the work of the many who came before me. It is thanks to them that I have been able to write a cultural history of what are ostensibly invisible things. Flying saucers, LSD, and atomic radiation all tend to operate outside the established spectrum of human sensory experience: we only ever come to perceive them through their effects. Such secrecy communicates itself to the public through coincidence, odd connections and confluences, hitherto undetected lines of influence. Like the writing on Cocteau's impalpable fourth wall, these are the only signs we have of what is unseen, unheard, unexpected. I have merely fashioned them into a coherent order.

Allowing for a certain slippage from fiction to nonfiction and back again, narrative remains little more than organized perception. This book owes its current form to the live twelve-part radio series of the same name I presented on Resonance FM from March through May 2006, the only difference being that the events of 1948 and 1949 were dealt with in one program rather than two separate chapters. I am extremely grateful to Richard Thomas at Resonance FM, who invited me to put the series together in the first place, and to Simon James, my producer and sound designer, who suggested that each show be presented live and unscripted. With Simon's calm presence in the studio and the appropriately strange soundtracks he conjured up during the course of each broadcast, I was free to compose my thoughts and deliver my ideas straight to the microphone with the utmost assurance. The results are still being downloaded from iTunes to this day and continue to attract a widening international audience.

When I later spoke to Mark Pilkington of Strange Attractor Press about my desire to rework the series into a book dealing with the same themes and narratives but in considerably more depth and detail, he immediately offered to publish it. In many ways this made the writing of *Welcome to Mars* a much surer and happier prospect, as I could not imagine a better publisher or editor for the final outcome. His insight and quiet confidence have both proved invaluable, and for that I thank him. I am also grateful to Anthony and Irene Newton of the NJL Foundation for their generous support in the completion of the original manuscript, and to North Atlantic Books for publishing this U.S. edition. While all of the individuals mentioned have proved in their own way that no one really writes a book on their own, there is still one more that I must name.

It may seem perhaps that the biggest commonplace to affect any work of literature is the moment when the author thanks his or her partner for all the loving support and patience they have shown during the writing of it. However, anyone who has ever had to share their life with someone who is in turn sharing their life with a book will know that mere words cannot express the gratitude and appreciation the acknowledgment of such a bond inevitably brings with it. That my wife Rachel understands the sincerity and depth of feeling behind such words is something for which I shall never stop giving thanks.

Ken Hollings
London/2014

# 1947: REBUILDING LEMURIA

## From the Suburbs to Outer Space

*Levittown*—You can imagine how it will look from space: the houses and roads and backyards arranged in neatly ordered rows, a framework of streetlights and driveways in a perfectly arranged grid at night. Located on what was once an expanse of potato fields, midway between New York City and the munitions plants of Long Island, the first Levittown, formerly known as "Island Trees," is opened to the public in February 1947. A planned community of six thousand households offering affordable housing in the form of small, detached single-family units, this new conurbation quickly expands to embrace a further eleven thousand homes, each situated sixty feet apart on their own patch of ground. Constructed from prefabricated sections and components, Suburbia has at last begun to extend its grand conformity into space.

An accomplished publicist, William J. Levitt trades in myth as much as in real estate. To help his community grow, he presents it as a new form of American life: one that offers the comfortable ideals of middle-class existence, with no money down. To thousands of returning servicemen, most of whom are young and raised in the big cities, this represents a sweet deal for both them and their families. A white picket fence, a front lawn, and a backyard to call your own, far from the crowded urban squalor of the streets, and all at such low, low prices: how can William Levitt and Sons afford to do it?

Simple.

Levittown's original inspiration is the planned community created in secret at Oak Ridge, Tennessee, to house the technicians and scientists of the "Manhattan Project" busily engaged in developing the first atomic weapon. For ease of orientation, the identical housing units that make up Oak Ridge are arranged along a series of precise grids and identified by numbers and colors. Levitt developed the basic models and techniques for preparing low-cost suburban homesteads out of prefabricated units while fulfilling military housing contracts during the closing years of World War II when storage facilities, dormitories, and administrative buildings had to be built quickly, cheaply, and in vast numbers.

From the start Levittown constitutes a strategic response to modern warfare. The Atomic Bomb has done its job too well. A future conflict in which whole cities might be obliterated does more than demoralize the enemy: it demoralizes everyone. The masses are defined and affirmed to the point of their own destruction. As a result, the politics of Total War, in which the entire resources of one nation are pitched against those of another, don't just call for proliferation but diffusion as well. A dispersed population is so much harder to find.

William Levitt's new suburban grid and the existing global one are becoming superimposed. What the Marshall Plan and the Truman Doctrine both have at their core is the concept that there is just one world, a single sphere of influence. The same month Levittown opens its gates to the public, the Voice of America starts broadcasting to the Soviet Union for the very first time.

An ever-expanding, subdivided tract of land, the suburbs constitute the location for a project that will connect humanity directly with outer space, with the future, and with its own emergent inner self. The possibilities are limitless. Levittown homes come with a television set already installed. What was formerly designated the "living room" is now a domestic environment, irradiated by the blue-gray glow of the cathode ray tube.

High-fidelity stereophonic sound systems will extend the boundaries of this new sensory laboratory even further. In 1947 Capitol Records releases *Music Out of the Moon,* a suite of compositions on a set of 78 rpm platters with characteristically mellifluous arrangements by Les Baxter. This sequence of six themes features the mysterious sounds of Dr. Samuel Hoffman at the Theremin, the electronic musical marvel from the Soviet Union that can be played by the simple expedient of waving one's hand in what appears to be empty space. Even more otherworldly in their effect are the wordlessly lush close-harmony choruses Baxter has set running through the course of each song. Eerily streamlined and enigmatic, they flesh out what titles like "Lunar Rhapsody," "Moon Moods," and "Celestial Nocturne" can only hint at. More importantly, as the sleeve notes suggest, the record requires its own specific setting.

"Take it home," the listener is advised. "Set the stage, in the evening when you are perhaps a little weary of the work-a-day world; its hypnotic beauty assures a unique musical experience." More specifically, it articulates the concept of encountering space-age technology in a space-age home. In its self-contained isolation, the suburban colony becomes a model for life not just on this planet but on all the others too. At the same time, this self-contained isolation will eventually establish the suburbs as a complex psychiatric community where aberrations such as alcoholism, schizophrenia, and sexual deviancy can be studied in clinical depth by an increasing number of sociologists, psychiatrists, and cultural anthropologists. It will also supply the pharmaceutical companies with a growing number of customers for a new generation of drugs. In other words, Suburbia will not only radically transform methods of perception but models of behavior as well.

If the skies above Levittown seem particularly dark in 1947, it's because the Nuclear Clock has been set running for the first time on the front cover of *The Bulletin of Atomic Scientists*. Intended to show the close proximity of humanity to total annihilation, the clock's minute hand is periodically shown edging its way toward ultimate midnight. Featureless and brand new, standing where there had once been only fields and wasteland, the suburbs seem not so much isolated in space but in time as well.

There is, after all, something mythic about the idea of an advanced civilization perishing overnight in some single vast cataclysm. Named after the lemurs that once populated it, the lost continent of Lemuria is said to have disappeared beneath the Indian Ocean centuries before the start of recorded history, an early utopian center that had managed to combine technical achievement with advanced spiritual knowledge.

Like another Atlantis, Lemuria's submerged contours mean that it is no longer subject to the physical confines of normal geography: Lemuria can be everywhere and nowhere, even here on this former stretch of agricultural land between Long Island and New York City. Lemuria is a phantom island, one of those agreements made with the facts that can sometimes go on, untroubled, for centuries. In fact, the enormous timescale involved, the passage of entire millennia ruptured by the devastating events of a single night, has pushed the Lemurians and all their works far beyond the narrow calibrations of human progress.

Which is fine for a bunch of backward foreigners, but this is the United States of America, and things are done a little differently around here.

In 1947, at the same time as Levittown is being constructed, David Henken locates a ninety-seven-acre site in Pleasantville, Westchester County, New York, for a cooperative housing project. The Pleasantville community is to be called "Usonian Homes II," its name and design both derived from architect Frank Lloyd Wright's plan for "Usonia," a colony of simple but elegant single-family homes to be built on circular one-acre plots of land. Wright came up with the name by combining the words "utopia" and "USA," thereby expressing precisely the kind of spiritualized manifest destiny Henry R. Luce would have applauded. "The Usonian dwelling seems a thing loving the ground," declares Wright in *The Natural House*, "with a new sense of space, light and freedom to which our USA is entitled."

Mathematical logician Albert Wohlstetter, a close friend of the modernist architect Le Corbusier, following the example of William J. Levitt and Frank Lloyd Wright, also immerses himself in prefabricated house design. Having worked at the National Housing Agency on a program to develop prefabricated modular living units that can be easily transported and quickly assembled into low-cost homes, Wohlstetter moves to Los Angeles in 1947 to start a private company that applies the rigorous architectural ideals of the International Style and the Bauhaus to the same basic approach.

That November the Broadway-Crenshaw Center opens to the public in south Los Angeles. Occupying 550,000 square feet, with thirteen acres of parking, a Broadway department store, a Woolworth's, a cluster of smaller shops, and Von's supermarket, it can claim to be the first outdoor shopping mall in existence. At the other end of the timescale, carbon dating is used for the first time in 1947 to establish the antiquity, and in many cases the reality, of historical artifacts. It's a tacit reminder that each fabulous new age that dawns, each great new city built, comes shadowed by its own loss. But for now let us content ourselves with the fact that Lemuria really does exist once more, reconstructed out of prefabricated concrete, mass-produced shingles, and precut drywall. The dream can be yours, no money down.

**From Outer Space to the Military-Industrial Complex**

*Organizing the Future*—Mere progress is the preoccupation of lesser beings. Lemuria begins and then it ends: it neither grows nor develops. Marvels of the modern age require more than that. The first Polaroid Land camera goes on public display in New York in 1947. In California, the Ampex Electrical Corporation demonstrates its Model 200 tape recorder, the first professional machine designed for commercial studio use, at Hollywood's Radio Center.

Quickly finding a home for themselves in the suburban environment, thereby helping to usher in the Pushbutton Age, such devices require the marshaling of considerable resources, capital, specialized equipment, and man-hours. It's not surprising therefore to note that some of the major organizational structures of what will be denounced by decade's end as the "military-industrial complex" suddenly start falling into place in this year of miracles.

The Atomic Energy Commission assumes active civilian control of America's nuclear program from the very first day of 1947; and Project RAND, an Air Force think tank of scientists and mathematicians, starts its slow move toward incorporation as a nonprofit business venture based in Santa Monica, California. Established at the end of 1945, Project RAND became an independent division of the Douglas Aircraft Company in March 1946. Retaining its original Air Force name, a streamlined modernist shortening of "Research and Development," RAND is the first organization to bring those two concepts together formally. Its first official publication, commissioned by Major General Curtis E. LeMay, on the feasibility of earth-orbiting satellites, was published in May 1946. As Deputy Chief of the Air Staff for Research and Development, LeMay sees United States airpower extending beyond the sky into outer space, ultimately reaching into the future itself, thereby fundamentally altering the way in which the Earth itself is viewed, and at what remove, in the decade to come.

Speculating on the potential design, performance, and possible use of a manmade satellite, *Preliminary Design of an Experimental World-Circling Spaceship* is only the first of many RAND reports exploring the possibilities of man in space. Its cover art shows a missile, the world, and a mathematical grid in an abstract freestanding relationship with one another. One of the simplest yet also the most elegantly complex expressions of human thought and ingenuity, the grid offers up a perfect reflection of the times. Precise and potentially limitless, it contains within its blank uniform spaces all the possibilities of the future; its vectors reaffirm the connection between Levittown's suburban divisions and the lines of latitude and longitude encircling the globe itself.

One person to look more deeply into the grid than the rest is James Lipp, head of Project RAND's Missile Division. "Since mastery of the elements is a reliable index of material progress," he declares early in 1947, "the nation which first makes significant achievements in space travel will be acknowledged as the world leader in both military and scientific techniques. To visualize the impact on the world, one can imagine the consternation and admiration that would be felt here if the United States were to discover suddenly that some other nation had already put up a successful satellite."

Lipp's observation indicates the extent to which it is not the unpredictability of the future but the changeability of the present that concerns industrial society. Capable of constructing its own world, the future is already here. It's merely a question of dealing with it.

Primarily concerned with defense strategy, bombing patterns, and long-range military planning, the experts at RAND are less interested in hardware than in behavior: how systems develop and take on a creative life of their own. To this end, Project RAND holds a symposium in New York in 1947 as a first step toward enlisting economists and social scientists in its work on national defense. "I assume that every person in this room is fundamentally interested in and devoted to what can broadly be called the rational life," mathematician and RAND consultant Warren Weaver declares in his keynote address. "He believes fundamentally that there is something to this business of having some knowledge, and some analysis of problems, as compared with living in a state of ignorance, superstition and drifting-into-whatever-may-come."

Responsible for organizing this event, having also coauthored parts of RAND's *Preliminary Design of an Experimental World-Circling Spaceship*, is the writer and political analyst Leo Rosten. The man who persuaded Walt Disney to make animated propaganda films for the Pentagon during World War II, Rosten is asked by John Williams, head of RAND's Mathematics Division, to invite key figures from the social sciences to attend. This Rosten proceeds to do while working at night on the screenplay for *The Velvet Touch*, a murder mystery for RKO Radio Pictures starring Rosalind Russell.

When finished, the movie will tell the story of a Broadway actress who murders her producer and then, conscience-stricken, helps the investigating detective to uncover the clues that will solve the case. Its cat-and-mouse plot owes more than a little to the mathematically precise methods of determining rational strategies in the face of uncertainty developed by John von Neumann, consultant to the Theoretical Division at Los Alamos National Laboratory. Known informally as "game theory," its principles have been outlined in *Theory of Games and Economic Behavior*, written by von Neumann in collaboration with Princeton economist Oskar Morgenstern and first published in 1944. A seminal work that will influence the thinking of corporate executives and military planners for decades to come, it suggests how game theory might be applied to both economic theory and the social sciences. Among the book's more enthusiastic readers is RAND's John Williams, who persuades von Neumann to join Project RAND as a part-time consultant in December 1947.

The adoption of game theory at this time indicates a moment of transition: one in which the physicists and mathematical logicians at RAND are no longer obliged simply to predict the random motion of subatomic particles but to contemplate how their effects might influence human outcomes. Arthur Raymond, chief engineer at Douglas Aircraft, further articulates this shifting relationship in 1947 when he defines RAND's main preoccupations as "systems and ways of doing things, rather than particular devices, particular instrumentalities, particular weapons, and we are concerned not merely with the physical aspects of these systems but with the human behavior side as well." A quantitative approach to the unpredictable complexities of human psychology, behaviorism is still a relatively new science; assessing its subject as little more than a species of responses, it helps place the rat inside the maze and pit the cat against the mouse.

In its impact on such soft sciences as economics and sociology, game theory represents the mechanization of policy by other means: the hardwiring of strategists and soldiers, mathematicians and logicians into the decision-making process. More importantly for those wishing to see an evolutionary process at work within the technological advances of progress, it reveals how the short-term and the long-range have become closely related by the same factors. Game theory's interdisciplinary applications eventually prompt John Williams, despite some initial resistance from Major General LeMay, to broaden RAND's range and scope by creating divisions at Santa Monica for the study of economics and the social sciences.

The analysts RAND subsequently brings into these new departments represent a cross-section of the very sociologists, psychologists, and anthropologists who will descend upon the suburbs, testing and probing its inhabitants. Top wartime psychiatrist Brigadier General William Menninger makes this clear in his keynote address as newly elected president of the American Psychiatric Association at their 1947 conference, held at the Pennsylvania Hotel in New York that year. Although there are still fewer than five thousand practicing psychiatrists in the United States, Menninger takes great pains to spell out to his colleagues the vital importance of bringing the potential benefits of psychiatry to the masses and of his ambition to "offer its therapeutic effort to a world full of unhappiness and maladjustment."

Under Menninger's kindly interest, the suburbs will gradually be transformed into Suburbia: as much a state of mind as a dispersed geographical location. As such, Suburbia can only give birth to itself. Its inhabitants, their expectations, and the way they intend to live their lives are merely by-products of that process, the raw material of social engineering. In relocating from the cities, the new suburbanites have left their extended families behind, together with their traditional values and knowledge. The door is thus left wide open for the psychologists and social scientists to walk in and take a look around.

Those who view with alarm the bodying forth of the military-industrial complex might do well to consider for a moment the third part of this descriptive proposition. That military and industrial interests should be seen coming together so intimately to form a "complex" says a great deal at a time when the nation's psychiatric elite is set to exert greater public influence. Such a thorny interlocking of drives and inhibitions, obsessions and barely suppressed urges is sure to have a deleterious effect not only on the physical aspects of these systems, to paraphrase Arthur Raymond of the Douglas Aircraft Company, but also on the human behavior side as well.

It is perhaps not altogether surprising, therefore, to discover that it is a pilot who is destined to report one of the most aberrant pieces of technological behavior to take place in this modern age.

"They flew like a saucer would if you skipped it across water," Kenneth Arnold tells Bill Bequette of the *East Oregonian*, referring to the nine unidentified flying objects he has seen speeding through the skies toward Mount Rainier on the afternoon of June 24, 1947. According to Arnold's written report submitted to the US military, they moved "in a definite formation but erratically" in a "diagonal-like chain, as if they were linked together." It is the image of the "flying saucer" that sticks in the popular imagination, however; its flashing and darting establishes an erratic but discernible visual rhythm that will continue to reverberate for years to come. A few weeks later, when the July 8 edition of the *Roswell Daily Record* appears in New Mexico with the headline "Army Air Force Captures Flying Disc in Roswell Region" spread across five columns of its front page, the transformation of motion into archetypal form is complete.

Although both stories have originated from local newspapers, they are quickly picked up all over the world, following the global grid now being comfortably imposed upon the Earth's surface. Never has a message been so clear, or its implications so ambiguous. "They're more than atom bombs or falling stars," runs the stark warning in "When You See Those Flying Saucers," a hillbilly ballad written in 1947 by Charles Grean and Cy Coben. Released as a 78 rpm disc on the RCA Victor label, the song links religion and atomic devastation with the "trouble and unrest brewing" on the far side of the Iron

Curtain. If it came out of the sky, the assumption goes, it can only be a judgment from on high. The other assumption, exemplified by the lack of a conditional preposition in the song's title, is that it's only a matter of time: of "when," rather than "if."

Both Arnold's Mount Rainier sighting and the crashed saucer in Roswell will go on to assume mythic status, subject to endless lines of speculation, research, and argument. It is worth reflecting at this point, however, upon just how close both these incidents are to the ragged edge of aviation technology as it exists at this time. According to his own account, Arnold was piloting his "specially designed mountain airplane" in search of a crashed C-46 Marine transport. The flying disc reported to have come down in the New Mexico desert is investigated by officers from Roswell Air Force Base, home to the US nuclear bomber wing. Less than two years previously the *Enola Gay* took off from Roswell AFB into the blinding light of summer on its way to Hiroshima.

The Atomic Energy Commission and Project RAND are soon studying the flying saucers, AEC chairman David Lilienthal going so far as to make a public statement discounting any direct relationship between such sightings and the effects of atomic radiation. However, the main connection between the saucers and the emergent military-industrial complex will inevitably be supplied by the United States Air Force: an organization that has had to wait until now for an Act of Congress to bring it into being. The 1947 National Security Act does as much to recalibrate the American war machine as von Neumann and Morgenstern's *Theory of Games and Economic Behavior*. It establishes the Department of Defense, creates the National Security Council, and separates off the United States Air Force as an independent entity from the rest of the Armed Forces. More importantly, it replaces the old wartime Office of Strategic Services with a brand new organization: the Central Intelligence Agency.

Great organizations create themselves out of confusion, and the United States Air Force is no exception. Glimpses of the future start to flash up at random. Over one weekend in the summer of 1947, a bunch of bikers go on a drunken rampage through the little town of Hollister, California, establishing the renegade motorcycle gang as another modern myth. Most of these mechanized outlaws are ex-servicemen, many of them former Army Air Force, bored with peacetime and looking for excitement. They are clearly not alone in their frustrations. At exactly the same time as Kenneth Arnold's account of flying saucers over America is making headlines around the world, the May 1947 issue of *Mechanix Illustrated* devotes its cover to the US Navy's "Flying Flapjack": a disc-shaped twin-propeller aircraft boasting a bold new arrangement of cockpit and engines within a circular fuselage. "It hovers like a helicopter: will it fly faster than the speed of sound?" the magazine wonders. Painted bright yellow with a futuristic silver undercarriage, the airplane's advanced "discoidal" shape is tested in June 1947 along Long Island Sound for a Navy Day display, causing excited bathers to report seeing a "flying saucer." It is the Flying Flapjack's first and only public flight. The Navy quickly drops the project to concentrate on jet-propelled craft instead.

The chaos continues.

On June 21, 1947, a marine salvage operator in Puget Sound sees a group of flying saucers over Maury Island, three miles out from Tacoma, Washington. Seemingly in distress, one of the saucers scatters hot debris over the island's bay area in the form of light metal and black, rock-like slag. Investigating the incident, Air Force intelligence officers Lieutenant Frank M. Brown and Captain Davidson dismiss it as a hoax. They are transporting some of the debris back to Hamilton Field AFB on August 1, when their B-25 crashes, killing them both. All the remaining pieces of saucer debris are then immediately impounded by Major Sander of S-2 Army Intelligence, McChord Field AFB.

Although the Maury Island incident is soon dismissed as a tragic hoax, it indirectly helps the USAF and the flying saucers to extend and define their presence through each other. Just as LeMay predict-ed, issues of air supremacy and the threat of outer space have helped to position the USAF ahead of all the other organizations, especially in a year when the prototype Bell 47 helicopter gets wheeled out of the hangar and the jet plane is offering unprecedented levels of speed and maneuverability. It is the flying saucer's shape, however, that really speaks of the future. For those on the ground, the flying saucer doesn't appear to depend on the same stresses and strains as the helicopter or jet plane do to get into the air. Rather than heaving itself up toward the sky, it seems to swoop effortlessly down from above. Its rounded design continues to mock the forward momentum of the jet plane, even after Chuck Yeager, piloting the Bell X-1 research plane, breaks the sound barrier for the first time in October 1947.

But where exactly does it come from? Initial speculation is that it may be the Soviets at work. Or it could be some secret project whose existence is hidden somewhere in the small print of the National Security Act.

At the end of 1947, the US Air Force sets up Project SIGN to investigate public sightings of strange things in the sky. As the name suggests, SIGN is an indication of that which has hitherto gone unnoticed: a signifier for what has so far passed without comment. By determining the significance of what may or may not exist in the skies over America, the Air Force impresses itself with greater clarity upon the popular imagination.

Except that at the very beginning it is movement and speed that define the flying saucer as a mass phenomenon, not its shape. Its overall visual appeal is one of metallic lightness, of reflective surfaces that glint and flash as the saucer maneuvers at high speeds. It has no stabilizing tail and leaves no trail.

The Maury Island saucer inadvertently marked itself out as a fraud by leaving that blackened trail of slag and scrap metal behind. While such a display may not be out of place among the ore-smelting operations of Tacoma Bay, slowly poisoning the islands in Puget Sound with toxic deposits of arsenic and lead, this saucer's sheer physicality denies it a presence in the future. It is only by removing all trace of its existence from the scene that the Air Force belatedly confers significance upon the incident.

The flying saucer becomes associated with forms of technology so superior that they can no longer be adequately detected by the human senses. As such, it is the elusive representative of an emergent invisible order of energy: of rays and beams, wireless transmissions and radiation bursts.

In a year when technicians at Bell Laboratories begin tests on an early model transistor, the US government formally takes control of

General Electric's cloud seeding experiments, and military contractors Raytheon come up with a basic idea for the microwave oven, the appearance of the flying saucer in popular culture marks a transition from mechanical forms of energy transfer to electronic ones. Like radio waves, TV signals, and atomic energy, whatever powers and steers the flying saucer remains a strange and unseen mystery. As the pragmatic Era of Edison appears to give way to a visionary Age of Tesla, the flying saucer also marks the deep gulf that has opened up between the actual accomplishments of technological progress and those who feel the future really can't get here fast enough. Suddenly the Raytheon microwave oven may not seem so humble anymore.

**From the Military-Industrial Complex to Inner Space**

*Flying Saucers over Lemuria*—"Call me Einstein, Flash Gordon or just plain crazy, but I know what I saw!" Kenneth Arnold declares in defense of his Mount Rainier sighting, thereby setting the mood for the next decade and a half. The strategists at Project RAND are absolutely right: the future is all about developing different ways of thinking rather than specific technological applications. Arnold's statement merely anticipates this shift at the public level, articulating it in the most specific terms. On July 29, 1947, Arnold's private plane touches down at Barry's Airport outside Tacoma Bay. He is here at the request of Ray Palmer, the publisher of *Amazing Stories* magazine, who has wired him $200 in expenses to investigate the Maury Island sighting.

Founded by the father of American science fiction Hugo Gernsback back in 1926, *Amazing Stories* was the first publication to feature the exploits of Buck Rogers amid the rocket ships, atom blasters, and alien worlds of the twenty-fifth century. More recently, however, it's been offering its readers another kind of adventure. Still on the newsstands when reports of Arnold's sighting hit the headlines is a special issue of the magazine dedicated entirely to what has become known as the "Shaver Mystery." Beginning in March 1945 with "I Remember Lemuria!" Palmer has been boosting circulation by publishing the writings of one Richard S. Shaver, an autoshop welder from Arkansas who claims to be receiving thought messages from the last descendants of the Lemurian race.

Unfortunately, all that remains of this once advanced and noble civilization are the Deros or "Detrimental Robots": a misshapen breed of bestial degenerates who are using the superior technology of their ancestors to spread havoc throughout the human world. What sets Shaver's writing apart from the usual fantasies to be found in *Amazing Stories* is Palmer's insistence that every word of it is true.

Immediately letters start flooding in from excited readers, offering further evidence in support of the Shaver stories, describing weird objects they have seen in the sky or detailing strange encounters with alien beings. "For heaven's sake, drop the whole thing!" urges one correspondent in the June 1946 issue of *Amazing Stories*. "You are playing with dynamite." The letter goes on to describe a wartime encounter with the Deros in the South Pacific that left its writer with "two nine-inch scars on my left arm that came from wounds given me in the cave when I was fifty feet from a moving object of any kind and in perfect silence. How? I don't know."

What makes this particular testimony of interest is that its author, Fred Crisman, is a business partner of the marine salvage operator who reported seeing the distressed flying saucer scattering debris over Maury Island. It is also Crisman who originally sent Ray Palmer some samples of black slag, prompting him to ask Kenneth Arnold to fly down to Tacoma Bay and investigate.

Palmer has noticed that whenever he features Lemuria on one of his covers, sales always increase dramatically. At 250,000 copies per issue, it has the makings of a collective hallucination. Seen from a behavioral point of view, the Detrimental Robots represent the dissolution of the human psyche into the systems that maintain it: the point at which there is nothing left but the workings. At the same time, the Deros are also the tiny voices living inside your head, making you do things. "The voices came from beings I came to realize were not human," Shaver has revealed, "not normal modern men at all." Perceived as a series of invisible forces, unseen technologies, death rays, and cosmic beams, the future is suddenly something received rather than transmitted. Under such circumstances, the belief expressed by RAND consultant Warren Weaver in "what can broadly be called the rational life" starts to appear a little shaky. Perhaps Delysid will help.

When administered in "very small doses," Delysid can cause "transitory disturbances of affect, hallucinations, depersonalization, reliving of repressed memories and mild neuro-vegetative symptoms," according to the trade literature prepared by Sandoz Laboratories. Four years after Dr. Albert Hofmann's wayward bicycle ride through the streets of Basel, Switzerland, LSD is marketed commercially for the first time in 1947 under the brand name Delysid. According to Sandoz, Delysid can be effective in the treatment of alcoholism and sexual deviancy. In fact, there seems to be no end to what it can do.

"By taking Delysid himself," the trade literature enthuses, "the psychiatrist is able to gain an insight in the world of ideas and sensations of mental patients. Delysid can also be used to induce model psychoses of short duration in normal subjects, thus facilitating studies on the parthenogenesis of mental disease."

That same year the first research paper on LSD appears in the *Swiss Archives of Neurology*. It is written by Dr. Werner Stoll, a close friend of Albert Hofmann and the son of Sandoz president Arthur Stoll. According to his findings, the drug causes hallucinations, promotes alterations in thinking, and can render schizophrenics more open to treatment. It is also odorless, colorless, and tasteless.

Undetectable by the normal senses, LSD exists outside their range in just the same way as flying saucers do. At a time when the "chemical brain" is beginning to be explored, starting with the discovery of nor-adrenaline in 1946, Stoll's paper on LSD is the equivalent of Arnold's reported sighting over Mount Rainier. There are no limits to its implications because—call those who take it Einstein, Flash Gordon, or just plain crazy—no one as yet knows what ingesting Delysid means.

Those two tiny words "as yet" sum up both the promise and the stark warning of this age. The US Navy is already setting up Project CHATTER by 1947, an early "offensive" program investigating the various means of obtaining information from subjects against their volition. One potential "truth drug" being tested on animals and humans at the Medical Research Institute in Maryland is mescaline, a hallucinogen with properties similar to those of LSD. The only absolute guarantee of truth under such circumstances is the weakening or the elimination of free will in others. "Suffice it to say," Shaver remarks of his conduct at the hands of the Deros, "that my enforced escapade, which I was blindly urged into by the subtle energy of the telepathy machines and other incomprehensible mechanisms using rays and forces that surface men had never heard of, ended with my arrest and sentence to a state prison. To this end, I, a well-intentioned human being, had been brought, by those potent rays in the hands of evil idiots, in earth's hidden caverns!"

While a cluster of eleven caves ranged to the northwest of the Dead Sea yield up their secrets in the form of ancient scrolls, other hidden caverns are being explored for the first time. In the final days of December 1947, advance copies of *Sexual Behavior in the Human Male* by Alfred C. Kinsey, Wardell B. Pomeroy, and Clyde E. Martin go on sale at the American Association for the Advancement of Science convention in Chicago. That same year the Kinsey Institute for Research in Sex, Gender, and Reproduction incorporates itself into a limited company to further pursue its inquiries. The "Kinsey Report," as it becomes familiarly known, offers the first statistical survey of activities usually pursued behind firmly closed doors. So shocking are its findings to the American public that no one really bothers to consider how these discoveries were made. Although Dr. Kinsey harbors a deep horror for most forms of modern technology, refusing to speak on the radio and grudgingly using a telephone only when absolutely necessary, he seems to have taken to early computational machinery without a second thought. His offices at Bloomington, Indiana, are equipped with the latest adding and tabulation machines, which are used for processing the massive amounts of data Kinsey has collected from thousands of personal interviews. The deployment of a standardized questionnaire means that the widest possible spectrum of sexual behavior can be separated out into a coherent form, revealing the extent to which the accepted and the aberrant are both part of the same human continuum. Kinsey's controversial findings also help to establish the electronic tabulation of human behavior in a year when ENIAC, the first digital computer, comes back online with a memory upgrade to remain in continuous operation until October 1955. Meanwhile, German rocket scientist Wernher von Braun marries his eighteen-year-old cousin, Maria von Quirstorp. At the time, von Braun is still a "prisoner of peace," quietly testing V2 rockets at the White

Plains proving grounds in New Mexico while the US military figures out what to do with him.

During a period of extreme transition such as this, it seems appropriate to mark the death near year's end in 1947 of an old, burned-out drug addict in a boarding house in Hastings on the southeast coast of England. Alone and perplexed and taking up to eleven grains of heroin a day, the Great Beast of the Apocalypse, Aleister Crowley, has finally quit this fleshly dimension. His final months are occupied in part with an extensive correspondence on the subject of Jack Whiteside Parsons, a rocket scientist at the California Institute of Technology who has been busy trying to create a "Moon Child" at his Pasadena home by magical means. Assisting him in this occult enterprise is an ex-naval officer and writer of pulp science-fiction tales for magazines such as *Amazing Stories*, known to his readers as L. Ron Hubbard.

In one letter Crowley describes himself as "fairly frantic" over their efforts, but it is also possible that his unease may have another cause. Crowley's time is almost at an end. The Kinsey Report on sexual behavior in the human male has revealed that the beast can be found rampaging through suburban bedrooms as well as the Temple of Pan; and strange drugs are now being marketed under sophisticated brand names as a potential panacea for mental health. Finally, machines are becoming a key part of human transcendence as rocket scientists and science-fiction writers start to force the evolutionary pace. No myth ever depends upon notions of good taste in order to survive. It remains a question of unspoken necessity, not propriety. Shaver's Deros operate within the shadow of that most slippery of progressive ideas: the perfectibility of the human animal. The fact that, according to Shaver, the Deros are descended, in the most literal sense, from space gods, collapses the notion of human progress in a highly suggestive manner.

What exactly does that now leave for Crowley, the wickedest man in the world, to do? Nothing, perhaps, except to look out over the orderly streets and lawns of Levittown and exclaim in wonder, as Richard S. Shaver once did: "I remember Lemuria."

# 1948: FLYING SAUCERS OVER AMERICA

## Insignificance

*January 7, 1948*–Captain Thomas F. Mantell, pilot with the Kentucky Air National Guard 165th Fighter Squadron, plummets to his death while pursuing what he describes as a flying saucer over Fort Knox, Kentucky, in his F51. "The object is above and ahead of me, moving at about my speed or faster," he reports shortly before blacking out from lack of oxygen. "I'm trying to close in for a better look." His plane continues its climb to thirty thousand feet before leveling off and spiraling back down to earth in a tragic scattering of debris. Taking a rather romantic view of the incident, the newly formed United States Air Force claims that Flight Leader Mantell was actually chasing the planet Venus.

Mantell's crash takes place within a week of Project SIGN becoming operational. Not everyone involved with SIGN's investigation of the incident is happy with the official version of what happened. At this point, however, no one really knows for certain what is going on up there. "We have a new project," writes Colonel H. M. McCoy, chief of intelligence for the Air Materiel Command at Wright-Patterson AFB, that March, "Project SIGN–which may surprise you as a development from the so-called mass hysteria of the past summer when we had all the unidentified flying objects or discs. This can't be laughed off ... We are running down every report. I can't even tell you how much we would give to have one of those crash in an area so that we could recover whatever they are."

A thorough examination of the F51 wreckage will reveal what happened to Mantell and his plane by the time they hit the earth but not what he may have actually encountered up there. This aspect tends to disappear beneath a plethora of timings and velocities, distances and angles of inclination: pieces of information that remain congruent with each other but not with the actual event itself.

What has been observed with the naked eye still remains disturbingly elusive. Kenneth Arnold testified to seeing a series of indistinct

curved flying wings over Mount Rainier. The marine salvage operator claimed he saw six very large "doughnut-shaped" craft over Maury
Island. Eyewitness reports made from the control tower in Kentucky
sent Mantell after something that resembled "an ice cream cone topped
with red."

Never actually present as anything more than a descriptive idea,
the "flying saucer" flits in and out of these differing accounts: a
hallucination that exists independently of the senses at a time when
radar and sonar are in the process of electronically extending the range
of human perception. An exhaustive review of such encounters tends
only to exhaust, however. The existence of flying saucers is unlikely
to be verified by an accumulation of facts and figures, dates and times,
which, if anything, tend to dull and distract the creative intelligence,
obscuring more than they reveal. Perhaps sightings should be studied
instead from the perspective of—and in terms of—Arnold's original
assertion: *"I know what I saw!"* Can such a speech act be any stranger
than declaring that one of your pilots met his death while trying to
reach Venus in a single-engine airplane?

The simple truth of Arnold's declarative statement will remain largely
overlooked. As the researchers engaged upon Project CHATTER are beginning to understand, truth and human volition are inextricably linked.

Which still leaves the investigators of Project SIGN asking themselves
the same question with each new report that comes in: which is the
bigger threat, superior technology from somewhere else in the universe,
or just somewhere else on Earth? That depends, of course, on where
you find yourself on the evolutionary timeline. After Lieutenant Brown
and Captain Davidson at Maury Island, Captain Mantell is the third
Air Force officer to be killed in a plane crash directly connected to a
reported flying-saucer sighting in less than six months.

Meanwhile green fireballs are seen in the night skies above New
Mexico. Considering how significantly alive the airspace is over this
particular expanse of desert, a vast white tract that still bears the
marks of settlers' wagons from the previous century, it is surprising
that such sightings have attracted any attention at all. A huge mir-

ror held up to the heavens, the desert landscape of New Mexico is also home to von Braun's team of rocket scientists, the Los Alamos atomic research center, the AEC Sandia Base, and the "DP vault" at Kirtland Air Force Base, near Albuquerque, where America's nuclear weapons are being stockpiled.

A phenomenon that might once have portended the end of kingdoms in the age of John Dee, Robert Fludd, or Edmund Spencer, or called forth nature's more mysterious forces in that of Lavater, Boyle, and Newton, has now become a troubling blip on the radar screen. Interpreted according to specific geopolitical sensitivities, green fireballs in the sky now represent the extent to which the military-industrial complex, even as its principal components are locking themselves into place, constitutes a new model of reality. What will be known retrospectively as the "Age of Confusion" in the history of flying-saucer culture is also the age of organizational emergence.

The establishment of a national Air Force marks the end of more traditional notions of combat. Specialist training and specialized technology also signal the disappearance of the warrior caste, to be replaced by a professional military elite. "Progression from the spear through the bow, musket, rifle and artillery to weapons of World War II was simply a matter of ever-increasing firepower," declares the Air Force's *Doctrine of Atomic Warfare*, a top-secret briefing document circulating in 1948. "The atomic bomb does not appear to have deviated from this evolutionary trend."

A significant event in the development of a new language with which to express this emergent technological order, Norbert Wiener's *Cybernetics: Or Control and Communication in the Animal and the Machine* is published in October 1948. Not only does Wiener's book establish the universal principle of feedback in the regulation of mechanical, electronic, and biological systems but also how it applies to larger social structures and organizations. The "fundamental notion of the message," argues the eminent MIT mathematician and physicist, applies equally to animals, machines, and humans. From this point on, command and control have a terminology of their own.

Unfortunately, the first edition of *Cybernetics* is riddled with mathematical errors. Wiener's eyesight is too poor to allow him to proofread the typesetting himself, so he entrusts the task to his most gifted doctoral students at MIT, Walter Pitts and Oliver Selfridge, who complete the assignment but then inadvertently send back an uncorrected set of galleys to the printers. It seems appropriate that Wiener, whose interest in feedback can be traced to his work during World War II developing a device to track the evasive action of enemy planes, should be undone by his inability to perceive accurately with the naked eye. As the number of sightings piles up at Project SIGN, the elusive nature of the flying-saucer report allows both the civilian and military populations to redefine their relationship with one another. The organization itself becomes a communications medium.

A systematic approach to the mechanics of communication is outlined for the first time in successive issues of the *Bell System Technical Journal,* published during the course of 1948. Written by Claude Shannon, a Bell Labs employee, and former member of Norbert Wiener's inner circle at MIT, "A Mathematical Theory of Communication" gives early expression to what will eventually become known as "information theory." Shannon's two-part paper clarifies the relationship between signal and noise in the transmission of a message at a time when investigators at SIGN are having a particularly tough time telling them apart. More importantly, Shannon keeps his technical definition of information rigorously apart from any consideration of the actual meaning a message might contain. "These semantic aspects of communication are irrelevant to the engineering problem," he declares in a gesture that leaves Project SIGN more aptly named than ever.

When human perception becomes a war zone, everyone is a potential enemy. In an age of confusion, increasingly dominated by specialized elites, who are the real experts when it comes to flying saucers? Is it the people who, like Kenneth Arnold, know what they saw? Or is it the investigating officers of the Air Force, the intelligence experts at the CIA, or the technicians at the Atomic Energy Commission?

In May 1948 Project RAND is incorporated as a nonprofit operating foundation under the laws of the State of California. The Articles of Incorporation set forth RAND's purpose in the simplest terms imaginable: "To further and promote scientific, educational, and charitable purposes, all for the public welfare and security of the United States of America." Where does such a promotion leave the public when it comes to the outer edges of science except, perhaps, for in the way? "Information is information," Wiener announces in the pages of *Cybernetics*, "not matter or energy. No materialism which does not admit this can survive at the present day." Flying saucers help these new emergent organizations to define themselves. The clash between professional investigators and amateur eyewitnesses over what is being seen in the skies above America indicates the extent to which these newly emergent institutions are also attempting to define not just what is identifiable, but how it should be identified. Meanwhile Louis Ridenour of the RAND Corporation continues to encourage institutional interest in an earth-orbiting spacecraft, arguing that "the development of a satellite will be directly applicable to the development of an intercontinental rocket missile," the initial velocity required for launching the latter being "4.4 miles per second, while a satellite requires 5.4." When *The First Annual Report of the Secretary of Defense* appears at the end of 1948, containing a brief paragraph indicating that each of the three armed services is now engaged upon studies for an "Earth Satellite Vehicle Program," there is a public outcry over the apparent waste of tax dollars.

Like any mystical order, belonging to an organization can determine a lot about your place in the universe. In 1948 technicians at the California Institute of Technology, where Jack Parsons is employed in the Jet Propulsion Lab, complete work on the Mount Palomar Observatory telescope in California. Aleister Crowley's Ordo Templi Orientis, of which Parsons is a member, is also rumored to have established a temple on Mount Palomar, believing it to be a vortex of powerful earthly energies. Wander a few miles down the road from the observatory itself, and you'll eventually come across Palomar Gardens, a lunch counter run by an ex-Theosophist and Prohibition rumrunner named George Adamski. We'll be hearing a lot more from him in due course.

In the meantime Ray Palmer quits *Amazing Stories* in 1948 after publishers Ziff-Davis refuse to let him bring out an issue dedicated entirely to flying saucers. Nothing if not sensitive to his times, Palmer starts *Fate* magazine. Its first issue contains Kenneth Arnold's account of the Mount Rainier sighting, "The Truth about Flying Saucers," in which he once again affirms that "I Did See the Flying Discs!" Other contributions to *Fate*'s debut issue include "Invisible Beings Walk the Earth" and "Twenty Million Maniacs."

More significantly, Ray Palmer has also split with Richard Shaver over the origins of the flying saucers. Shaver insists that they come from below ground. Palmer looks more toward the heavens. Do they still come from underground labyrinths haunted by the Deros, or from out of the sky? And if from the sky, from how far up? Subsequent Kenneth Arnold articles for *Fate* that year go further in linking flying discs to outer space rather than the Soviet Union or the United States.

It is by no means an accident that military and commercial pilots are among the first to see saucers over America. A lot closer to the skies than most of the populace, they are also trained to know what they're looking at: another reason why their testimony is of such interest. From the cockpit of Eastern Airlines Flight 576, Clarence Chiles and John Witted see a cylindrical object traveling at high speed over Alabama. In North Dakota, Second Lieutenant George F. Gorman of the Air National Guard gets into an aerial dogfight with a glowing ball of light.

Potential levels of boredom in a time of peace after such an intensely protracted period of war may well be an important factor here. Even the disastrous encounter with the Deros that Fred Crisman recounted in his letter to Palmer in 1946 begins with him being shot down on "my last combat mission." There is a need for excitement that heightens one's sense of reality and sends pilots chasing after the planet Venus. And they are not alone. As Ray Palmer and Richard Shaver argue over the origins of the flying saucers, the Hells Angels Motorcycle Club is formed in the wake of the 1947 Hollister biker riot, their name establishing a direct link between what exists high above the sky and that which dwells far beneath the earth.

### The Enigma of Dr. Cameron

*The Allan Memorial Institute of Psychiatry, Montreal*—Dr. Ewen Cameron is nothing if not a confident man. Even after being appointed director of a Canadian psychiatric hospital, he refuses to give up either his American citizenship or his American network of professional contacts. In fact, he keeps his home and his family life firmly on the American side of the border in upstate New York and discourages members of his staff from visiting him there.

Dr. Cameron has recently returned from Nuremberg, where, together with his senior colleague at the Allan Memorial, the celebrated neurologist Dr. Wilder Penfield, he formed part of the American team of psychiatrists selected to determine whether Rudolf Hess was mentally fit to go before the International Military Tribunal and answer for his crimes.

That the Allies chose to convene some of the most prominent figures in the psychiatric community at Nuremberg gives some indication of their newfound status as a progressive force. Their primary directive, however, was to evaluate rather than to diagnose. It was the Nazis, after all, who had publicly burned the writings of Sigmund Freud as pornographic trash and who had eventually forced their author into reluctant exile in London. Mental health under the Nazi regime had consequently devolved into questions of racial hygiene, selective breeding, and finally "medical killing." Why bother treating your patients, the Nazi mind doctors had argued, when it was simpler to have them sterilized? As for the difficult cases: well, they were even more easily disposed of. The extermination techniques used in the death camps had first been tested in Germany's mental hospitals.

Reflecting on his time in Nuremberg, Dr. Ewen Cameron grimly remarks that such a "psychological epidemic" as Nazism could only occur "when man had lost confidence in a design for living which had seemed sufficient for decades."

There is a lot riding on the words "seemed sufficient."

As a historical event, Nuremberg represents a moment when progress became momentarily blinded by its own clarity. Declared by the Allies to be 90 percent dead, its population living in cellars beneath piled-up rubble, what has been revealed in Nuremberg's dark mirror is enough to unsettle anyone who stares into it for too long. The shabby bunch of unemployed state functionaries that stand before the Tribunal represent a great deal more than their rather unprepossessing appearance might at first suggest. More than one reporter has gazed at this drab collection of mediocrities and wondered how on Earth they ever came to wield such monstrous power. Crimes against humanity must, by definition, be committed by other human beings.

Having established to their satisfaction that Rudolf Hess is clearly aware of the nature of the charges brought against him and what the mechanisms of the trial entail, Cameron and his associates pronounce him completely sane. On the slightly more troubling question of Hess's "hysterical amnesia" they are not so certain.

How strange that the issue of one man's memory should cause so much concern in Nuremberg of all places. It was here in 1828 that the mysterious Kaspar Hauser first made himself known to the outside world after having been kept locked up in a cellar for the first seventeen years of his existence. During what should have been the formative period of his life, young Kaspar had been shut away inside a windowless basement room, denied all contact with other human beings, and fed a meager diet of bread and water. Deprived even of enough room to stand up, Kaspar Hauser's basic coordination and locomotive skills were, at the time of his release, virtually nonexistent. He moved like an alien in an alien world, refracting everything he saw through startled, uncomprehending eyes. Knowing nothing, remembering little, rendered a human blank by his enforced solitary confinement, Kaspar Hauser remains a puzzling and enigmatic challenge to the measure of man.

For what now is the measure of man?

As the results of Rudolf Hess's Rorschach tests begin to circulate clandestinely among the psychiatric community in North America, there are some who believe that his responses reveal distinct signs of schizophrenia. If indeed that had been the case, they argue, why was Hess allowed to stand trial at all? More importantly, one of Dr. Cameron's colleagues at the Allan Memorial wants to know, why hasn't the patient been properly treated for his condition?

Good question. On his return to the Allan Memorial, Dr. Cameron begins experimenting with the most recent design in tape recorders as a means of automating the therapeutic process. Not much given to either socializing or small talk, the two great passions in Cameron's life are new gadgets and even newer cars. Technological visions of the future fascinate him, and he likes to indulge himself each year by acquiring the latest model automobile. "He read science fiction novels every night before he fell asleep," his son Duncan later recalls. "He called them his blood."

In the hope of discovering a quick and clean method of treating mental illness, Cameron is soon fooling around with a gizmo known commercially as the Cerebrophone. A modified playback system devised by Max Sherover, the Cerebrophone has sparked off a national fad for "Sleep Learning." Capable of relaying up to six hundred repeated instructions via a special loudspeaker that can be inserted beneath your pillow, the Cerebrophone will help you learn languages, mathematical formulae, and music while you sleep. In one experiment conducted during the summer of 1946, twenty chronic nail-biters were persuaded to kick the habit after hearing the message "My nails taste terribly bitter" endlessly repeated during the night.

Sleep Learning may not have caught on, but its take on education as a form of behavioral modification stays with Dr. Cameron, who starts experimenting with the basic mechanisms behind the process in the hope of finding a quick and easy automated method of treating mental illness. His passion for new cars is apparent in the term he derives for this new process: "psychic driving." It quickly becomes clear that, at the time when the first parkways and interstates are being built across America, the correct model for treating the human mind is no longer the Freudhaus in Vienna but General Motors in Detroit.

**The Snake Pit**

*Dr. Kik's Office—*Examined epistemologically, the Cerebrophone unites the brain with the voice in a way that Thomas Edison would appreciate. But is it possible to automate psychiatric therapy without actually reducing the human subject to a set of mechanical procedures in the process? In a bleak reversal of Kaspar Hauser's early years, Rudolf Hess's mind will be allowed slowly to erase itself in the lonely confinement of his cell in Spandau. Meanwhile the overriding concern facing the West at the moment is the mental stability of the many rather than the few. United States Congress has already signed the National Mental Health Act into law, freeing up millions of dollars for a "Manhattan Project" to research the cause, diagnosis, and treatment of neuropsychiatric disorders.

The countless examples provided by the war of soldiers cracking under the stress of combat suggest that strength and heroism, together with the possession of a strong moral or ethical character, don't guarantee anything. The mental equilibrium of America's fighting forces has become such a sensitive issue that a 1946 Army information film, *Let There Be Light*, dealing with the treatment of soldiers psychologically damaged by the conflict, is considered too disturbing for public consumption and promptly banned upon completion.

So Hollywood decides to let the women go mad instead.

As a contrasting alternative to *Let There Be Light*, moviegoers in 1946 have been treated to *The Dark Mirror*: a psychological thriller in which Olivia de Havilland, in the dual role of identical twins, is subjected to a bewildering array of Rorschach inkblots, word-association games, and lie-detector tests in order to determine which of them is a murderer. "One of our young ladies is insane!" the cop in charge of the investigation announces, but which one? The twins even come ready labeled as test specimens, each wearing a big, clunky-looking necklace spelling out her name.

The psychiatric movie is taking over from the classic horror film, a genre that effectively buried itself right at the very end of World War II with the release of Universal's *House of Dracula*. That same year Alfred Hitchcock's *Spellbound* hit the screens: a murder mystery in which Ingrid Bergman uses psychoanalysis to unmask the killer. The inclusion of a dream sequence designed by surrealist painter Salvador Dali and the addition of Dr. Samuel Hoffman's Theremin to the soundtrack help give the movie an extra futuristic frisson.

In 1948 Olivia de Havilland makes a return trip to the outer edges of madness playing a woman who hears voices inside her head in *The Snake Pit*: a crusading film about the treatment of mental patients in the state institutions. "Robert, there's something wrong with my head," she confides in her husband before being whisked off to Juniper Hill State Hospital.

"You had a nervous breakdown," she's informed by kindly Dr. Kik upon her arrival. "A nervous breakdown," Olivia replies. "That doesn't sound so bad, does it?" Well, certainly not as bad as the cure. Pretty soon she's being fed into the system: hydrotherapy, electroshock therapy, and Thorazine injections in shadowy rooms filled, like Dr. Frankenstein's laboratory, with dials and switches, canvas restraints, and sparking electrodes.

By 1948 the surgical treatment of mental disorders is already coming under mounting criticism by behaviorists, who see the mind as a series of programmed routines, and those who advocate the study of the chemical brain. To believe that madness can still be carved out of your patients puts you on the same level as the Nazi doctors standing trial in Nuremberg or the mad scientists still to be found prowling low-budget movies of the period. After making their names playing monsters for Universal Pictures, stars like Boris Karloff and Bela Lugosi settle into careers that require them to go bonkers in basement labs on a regular basis for cut-price outfits like Monogram and PRC. Wearing costumes no more outlandish than a white coat or a sturdy business suit, they breed devil bats, revive ape men, construct mechanical hearts, and inject themselves with murderers' blood until no law of nature has been left unviolated.

If such antics are starting to look a little corny by 1948, it's because psychiatrists like Dr. Kik are becoming increasingly aware that the mind can breed monsters of its own. "Dr. Kik, when am I real?" Olivia asks as the flashbacks pile up and she sinks further into madness. Meanwhile Sigmund Freud looks on from the wall in Dr. Kik's office.

Another interesting feature of this room is the glass door leading into it: this is the only place in the movie where Dr. Kik's real name can be read. Spelled out in reversed lettering, as if reflected in a dark mirror like some evil twin, the man responsible for Olivia's cure is revealed to be one Dr. H. M. Van Kensdelaerik. Such reversals occur throughout the film. Hardened inmates soaking in the hydrotherapy room crudely refer in Pig Latin to their chances of becoming "anesay" again. The "Snake Pit" itself, a horrific holding tank where insane patients are left to babble and lash out at each other, is also a reflection of the reversed logic to be found in the physical treatment of psychiatric disorders. "I think they figured that what might drive a normal person insane might shock an insane person back into sanity," Dr. Kik explains. "Did you ever hear of that?"

In a movie made up of missing time, flashbacks, and regressions, what's said and what's heard are of increasing importance. Talk itself is therapeutic: answering the doctor's questions helps chart your progress toward sanity. "Don't be afraid to talk and you'll get well too," Olivia is advised by one of the other patients. The weird and old-fashioned practices of bearded, foreign-born doctors have long since been replaced in America by the more modern, streamlined techniques of personality tests and IQ ratings. Already used in schools, big business, and the armed forces, such techniques have endowed psychology with the status of a progressive science. They also ensure that, in a forward-looking democratic society, psychiatry is for the masses and not just a privileged elite. Thus does the unspeakable H. M. Van Kensdelaerik become the conversational "Dr. Kik": spelled out on a lined stenographer's pad for all to see.

# 1949: BEHAVIOR MODIFICATION

**Sell Your Soul to Science**

*The Human Subject*—Psychiatrists were present at Nuremberg not only to judge the suitability of war criminals to stand trial; they judged their fellow scientists as well. As the twelfth and final hearing rumbles toward its conclusion in the spring of 1949, the US Government Printing Office publishes *Trials of War Criminals before the Nuremberg Military Tribunals under Control Council Law*, number 10, volume 2. Included within its pages are ten Directives for Human Experimentation drawn up by American psychiatrist Leo Alexander and commonly referred to as "The Nuremberg Code."

"The voluntary consent of the human subject is absolutely essential" is its primary stipulation. This truth, however, is not held to be particularly self-evident until German doctors and medical administrators, charged at Nuremberg with crimes against humanity, claim in their defense that no international law or formal agreement exists that clearly defined what constituted illegal human experimentation. Drafted as a response to such claims, Dr. Alexander's directives establish scientific practice as a series of differentiations, defining not only what makes good science but a good scientist as well. The Nuremberg Code consequently establishes itself as a series of contraventions, its existence affirmed mainly by the actions of those who don't follow its statutes.

And by 1949, their number is growing.

By the time Dr. Alexander's Directives for Human Experimentation are published in America, around eighteen pregnant women will have received doses of radioactive iron in a government-backed experiment at Vanderbilt University, Tennessee. The objective is to gauge the effects of radiation on fetal development. A follow-up study will find a higher than normal cancer rate among the women's children. Similar experiments using injections of radioactive calcium are conducted on terminally ill cancer patients in New York. Eighteen patients with dangerous illnesses will be injected with high concentrations of plutonium in experiments conducted at Chicago University. Manhattan Project researchers will

inject a further five human subjects with polonium and six other human subjects with uranium to obtain metabolic data relating to the safety of those working on the production of nuclear weapons. All of these experiments are apparently carried out without the patients' consent.

Informed and voluntary consent becomes even less of an issue in December 1949 when the AEC carries out the largest release of radioactive chemicals to date from their Hanford nuclear processing plant in Washington state, the thick plume of radioactive iodine covering hundreds of miles, extending as far as Seattle, Portland, and the California-Oregon border, and irradiating thousands of people. One of America's oldest nuclear facilities, responsible for manufacturing the plutonium for the bombs dropped on Hiroshima and Nagasaki, Hanford is one of the most heavily contaminated as well. Its reactors are cooled by water from the Columbia River; children swim in the hot currents streaming back out of the Hanford facility, while farmers working the land along the river's banks make jokes about the increasing numbers of deformed sheep born every year.

Located not far from Maury Island in the Puget Sound, there's also a distinct possibility that the "flying saucer debris" impounded by Major Sander of McChord Field AFB is actually nuclear waste from Hanford that has been illegally dumped on the island. In an account published in *Fate* magazine of his investigation into the Maury Island sighting, Kenneth Arnold describes handling some of the saucer debris brought to his Tacoma hotel room by Fred Crisman. "Someone suggested that these fragments could have been the lining of some kind of power tube," he writes. "When we lined up all the pieces, following the curve of the smooth surface, we saw that they could have been a lining of a tube of some kind about six feet in diameter." On the cover of the February 1949 issue of *Popular Mechanics* two prospectors are shown intently studying a Geiger counter: "Build Your Own Uranium Detector—page 238" reads a box in the lower left-hand corner.

Dr. Alexander's primary directive on voluntary consent ends with the following stern provision: "The duty and responsibility for ascertaining the quality of the consent rests upon each individual who initiates, directs or engages in the experiment. It is a personal responsibility, which may not be delegated to another with impunity." Not bound by this edict, however, are those who ultimately have access to the results of such experiments.

It all becomes a matter of usefulness. Do the findings have anything of value to offer, supposing it were possible, even for a second, to close one's eyes to the information that the bland initials "TP" contained in the Nazi doctors' notes stand for "Test Person"? The term "aviation medicine" sounds equally innocuous until you consider the physical and mental extremes embraced by these two relatively simple words.

Aerospace is humanity's outer limit. Until two years ago the sound barrier was thought to be impenetrable, at least by anyone who might live to tell the tale. Aviation takes the human form further and faster than it has ever been before—into the coldest and hottest environments, subject to the most intense pressures and distorting forces. Under the directorship of Dr. Hubertus Strughold, the inmates at Dachau were given firsthand experience of these nightmarish extremes, their bodies tossed about and discarded like rag dolls on behalf of the Luftwaffe's Aeromedicine Institute and to the greater glory of modern science. The quality of their consent was never really an issue at any time.

"The experiment should be such as to yield fruitful results for the good of society," runs Dr. Alexander's second Directive for Human Experimentation, adding that such results should also be "unprocurable by other methods or means of study, and not random and unnecessary in nature."

Dr. Strughold now resides in Texas, assigned in 1949 to head up the Space Medicine department at the School of Space Aviation at Randolph Air Force Base, San Antonio. He is considered second only to von Braun in importance as a government-employed scientist. Meanwhile the Air Force continues to sift through the results of his brutal researches at Dachau.

Of equal interest to US Naval Intelligence is the work of Strughold's Luftwaffe colleague, Dr. Kurt Plotner, who injected prisoners in Dachau with mescaline to see if it could be used to "impose one's will on another person as in hypnosis." Researchers engaged upon Project CHAT-TER are soon diligently studying Dr. Plotner's findings. The will to truth cuts across all notions of voluntary consent: "sentiments of hatred and revenge were exposed in every case" runs one observation made during the course of the Dachau mescaline experiments. America's intelligence community is already well equipped to make use of this information. Responsible for "the planning, development, coordination and execution of the military programme for psychological warfare" during World War II, the Office of Strategic Services was the precursor to the recently established CIA. Under the gung-ho leadership of General "Wild Bill" Donovan, it had already begun to look into the mind-controlling effects of marijuana and cocaine. Donovan recruited an educated white-collar elite of scientists and technicians, encouraging them to fight dirty and deploy "every subtle device and every underhanded trick" in the book.

Head of OSS Research and Development Stanley Lovell even went so far as to declare his intention to stimulate the "bad boy beneath the surface of every American scientist and to say to him 'throw all your normal law-abiding concepts out the window. Here's a chance to raise merry hell!'"

Having been part of the newly created military Medical Intelligence Organization since the previous year, the CIA still follows Lovell's basic precept. Put in charge of "foreign, atomic, biological, and chemical intelligence, from medical science's point of view," the agency's Chemical Division starts testing psychotropic drugs in secret.

Behavior modification and mind control constitute new forms of biochemical warfare, and Lovell's bad boys are soon stripped and ready for action. The streets, living rooms, and offices of the United States become field laboratories in which strange new drugs are tried out on unsuspecting members of the public. Early experiments test the use of Seconal, Dexedrine, sodium pentothal, Desoxyn, Thiamine, scopolamine, atropine sulfate, sodium luminol, and caffeine sulfate as potential agents of influence. The effectiveness of these drugs is augmented by the use of medical techniques such as lobotomy, hypnotism, and sensory deprivation. So far, their influence remains hypothetical, their effects little more than speculative.

Meanwhile, as Sandoz makes LSD commercially available in the United States for the first time under the Delysid brand name, the Army Chemical Corps starts testing hallucinogens on its own men. Over seven thousand soldiers will become unwitting subjects of experiments conducted at Fort Detrick, Maryland, involving LSD and mescaline. The chemicals are sprayed inside oxygen masks, which the men wear while doing vigorous exercise. Over one thousand test subjects will go on to develop severe psychological problems and epilepsy, while several others attempt suicide.

The aim of such operations is to make the mind perform upon command a series of relatively simple tasks related to the basic processing of information: reveal, accept, remember, forget. The behavioral model invoked is closely related to that of Alan Turing's Universal Machine, in itself a simple table of instructions pertaining to the inscribing and erasing of data on a paper tape of infinite length. Formulated just before the outbreak of World War II, Turing's Universal Machine has not only supplied the theoretical basis for the computers currently being developed by games theorist John von Neumann at the Institute of Advanced Studies but also introduced the concept of the infinite tape as a metaphor for how human cognition works. Thanks to the postwar technological shift from paper to acetate, the magnetic tape recorder quickly establishes itself as a functioning model for consciousness.

In March 1949, the sixth Josiah Macy Jr. Foundation conference on "Circular, Causal and Feedback Mechanisms in Biological and Social Systems" takes place at the Beekman Hotel on Manhattan's Upper East Side. Those attending include John von Neumann, the eminent psychiatrist Lawrence Kubie, anthropologists Gregory Bateson and Margaret Mead, together with Medical Director of the Foundation, Frank Fremont-Smith, and the father of cybernetics himself, Norbert Wiener. Chairman of the group is neurophysiologist Warren McCulloch, one of the world's foremost authorities on the function and organization of the brain.

Started during World War II, the Josiah Macy Foundation conferences are designed as a series of informal interdisciplinary exchanges over questions relating to how the human mind processes information. Margaret Mead has already characterized its participants as an "evolutionary cluster" whose individual members are working "to make choices which set a direction." For the first time in its history the conference prepares to publish a transcript of the proceedings. "By preserving the informality of our conferences in the published transactions," Fremont-Smith argues, "we hope to portray more accurately what goes on in the minds of scientists and to give a truer picture of the role which creativity plays in scientific research." The results, however, often appear faltering, muddled, and repetitious, as each specialist grapples with terms and concepts outside their specialist discipline. Even so, the CIA starts to take an interest, sending along its own representatives to report on future conferences and occasionally channel funding into some of the delegates' more promising lines of research.

The Josiah Macy Jr. Foundation Conference on Cybernetics, as it will henceforth be known, marks a point of programmed convergence between man and machine at a time when the prospect of mind control presents itself as the newest weapon of the Cold War. In communist Hungary, now firmly part of the Eastern Bloc, Cardinal József Mindszenty goes on trial, accused of treason. Under Western eyes, his behavior in court seems oddly remote, as if the man has been transformed into some kind of functioning automaton: even the defendants at Nuremberg appeared a little more clued in than his eminence.

While *Popular Mechanics* boldly declares that computers in the future "may weigh no more than 1.5 tons" and Cardinal Mindszenty stands in a Budapest courtroom, displaying every sign of being either hypnotized or doped, the programming of the human computer appears to be an increasingly attractive proposition. In his introduction to Claude Shannon's *A Mathematical Theory of Communication*, now published as a single volume, RAND consultant Warren Weaver widens the author's concept of information separated from meaning to include "all of the procedures by which one mind may affect another … not only written and oral speech, but also music, the pictorial arts, the theatre, the ballet and, in fact, all human behavior." A paper by von Neumann entitled "The General and Logical Theory of Automata," published the same year, enlarges upon Turing's idea of a Universal Machine by proposing a tape-driven, self-producing "automaton whose output is other automata." Meanwhile Donald Hebb, chairman of psychology at McGill University and a senior member of Canada's Defence Research Board, publishes his own groundbreaking study on how the mind works. It is called *The Organization of Behavior*.

That it should be left to a psychiatrist to draw up the Nuremberg Code on scientific practice seems entirely appropriate. Leo Alexander extends the thinking behind his Directives for Human Experimentation in the July 14 issue of *The New England Journal of Medicine*. In it, he argues that medical killing "represents the eruption of unconscious aggression on the part of certain administrators" as well as those more closely related to the human subject. "The hostility of a father erupting against his feebleminded son," he writes, "is understandable and should be considered from the psychiatric point of view, but it certainly should not influence social thinking."

Except that, thanks to Stanley Lovell's bad boys, such psychiatric understanding is clearly beginning to affect social thinking. However, at a time when the stipulations of the Nuremberg Code are largely being ignored, the ensuing shift in attitude is more likely to reflect the hostility of the son erupting against a feebleminded father than the other way around.

### The Opticon Scillometer

*Cosmic Rays*—In another issue of *The New England Journal of Medicine*, appearing in September 1949, two essays appear back to back on the same subject: "Radiation Exposures from the Use of Shoe-Fitting Fluoroscopes" by Charles R. Williams, PhD, and "Potential Dangers in the Uncontrolled Use of Shoe-Fitting Fluoroscopes" by Louis Hempelmann, MD. Both concern themselves with the high levels of radiation to which customers and clerks are being exposed by in-store X-ray devices. The sight of mothers, children, and sales assistants happily grouped around these machines to check the possible pinching of a new pair of shoes on developing feet has been a familiar one since the 1930s. Now, in a time when public anxieties over the harmful effects of radiation are mounting, *The New England Journal of Medicine* comes down firmly on the side of watchful ignorance. "Since the maximum amount of radiation that the foot can tolerate at intervals of several months is not known," concludes Dr. Hempelmann, "it seems advisable to reduce the foot dosage to the minimum that is compatible with satisfactory use of the fluoroscope."

Children are in any case being irradiated from a different source by 1949, as the cathode ray tube begins its steady takeover of suburban living rooms throughout America. Its effects on a developing population of young consumers will be more mysterious and far-reaching than *The New England Journal of Medicine* can possibly imagine.

Early audiences watch in amazement as a nameless lawman from the Old West, having been wounded and left for dead by a gang of outlaws, is sheltered in a cave by an American Indian. A few days later, the mysterious stranger emerges blinking into the bright California sun only to discover that his Stetson has been bleached white by its rays. One black mask later, and the Lone Ranger's spiritual rebirth is complete. The transfer of *The Lone Ranger* adventure serial from the radio to television in 1949 adds a new mythical dimension to what was already a very successful franchise.

For a start, children get to see the mask. To ask "Who was that masked man?" of a voice on the radio is to share a watchful ignorance with the listener at home. Once televised, however, the question of the Lone Ranger's hidden identity becomes one of mystery, transformation, and initiation, thanks to the new medium.

The cave in which this personality-changing shamanic experience takes place is also of great mythical significance. The transformation from nameless dying lawman to the Lone Ranger actually occurs in a remote area of Los Angeles known as Bronson Canyon, a former gravel quarry located along the sprawling westerly edge of Griffith Park, the largest municipal recreation area in the world. The Union Rock Company started digging here back in 1903, burrowing into the Hollywood Hills to supply crushed rock for the expanding network of boulevards, roads, and railways required by the thriving city below. In the process of helping to make Los Angeles the capital city of the twentieth century, Bronson Canyon has been turned into an alien landscape of barren rock, scrub, and exposed peaks.

When mining operations ceased in the 1920s, the film industry moved into its manmade caves and tunnels and has been there ever since: the canyon proving to be an inexpensive backdrop for cheap westerns and low-budget space operas. It is a place of simple illusions. The Lone Ranger's cave isn't even a real cave, for example, but a large tunnel linking the canyon's interior with the outside world; but it will appear in an increasing number of movies, especially independent productions from companies that have come into existence following the collapse of the old Hollywood studio system.

Thanks to a 1948 Supreme Court ruling, the film industry's major players are being forced to divest themselves of their theater chains, thereby altering forever the way in which movies are to be financed and distributed. Worse still, from the point of view of the big studios, people's viewing habits are also starting to change. Population dispersal into the suburbs is creating a style of living that is antithetical to the notion of spontaneously going "downtown" to watch a movie. When the public sees movies, how it sees them and what it wants to see are already in a state of flux, and this is still at a time when less than half of 1 percent of all households in the United States owns a television set.

It therefore seems appropriate that another highly popular TV series begins in 1949, one that pinpoints the relationship between the viewer and the newly emergent technology. Premiering on June 27 on the DuMont Network, *Captain Video and His Video Rangers* is all about the science. The format, structure, and characterization may alter over the coming seasons, but Captain Video remains a technological genius, a "Master of Science" whose inventions reflect a rapidly overheating order of new communications media. Among his most popular devices are the Opticon Scillometer, a long-range X-ray machine that allows him to see through walls; the Discatron, a portable television that functions as a communicator; and the Radio Scillograph, a handheld two-way radio. Captain Video's futuristic range of weapons also includes the Cosmic Ray Vibrator, a beam of static electricity capable of paralyzing its target; the Atomic Disintegrator Rifle; and the Electronic Strait Jacket. Simply by having a television set in your living room, you put yourself and your children directly in touch with this fabulous new world.

Such devices have, of course, been around for a while. Like the "Shoe-Fitting Fluoroscope," movie serials and chapter plays have, since the 1930s, featured rays and gases, bombs and radio waves, usually in the hands of villains and almost always for the purposes of conquering the world. What has changed is the context. Captain Video's gizmos present the possibility of mass destruction within the shadow of mass destruction. Even as he circles the globe in his X-9 jet, fighting mad scientists and alien invaders, Captain Video's followers, his "Video Rangers," help to connect the mythically transformed Wild West of *The Lone Ranger* with the missile ranges and test sites that constitute America's newest frontier. No wonder *New York Times* critic Jack Gould accuses everyone associated with the show of keeping its young audiences "emotionally hopped up."

**Twilight's Last Gleaming**

*From SIGN to GRUDGE*—In the middle of February 1949, a two-day conference is held at Los Alamos to discuss the green fireballs that have been seen over the missile ranges, radar installations, fighter bases, and atomic storage facilities of New Mexico during the course of the previous year. Among the military officers, rocket scientists, and Los Alamos technicians in attendance are "world renowned expert on the physics of the upper atmosphere" Dr. Joseph Kaplan and Dr. Edward Teller, who is currently engaged with mathematician Stanislaw Ulam upon developing the first Hydrogen Bomb. What makes this conference of particular interest, however, is that everyone present has seen the green fireballs. Confronted with a lack of photographs and other physical evidence, Kaplan and Teller declare them to be a natural phenomenon; others are not so sure. Delegates leave the conference having agreed upon very little except that the Air Force Cambridge Research Laboratory will initiate Project TWINKLE during the summer to photograph and study the fireballs.

This may seem like a strange undertaking, considering that the USAF is in the process of radically altering its internal policy regarding flying saucers. Even before the Los Alamos conference has broken up, Project SIGN is preparing to issue its last report at the end of February, by which time it will officially no longer exist. Open-minded on its best days, factional on its worst, overseen from Wright-Patterson AFB by the Air Materiel Command, SIGN's organizational behavior has increasingly included the thoughts and opinions of those who embrace what has come to be called "the Extraterrestrial Hypothesis"—that flying saucers come from outer space. Unimpressed by their arguments, Air Force Chief of Staff General Hoyt S. Vanderberg has rejected their best case-history evidence. Fears that the freethinkers inside Project SIGN are going to wind up embarrassing the United States Air Force have subsequently led to both a change of name and a change of policy. SIGN had become "compromised"; from February 11 onward it shall be known as GRUDGE. The primary objective of the project will henceforth be to explain all public reports of flying saucers as evidence of any number of perfectly natural phenomena, ranging from meteorological anomalies to mass hysteria and "war nerves."

Meanwhile Project SIGN's final report is being readied for release at the end of February. Among its appendices is a "Scientific Overview" from Professor James Lipp of the RAND Corporation's Missile Division. Professor Lipp is once again taking the widest possible view of events. Is it possible, he wonders, that the arrival of flying saucers in our skies is a sign that our use of atomic weapons is attracting attention from elsewhere in the universe?

"The first flying objects were sighted in the Spring of 1947," he writes, "after a total of 5 atomic bomb explosions, ie Alamogordo, Hiroshima, Nagasaki, Crossroads A and Crossroads B. Of these the first two were in positions to be seen from Mars, the third was very doubtful (at the edge of the Earth's disc in daylight) and the last two were on the wrong side of Earth."

Leaving aside the possibility that, depending on your location at the time, all five atomic explosions took place "on the wrong side of Earth," Lipp's speculation has a logical charm all of its own. "It is likely," he continues, "that Martian astronomers, with their thin atmosphere, could build telescopes big enough to see A-bomb explosions on Earth, even though we were 165 million and 153 million miles away, respectively, on the Alamogordo and Hiroshima dates."

Lipp also notes, however, that flying-saucer behavior doesn't fit any rational system or approach commensurate with such an observation. If the Martians are technically superior, he argues, why not just walk right in and take over? If, however, they're just feeling us out, gauging our reactions to their presence, what can possibly be gained by running the same play over and over again?

While the RAND Corporation uses game theory to second-guess the activities of intelligent life elsewhere in the solar system, it may be worth pausing here to note that, while anyone can see a flying saucer, not everyone can observe one. To observe something is to alter it, subtly modifying its behavior even at the most superficial level. Open-minded speculation of this kind, especially when bearing a "Top Secret" stamp on its cover, is possibly not the best way to proceed. Back in the summer of 1947, when flying saucers still constituted little more than a heightened form of popular hysteria, Gallup polled the American public on the subject. While 33 percent of respondents had no clear idea of who or what was responsible for the plethora of flying-saucer sightings, a combined total of 58 percent thought they must be due to one of the rational explanations now being offered to the public by Project GRUDGE. The "Extraterrestrial Hypothesis," if considered at all, made up only part of the remaining 9 percent who were prepared to entertain "other explanations," including the fulfilling of biblical prophecies and "radio waves from the Bikini atomic bomb explosion."

After one year of Project SIGN, this 9 percent now poses such a threat that Project GRUDGE has no other choice than to go on the offensive, even to the extent of withholding its new name from the public. It is consequently referred to simply as "Project Saucer" in a two-part article appearing in the *Saturday Evening Post* during the late spring of 1949, debunking popular beliefs about flying saucers. Written by Sidney Shalett with the full cooperation of Project GRUDGE, "What You Can Believe about Flying Saucers" paints a picture of the USAF reluctantly being dragged in to investigate sightings by a bunch of wild-eyed fanatics who think the Martians are coming. "The investigating authorities have learned," Shalett sadly notes, "that all the logic in the world will not convince the witness who wants to believe that the thing he sighted was something sinister or maybe interplanetary."

Which is an interesting statement, if only because it leaves the reader wondering who exactly is being addressed here, in an article devoted to so elective a matter as personal belief.

Not only does the *Saturday Evening Post*, for whom Norman Rockwell painted pictures of boys and their dogs, small-town events, and family gatherings, become the first publication in America to feature the term "UFO" during the course of this two-part feature, but it also gets to inform its readers on what they can and can't believe. At the same time, Project GRUDGE is allowed to determine not only the parameters of its investigation but also the legitimacy of the subject for study.

By officially separating out those who make the report from those charged with investigating it, the USAF has managed to make that 9 percent who believe in "other explanations" suddenly appear a lot larger than before.

However, Project SIGN is not yet done with either GRUDGE or the *Saturday Evening Post*. On April 27, three days before the first part of Shalett's article appears, a condensed version of SIGN's final report, including Professor Lipp's musings on Martian observers and atomic explosions, is released to the public. A couple of weeks later Major Donald Keyhoe receives a telegram from Ken Purdy, the editor of *True* magazine. Sent on May 9, just two days after the second part of Shalett's article hits the newsstands, it invites Keyhoe to investigate what Purdy's terse economical prose describes as a "gigantic hoax to cover up official secret."

Purdy has picked the right man for the job. A former Marine Corps pilot and a graduate from Annapolis Naval Academy, Don Keyhoe quickly demonstrates a fine feel for interpreting the behavior of large organizations. Why, for example, would the USAF collaborate on an article designed to ruthlessly debunk any notion that flying saucers might exist while simultaneously issuing a press release that more or less takes that existence as a given? Is it possible that the Air Force is deliberately distracting people from the truth while at the same time preparing them for its inevitable revelation? Could it be that flying saucers really do come from outer space?

"Beyond the low hills to the west I could see the stars," Keyhoe will later write of his first thoughts on the subject. "I can still remember thinking, If it's true, then the stars will never be the same again."

Like a number of former airmen at this time, from Captain Mantell to the Hells Angels, Donald Keyhoe is soon gripped by that sense of being picked up and carried over the hills and far away by something larger and more exciting than the events of daily life. During the summer of 1949, while members of the Project TWINKLE team forlornly chase green fireballs around the New Mexico desert in a vain attempt to photograph even one of them, Keyhoe starts his research.

Keyhoe's main strength as a writer lies in the imaginative leaps he makes in interpreting the reactions of Air Force officers and other intelligence operatives to something as essentially imponderable and intangible as flying saucers have so far proven themselves to be. Keyhoe doesn't see flying saucers, nor does he attempt to interpret what the skies might be concealing. What Keyhoe does best, as his remarkable publishing career on this subject will soon demonstrate, is to scrutinize the organization of behavior, the bureaucratic torque and drag, within the US Air Force. In other words, the main subject of his study is not the flying saucers themselves but the effect they have on institutional structures. His groundbreaking article, "Flying Saucers Are Real," in the January 1950 issue of *True* magazine rapidly becomes one of the most widely read features of all time. UFOs are now big news. Project GRUDGE is made to look foolish.

As the first copies of *True* are mailed out to subscribers just after Christmas 1949, GRUDGE attempts to counter Major Keyhoe's accusations that it has deliberately instigated a flying-saucer cover-up by issuing a final report on December 27, flatly denying the existence of flying saucers and effectively shutting itself down. An equally assertive statement from the RAND Corporation appears in the report's appendix: "We have found nothing which would seriously controvert simple rational explanations of the various phenomena in terms of balloons, conventional aircraft, planets, meteors, bits of paper, optical illusions, practical jokers, psychopathological reporters and the like."

It is clear, however, that RAND should not underestimate the powerful effect "bits of paper" can have, especially at a time when, according to the surveys, every household in the United States regularly receives a periodical of some kind. Printed statements, whether in the form of official reports, estimates of the situation, magazine articles, or newspaper headlines, are still what shape reality for the vast majority of people.

From "What You Can Believe about Flying Saucers" to "Flying Saucers Are Real," from SIGN to GRUDGE, this is still an age where wonders exist primarily on paper. Just as Ray Palmer switched coordinates from *Amazing Stories* to *Fate*, so too has the argument over flying saucers now relocated to a men's magazine that declares itself to be *True*. Whichever way you choose to read this shift, the line from *Amazing Stories* to *True* is a straight one. The operative word in the title of Keyhoe's article is "real": it links his readership back to Arnold's declaration and, a little further still, to Palmer's assertion that Shaver's memories of Lemuria were all true. In this same spirit, two small articles have already appeared in the October 12 and November 27 issues of *Variety* magazine. Written by entertainment correspondent Frank Scully, they allege that a crashed saucer, together with its occupants, has been recovered and is now in the possession of the US Air Force. From this point on the stars truly won't be the same again.

On the other side of the world, the Soviet Union explodes its first A-Bomb. Meanwhile a former World War II sharpshooter called Howard Unruh kills thirteen of his neighbors in Camden, New Jersey, with a souvenir Luger, thus becoming America's first single-episode mass murderer. It takes him just twelve minutes.

# 1950: CHEAPNESS AND SPLENDOR

**The Buchenwald Touch**

*Minimal Risk*—In the spring of 1950, parents of pupils attending the Walter E. Fernald School, a Massachusetts institution for children with learning difficulties, receive the following letter from the school's clinical director:

*Dear Parent:*

*In previous years we have done some examination in connection with the nutritional department of the Massachusetts Institute of Technology, with the purposes of helping to improve the nutrition of our children and to help them in general more efficiently than before.*

*For the checking up of the children, we occasionally need to take some blood samples, which are then analyzed. The blood samples are taken after one test meal, which consists of a special breakfast meal containing a certain amount of calcium. We have asked for volunteers to give a sample of blood once a month for three months, and your son has agreed to volunteer because the boys who belong to the Science Club have many additional privileges. They get one quart of milk daily during that time, and are taken to a baseball game, to the beach and to some outside dinners and they enjoy it greatly.*

*I hope that you have no objection that your son is voluntarily participating in this study. The first study will start Monday, June 8th, and if you have not expressed any objections we will assume that your son may participate.*

*Sincerely yours,*
*Clemens E. Benda, MD*
*Clinical Director*
*Walter E. Fernald School*

Happy the parents who read that their child now belongs to his school's Science Club; unhappy the child whose parents fail to register their objections to the proposed experiment. What is not made clear

# Life Aboard a Space Ship

An unstrapped crewman floats weightless in a space ship in the movie Destination Moon.

*Eating, washing and sleeping will be tough problems*
*for passengers on the first flights to outer space.*

## By Willy Ley, World-Famed Rocket Authority

"NEVER doze off without tying yourself down or you'll crack your head on something. If you feel a sneeze coming, hang on to something or you'll slam into the bulkhead. Don't try to pour from a bottle and don't smoke without turning up the air conditioner."

This advice may well be given to a space cadet in about 1980 by an experienced hand. All of it refers to the little tricks men will have to learn if they want to survive a trip through space and be reasonably comfortable while doing so. *Reasonably* comfortable; real comfort is not likely to come to the space lanes for many years.

in Dr. Benda's letter is that the main part of the "special breakfast" provided for the boys of the Science Club will be a bowl of oatmeal enriched with a generous helping of radioactive calcium. As well as the Massachusetts Institute of Technology, other more knowing participants in this experiment include the National Institutes for Health, the Atomic Energy Commission, and the good people at Quaker Oats. Ostensibly designed "to determine how the body absorbed iron, calcium, and other minerals from dietary sources and to explore the effect of various compounds in cereal on mineral absorption" the study will continue, unopposed and unchallenged, until 1953.

It is one thing to see your children glowing with health: quite another to discover that they can now glow in the dark. Federal regulations at this time allow for "nontherapeutic" research on children if an institutional review board of local citizens determines that the research presents "no greater than minimal risk" to the children who will serve as its subjects. There is, however, no clear definition of what constitutes "minimal risk," especially in cases where the children exposed to it are precisely those who are most in need of society's protection.

The breakfast table is not the only place in the United States that is no longer safe. Whole communities are also at risk. The Atomic Energy Commission has formulated a secret program of experiments in which atomic devices are deliberately detonated in the atmosphere over New Mexico, Nevada, Utah, and Washington in order to examine the spread and effects of radioactive fallout. After one such test in 1950, government scientists carefully measure radiation levels in the town of Watrous, NM, located barely seventy miles from the blast site. Although its inhabitants have been reassured that their lives are not at risk, the main purpose of the test is to develop an atomic weapon capable of killing enemy soldiers with its radioactive fallout.

Officially classified by the AEC as "low use segments of the population," those caught in the atomic backdraft are more commonly known as "downwinders." The CIA is authorized by the Scientific Intelligence Committee and the Joint Medical Science Intelligence Committee to engage in the recovery of over 1,500 bodies, not always with the permission of relatives, and the collection of tissue and bone samples from communities directly exposed to the nuclear fallout from tests in the Nevada desert.

Ethical issues quickly become diffused during this period into more practical questions of application, procedure, and selection.

Throughout the year, Shields Warren, director of the Atomic Energy Commission's Division of Biology and Medicine, together with Alan Gregg of the Advisory Committee for Biology and Medicine, attempts to block efforts made by the Defense Department and the AEC's own Division of Military Application to initiate an extensive program of Total Body Irradiation (TBI) experiments, using healthy human subjects taken from the nation's prison population, to further the development of a new nuclear-powered airplane. In full-throated support of such a procedure, however, is Robert S. Stone, Professor of Radiology at the University of California at San Francisco and a member of the Medical Advisory Committee to the Nuclear Energy Propulsion for Aircraft (NEPA) program. "Live prisoners," he counters, "are the one group of people that are likely to remain in one place where they can be observed for a great many years."

A memorandum circulated in 1950 by radiation biologist Dr. Joseph Hamilton to senior AEC officials warns that human experimentation of this order is probably unethical, possibly illegal, and perhaps a breach of the Nuremberg Code of Scientific Ethics. Were it to become public that such experiments are taking place, Dr. Hamilton points out, the AEC might well expect a lot of criticism "as admittedly this would have a little of the Buchenwald touch."

Well, perhaps just a tad.

Meanwhile, in September 1950, US Navy submarines spray sectors of the San Francisco Bay Area with the bacterium *Serratia marascens* to act as a biological tracer for a possible anthrax attack. A paper in the *Archives of Internal Medicine* describes eleven *Serratia marascens* infections observed in one San Francisco hospital alone between September 1950 and February 1951. Such infections are, as a rule, very rare. All the same, at least one elderly patient dies after being exposed to the bacterium cloud.

"A little of the Buchenwald touch": somehow Dr. Hamilton manages to make it sound like the design motif for some suburban home interior or a line of cover copy from an album of easy-listening favorites. Perhaps his choice of words isn't all that inappropriate after all. This is an age of undetected presences: tasteless, odorless, and colorless agents such as radiation and bacteria, along with the wide range of psychoactive drugs being researched behind closed doors, are completely off the sensory scale of things. What remains unknown is often barely suspected. It is up to popular culture, even at the most innocuous levels, to supply correlatives for what has so far been unarticulated. In a manner similar to the US Navy's dispersal of *Serratia marascens*, Kenneth Arnold's flying saucers rapidly come to serve as a biological tracer for this period of uncertainty and transition.

And with this new undetected order comes an equally new evolutionary agenda. What makes LSD, atomic radiation, and flying saucers such important subjects for study is the extent to which they establish a cultural technology for themselves: that is to say, a set of social mechanisms through which their more speculative effects can be perceived and used.

The last fifty years of the twentieth century will be unique in being so closely plotted and calibrated in terms of calendar time. Specific years will be celebrated, countdowns started, anniversaries observed, and decades scrutinized with increasing attention. There is a growing obsession with locating this current period of transition not just within the precisely measured cycle of decades and centuries but also upon a mythical timeline of planetary evolution. Robots and scientists, rulers and slaves, mindless beasts and disembodied brains will soon emerge from popular culture to form themselves into kaleidoscopic combinations within the public imagination, hinting at humanity's location within this evolutionary scheme. At the level of popular culture, the fact and fantasy of science both originate from the same social mindset, even when they appear so separate and isolated from each other. At first glance, a letter about Science Club activities at the Walter E. Fernald School doesn't seem to fit any specific preconceived notions of how a mad scientist might behave. But then, this is also the first year in which Bert the cartoon "Duck and Cover" Turtle explains to children what they should do in the case of nuclear attack. Will covering their heads with a newspaper really make that much of a difference? From this point on, it's all science fiction.

## Early American Space Age

*The Last Picture Show in Lemuria*—"Streaking out of the Unknown Comes a Strange New Terror," runs the poster copy. "The Flying Saucer … starring Mikel Conrad, produced and directed by Mikel Conrad, based on an original story by Mikel Conrad…." A film not only starring but also written, produced, and directed by an individual no one has ever heard of: that is always a quality sign. Out on national release in 1950, *The Flying Saucer* is no exception to this principle.

"You wake me up in the middle of the night, tell me to get on a plane to Washington, and now all this malarkey about flying saucers," Mikel Conrad emotes sourly in the role of Mike Turner, an ex-GI pressed back into active service to investigate the latest wave of sightings over America.

This being the first feature-length release to deal with the subject, Mike is soon set straight about the real threat posed by the flying disc. "It works on a revolutionary principle we can't even guess at," Mike's bureau chief in Washington admonishes. "It appears it was designed with one purpose: to carry the atomic bomb. Now the first country that learns the secret of the flying saucer will control the skies of the world. I don't want that country to be Russia."

Too late: the Soviets are already in Alaska, offering to buy the saucer from its inventor. "Instead of being used to serve the imperialistic designs of America," their leader announces, "your invention will now be employed for the good of the entire human race."

At the film's first public presentation in Ohio the previous year, Conrad claimed that its contents had been cleared for release by the FBI following a special screening. This is not the last time that an individual will claim to have received special clearance from a large federal agency to reveal some startling information about flying saucers or their occupants. As a promotional gesture it has much to recommend it. If the FBI stays silent, the bureau appears to be giving tacit approval to such a claim. If they strongly deny it, the public is left wondering what they're hiding. And even if the bureau gets the individual to retract their claims, the damage has already been done—plus the public is still left wondering what the FBI is hiding. Conrad will go on to state that his movie contains actual flying-saucer footage, while other sequences, including one of him talking with an alien pilot, have been confiscated.

Generating more heat than light, Mikel Conrad's flying saucer is still doing a lot better than Hollywood's first serious attempt to enter the Space Age. Based on a novel by Robert Heinlein, United Artists' *Destination Moon* can boast technical advice from the father of modern rocketry Hermann Oberth and its sorcerer's apprentice Wernher von Braun, plus astronomical art from illustrator Chesley Bonestell, whose interstellar vistas have become a staple feature of such magazines as *Life*, *Look*, and *Collier's*. The Moon consequently looks realistic, and the United States gets there first. More importantly, the story line involves an industrialist, a scientist, and a technician getting together with Army brass on the project. Unlike the power play going on in *The Flying Saucer*, these individuals understand that whoever controls the Moon controls life here on Earth. The military-industrial complex has made its first bold move into space. The future, however, remains located where it has always been: in America.

Von Braun and his spacemen are still at the White Sands Proving Ground in the New Mexico desert. The last of Germany's engineer heroes have moved as far west as they can possibly go, following in the tracks of the numerous writers, filmmakers, and artists who fled Nazi persecution in the 1930s. The only destination left to them, then and as now, is Hollywood; von Braun's visa application has already been skillfully retouched to remove all references to his Nazi past. His role as technical consultant for a film like *Destination Moon* indicates the degree to which space travel and mass entertainment will become linked in the coming decade. Isolated and shimmering in the heat, miles from anywhere, White Sands is the first Dream Factory of the Space Age.

This, however, is the wrong dream at the wrong moment.

*Destination Moon* may be scientifically accurate, but who really cares? The film makes little impact at the box office. Far more successful is *Rocketship X-M*, a cheap copy of *Destination Moon* filmed in the Mojave Desert and Palm Springs then rushed out before the bigger budget film can even get its name up onto the marquees. *Rocketship X-M* also goes one better than its rival by missing the Moon altogether and hitting Mars instead. There the spaceship's crew discovers the remains of an ancient civilization that has destroyed itself with atomic weapons, leaving only a few primitive warlike Martians as a grim warning for mankind. The whole crew may die at the end of the movie, and the meteorites they encounter may have been potatoes wrapped in aluminum foil, but *Rocketship X-M*'s narrative drive and lack of scientific gravitas both prove popular at the box office. The inclusion of "X" in its title doesn't hurt either, echoing as it does *Captain Video*'s X-9 rocket ship and reinforcing memories of the Bell X-1 research plane, piloted by Chuck Yeager through the sound barrier.

"X" also marks the spot where a battered public imagination gives way to the unheard of, the unseen, and the unspeakable. Another successful movie release in 1950 is *The Man from Planet X*; a cautionary tale about a representative from an advanced civilization who comes from outer space to Earth and meets with a hostile reception, it is directed by Austrian émigré Edgar Ulmer.

Meanwhile the new children's television series *Tom Corbett: Space Cadet* can boast Willy Ley as its technical advisor. Cofounder with Hermann Oberth of Germany's prewar Society for Space Travel (Verein für Raumschiffarht) and author of the classic *Rockets, Missiles and Men in Space*, Ley has just finished collaborating with Chesley Bonestell on *The Conquest of Space*, a lavishly illustrated depiction of mankind's technological future that will be cluttering up coffee tables in Suburbia later in the year.

At the same time an expanded version of Donald Keyhoe's *True* magazine article, "The Flying Saucers Are Real," goes into circulation as a Gold Medal paperback. The cover depicts a cluster of classic space ships familiar from science-fiction pulp magazines soaring above the darkened curve of the Earth, projecting strange beams of light. Keyhoe's position hasn't changed any: the Air Force is still covering up its findings on flying saucers. Weird meteorological conditions and skyhook balloons can't explain everything, can they?

Evidently not. In a sober blue-gray dust jacket, depicting a flying saucer so abstract, it is barely more than an innocuous parabola traced by a football through a night sky during the course of a friendly high-school game, Frank Scully's *Behind the Flying Saucers* comes out in hardback. Any resemblance to the safely familiar ends right there, however. The carnival has come to town, and there are plenty of rubes to be found wandering up and down the midway. Expanding upon the claims made in his *Variety* articles from last year, Scully now offers to take his readers around the back of the Flying Saucer Spook House to reveal some of the scams and cons taking place away from the public gaze. Even its title, *Behind the Flying Saucers*, hints at something lurking in plain sight. Things seem to be shifting and rearranging themselves behind the scenes, reminding us that the future is still very much a façade, a piece of stage machinery that constantly needs propping up. However dubious its claims to veracity may be, Scully's book at least points toward some of the props and flats that are currently being lowered into place.

Supposedly based on a lecture given at the University of Denver by millionaire oilman Silas M. Newton, *Behind the Flying Saucers* presents further startling information on the recovery of crashed flying saucers by the United States Air Force, as related by the mysterious "Dr. Gee," who claims to have been brought in to examine both the spaceships and their occupants. As the stage fills with figures from the worlds of higher education, big business, science, and the military, it is often hard to remain focused on who or what is being kept hidden behind the constantly changing scenery. Try not to be distracted by pieces of technical trivia, such as the dimensions of the crashed saucers all being divisible by nine, and keep a close eye on the occupants. This particular spook house is actually an old-fashioned peep show.

The flying saucers, according to Dr. Gee, are piloted by small humanoids, shorter than the average human, and dressed in a style reminiscent of the 1890s. More importantly, their bodily orifices have been taped, and an examination of their mouths reveals that they have perfect teeth, with no decay or fillings whatsoever. In a display of inverted prurience, Dr. Gee's flying-saucer occupants take their place in the evolutionary scheme as something more than human and yet also less so. Like true superior beings, they remain aloof from all physical acts and processes, no longer awash with their own body fluids the way mere humans are. They position themselves above us in the same manner as our grandparents do, Dr. Gee seems to imply, even sharing the same style of costume with them. At the same time, however, they are trapped by their own physicality: the fact that their orifices are taped shut indicates that their true function has merely been repressed, not transcended. His comment on their perfect teeth is a sly wink and a nod toward a barely concealed degree of sexuality in the creatures' appearance. Opening directly onto the world, the mouth is simultaneously the most public and most intimate of cavities, its contents remaining essentially sexual in nature.

Finally, and most damningly, the creatures are shown to be inept and corrupt, their bodies burned and damaged by a crash their superior technological skills were unable to prevent. In short, they are not our superiors but our hypocritical ancestors, caught in a grotesque display of physicality: an old-fashioned burlesque of clumsiness and ineptitude derived from the barely controlled repression of their bodily urges. No wonder the paperback edition of Behind the Flying Saucers dispenses with the homely abstractions of the book's original dust jacket in favor of a far more lurid cover image. Still dressed in their night attire, a frightened crowd of people have taken to the darkened city streets. Men in pajamas and robes point boldly toward the sky while women in clinging wraps and negligees cower in fear. Meanwhile the saucers quietly gather overhead. What happens next is probably best left to the reader's imagination.

Equally alarming, although presenting itself as a far more intellectual exercise, Aldous Huxley's old friend and intellectual collaborator Gerald Heard makes a strong case in The Riddle of the Flying Saucers for flying saucers being under the control of super-intelligent bees from Mars: these being the only creatures capable of piloting the craft at such enormous speeds while still retaining their bodily integrity. Like James Lipp at the RAND Corporation, Heard argues that their attention has been drawn to this planet by our increasing use of atomic weapons. Nuclear blasts on Earth have been known to trigger sunspots according to Heard, which, not unreasonably, may be considered as "warnings of indigestive troubles—as spots on our own face sometimes tell about our deep interior conflicts. Is it not possible that the Martians who have so much to fear from sun trouble may have read these signs?"

Heard's book will later be published under the far more ominous title *Is Another World Watching?* We'll be hearing from Gerald Heard and Dr. Gee again before too long.

Respected psychiatrist and cofounder of the Hebrew University of Jerusalem Immanuel Velikovsky also goes for the bigger galactic picture in the year's surprise best seller, *Worlds in Collision*, in which he describes how a bit of Jupiter broke loose many centuries ago and went careering off around the solar system. It passed close to Earth, Velikovsky asserts, then dallied with Mars before finally settling into solar orbit as the planet we now know as Venus. This erratic celestial behavior subsequently formed the core to most ancient myths and legends, including Greek and Egyptian mythology, plus Old Testament accounts describing pillars of fire and manna being strewn in the desert.

But what happens to our belief systems once gods and planets are brought into such chaotically close proximity to one another? McGraw Hill, the textbook division of MacMillan Publishers who originally brought out *Worlds in Collision*, is forced to withdraw the book when scientists and teachers threaten to boycott all of their other publications unless they do so. Doubleday subsequently rushes out a new edition, which continues to sell in remarkable quantities.

Hermitage House, a small publisher of psychiatric textbooks based in New York, also discovers that it has a runaway success on its hands when the initial print-run of L. Ron Hubbard's *Dianetics: The Modern Science of Mental Health* sells out and the repeat orders start flooding in. What on earth are the boys in the Science Club reading now?

**Chemical Engineering**

*Locked and Loaded*—The September 16 issue of *Publishers' Weekly* makes special mention of a resolution unanimously adopted by the American Psychological Association during the course of their meeting at State College, Pennsylvania, the previous week. "While suspending judgment concerning the eventual validity of the claims made by the author of *Dianetics*," the APA warned its eight thousand members, "the association calls attention to the fact that these claims are not supported by empirical evidence of the sort required for the establishment of scientific generalizations. In the public interest, the association, in the absence of such evidence, recommends to its members that the use of the techniques peculiar to Dianetics be limited to scientific investigations to test the validity of its claims."

With Hermitage House announcing that it has already sold fifty-five thousand copies of Hubbard's book since its publication on May 15, and the September 6 edition of the *Los Angeles Daily News* hailing Dianetics as "the fastest growing 'movement' in the United States," the APA has timed its resolution well. That same month the *Miami News* publishes an article by Edward Hunter entitled "'Brain-Washing' Tactics Force Chinese into Ranks of Communist Party."

This marks the first public use of the term "brainwashing" on record. As with "flying saucers," the concept owes its origins to a newspaper story. Hunter, a CIA propaganda operative working undercover as a journalist, made up the word from the Chinese *hsi-nao*, meaning "to cleanse the mind": an expression that has no specific political connotations in Chinese. With America now battling against the spread of communism in Korea, Hunter offers "brain-washing" as an explanation for the numerous confessions signed by captured American servicemen alleging that the United States is using germ warfare against its enemies. It also helps explain Cardinal Mindszenty's dazed appearance as he gave evidence against himself in a Budapest courtroom, and the self-incriminating confessions delivered in dull monotones by defendants in Soviet "show trials." According to Hunter, brainwashing has the power "to put a man's mind into a fog so that he will mistake what is true for what is untrue, what is right for what is wrong, and come to believe what did not happen actually had happened, until he ultimately becomes a robot for the Communist manipulator."

No wonder the APA has chosen this particular moment to denounce L. Ron Hubbard and his "Modern Science of Mental Health." What they potentially have before them is another crashed saucer. But whereas Dr. Gee discovered our own sexually repressed forebears lying amid the futuristic wreckage, it looks as if the man originally responsible for diagnosing their ills may be the victim this time. In an age of rocket ships and atomic physics, mass communication and mechanical reproduction, the writings of Sigmund Freud are starting to appear increasingly outmoded and outdated, a leftover from the previous century. Which is precisely what they are. By describing the unhappy subject of brainwashing as a "robot," Hunter merely confirms this prognosis.

Dianetics, on the other hand, is first brought to the attention of the reading public in the April issue of *Astounding Science Fiction* magazine, edited by the redoubtable John Campbell Jr. "No stranger adventure appeared in *The Arabian Nights* than Hubbard's experience, using his new techniques, in plowing through the strange jungle of distorted thoughts within a human mind," Campbell writes as a trailer for Hubbard's essay, due to appear in the next issue. "To find, beyond that zone of madness, a computing mechanism of ultimate and incredible efficiency and perfection!"

Is it possible that the implacably rigorous John Campbell Jr., who once rejected a story by Theodore Sturgeon because the fusion of light metals required in the plot was chemically impossible, may really be going for any of this?

"This is no wild theory," Campbell continues. "It is not mysticism. It is a coldly precise engineering description of how the human mind operates and how to go about restoring correct operation tested and used on some 250 cases."

Scientific accuracy is not without its drawbacks, however. Campbell spent a good part of 1944 being questioned by the FBI after *Astounding Science Fiction* published a story by Clive Cartell called "Deadline," which dealt with the development of an atomic bomb. Some of Cartell's descriptions had come a little too close to the Manhattan Project's closely guarded reality for comfort.

Campbell may, as a consequence, feel entitled to hold himself aloof from the likes of Ray Palmer or Frank Scully with their straight-faced appeals to public credulity, but does that necessarily mean he understands the nature of belief better than they do? You can't kid a kidder: anyone on the midway will tell you that. Sometimes it's the practical men of intellect who do the real damage. Albert Einstein himself is reputed to be among *Astounding*'s 150,000 regular readers.

Like Dr. Ewen Cameron of Montreal, Campbell has a fascination with gadgets and gizmos: Hubbard's mechanistic take on the workings of the human mind really appeals to him. Appearing in the May issue of *Astounding* magazine, "'Dianetics': A New Science of the Mind" begins, therefore, by proposing that the human brain functions in a manner very similar to Turing's Universal Machine: that is to say, as a computer with an infinite memory and "perfect function." Furthermore, like Turing's Universal Machine, it can do anything, conferring untold benefits upon its user, such as restoring sanity, establishing total recall, and curing all manner of bodily disease.

However, the mind inevitably becomes disabled by the large amounts of harmful data accumulated and stored from its time spent forming in the womb onward. When promoting his book, Hubbard will later compare this process to that of a "glorified tape recorder that files and retains pain and painful emotions as 'engrams,' and these engrams ... are impressions on cellular protoplasm itself, complete recordings down to the last accurate detail of every perception present in the moment of unconsciousness."

At the same time, the imprints on this protoplasmic tape constitute an individual's "time track": a highly detailed human recording that can be run backward and forward in a process called "auditing" so that harmful engrams can be removed in the same way that recorded sounds are erased or rerecorded by a skilled audio technician. Once these engrams have gone, Hubbard claims, complete recovery of both mental and physical health is absolutely guaranteed. Even missing teeth will grow back again.

As Dr. Gee has already demonstrated: a mouth may lie, but teeth never do. "Are your cavities filling up?" shouts a member of the audience during a Dianetics rally at the Shrine Auditorium in Los Angeles. Held in August at what was once the Al Malaikah Temple, Hubbard's followers fill its 6,500 seats to capacity, spilling out into the aisles in their eagerness to be a part of this new national sensation. *Publishers' Weekly* reports that more than 750 nonprofessional Dianetics groups have already sprung up in Suburbia. Like that other social ritual, the Tupperware party, it's a great way to get to know your new neighbors. While the suburbs continue to grow fifteen times faster than urban or rural communities, and the principal architect of that expansion, William Levitt, looks on benignly from the cover of *Time* magazine, reliving your birth trauma in a state of "Dianetic Reverie" becomes the latest craze.

"It's cheap. It's accessible. It's a public festival to be played at clubs and parties," observes *Look* magazine. "In a country with only 6,000 professional psychiatrists, whose usual consultation fees start at $15 an hour, Hubbard has introduced mass production methods." Freud can definitely take a backseat on this flying-saucer ride: the new model Ford is here. As Dr. Ewen Cameron will fully appreciate, therapy that can be done quickly can also be done economically. With mental health destined to become the next big consumer item, *Look* also notes that Dianetics parties have become a big hit in Hollywood.

The masses, however, are subject to the laws of inertia, needing direction, organization, structure, and, most importantly, inspiration. "Education, medicine, politics and art, indeed all branches of human thought, are clarified by Dianetics," Hubbard remarks to the man from *Look*. "And even so, that is not enough."

With Julius and Ethel Rosenberg arrested for their role in an atomic spy ring accused of passing secrets on to the Soviets, and America involved in a war with North Korea, it's worth recalling the starkly political slant to Edward Hunter's first article on brainwashing. From a behavioral perspective, it seems to imply, all overt ideology is a form of mind control.

Early memos on Chinese brainwashing techniques circulating among the intelligence communities during 1950 indicate a heavy reliance upon group dynamics: teams of interrogators take it in turn to interrogate their subject, repeatedly asking the same questions and scrutinizing every reply for lapses, hesitations, or inconsistencies. This deliberate overloading of the mind inevitably leads to the complete breakdown of the subject: "perfect function," to use one of Hubbard's phrases, is no longer possible. This is a cue for the interrogators to take the subject back along their "time track," removing all ideological "engrams" by reinterpreting every aspect of their lives in terms of Chairman Mao's teachings and precepts.

"Our object in exposing errors and criticizing shortcomings is like that of a doctor curing a disease," Mao himself has observed. "We cannot adopt a brash attitude toward diseases in thought and politics."

On April 20, while readers of *Astounding Science Fiction* eagerly await the first exciting revelations concerning L. Ron Hubbard's "New Science of the Mind," CIA director Roscoe Hillenkoetter approves funding for a hypnosis project, codenamed BLUEBIRD, whose object is to get an individual to do the agency's bidding "against his will and even against such fundamental laws of nature as self-preservation." Within one month of Edward Hunter's use of the term "brainwashing" in print, Project BLUEBIRD's first operations take place in Japan, where twenty-five North Korean POWs are given alternating doses of barbiturates and amphetamines throughout October, then hypnotized and questioned. Allegedly on hand to witness this experiment is Richard Helms, a high-ranking member of the CIA's "dirty tricks" department. At the same time Helms has been fooling around with some of the LSD Allen Dulles brought back with him from Switzerland at the end of World War II. "This stuff is dynamite!" Helms exclaims the first time he tries the drug.

That's an interesting choice of words: people used to be very afraid of dynamite. It has helped to establish a new balance of power in the modern world. More specifically, by linking LSD to explosives, he pushes the mechanistic take on the human mind to its outer limit, turning it into a weapon that can be locked, loaded, aimed, and finally fired. Meanwhile Dr. Werner Stoll publishes his second paper on LSD, entitled "A New Hallucinatory Agent: Active in Very Small Amounts." In their report to the American Psychiatric Association's annual meeting, Drs. Max Rinkel and Robert Hyde present their findings on the drug's efficacy as a "psychotomimetic," able to induce a "transitory psychotic disturbance" in their test subjects, thereby allowing for an objective study of mental disorders and how they affect the "integrity" of the mind.

This consequently seems to be exactly the right time for Norbert Wiener's *The Human Use of Human Beings*, an attempt to explain cybernetics to the general public, to appear in print for the first time. According to Wiener, people interact with machines to form a single entity, thereby opening up a "vast array of human proprioceptive and electrophysiological feedback systems" for examination. The human being is an information processing system; as such, we do not so much reproduce reality as calculate it. Wiener's "self-correcting model," used to describe this process, contrasts sharply with the linear one favored by those who adopt a more mechanistic take on how the mind functions. From the chemical engineers within the CIA and the APA through to the Red Chinese and the groups of excited suburbanites tracing the Dianetic time track back to the moment of their birth, the predominant notion is that the mind can be treated like a machine capable of responding to specific stimuli in a specific manner.

In other words, a technology of the mind is being formulated at exactly the time when we're just starting to ask ourselves whether machines will ever have the potential to think for themselves. In the summer of 1950, volume 59, issue 236 of *Mind* comes out, featuring Alan Turing's groundbreaking essay, "Computing Machinery and Intelligence."

"I propose to consider the question, 'Can machines think?'" the mathematician writes in his prefatory comments. "This should begin with definitions of the meaning of the terms 'machine' and 'think.' The definitions might be framed so as to reflect so far as possible the normal use of the words, but this attitude is dangerous."

No kidding.

"It can potentially do a great deal of harm," writes the former president of the American Psychiatric Association, Brigadier General Will Menninger, in a public denunciation of Hubbard and his new science of the mind. "It is obvious that the mathematician-writer has oversimplified the human personality." This is no small claim coming from a man who once described human consciousness in a newspaper article as "something like a clown act featuring a two-man fake horse."

"Nevertheless," Alan Turing will later write, "I believe that at the end of the century the use of words and general educated opinion will have to be altered so much that one will be able to speak of machines thinking without expecting to be contradicted." Least of all by Richard Helms, L. Ron Hubbard, Edward Hunter, or John Campbell Jr.

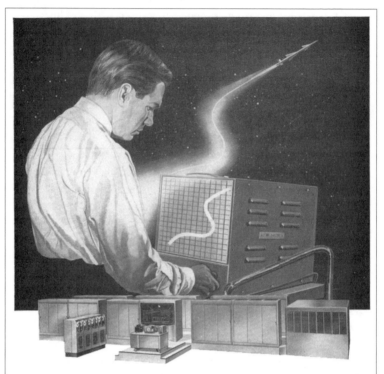

The Univac Scientific Computing System

# Operation in Real-Time . . .

In the field of missile development, there's *only one* commercially available digital computer capable of real-time performance – the famous Univac® Scientific. It's the ideal system for flight simulation and for on-line data reduction. It solves complex problems from purely sensed data at speeds that are compatible with real-time control.

Because of its ability to reduce large volumes of data at tremendous speeds, the Univac Scientific System easily handles even the most difficult research problems. Furthermore, it offers many other outstanding characteristics, including: superb operating efficiency, obtained through large storage capacity . . . great programming versatility . . . the ability to

operate simultaneously with a wide variety of input-output devices . . . and far greater reliability than any computer of its type.

For more information about the Univac Scientific System or for information about ways in which you might apply the system to your particular problems, write on your business letterhead to . . .

ROOM 1315, 315 FOURTH AVE., NEW YORK 10

## *Remington Rand Univac*

DIVISION OF SPERRY RAND CORPORATION

# 1951: ABSOLUTE ELSEWHERE

**First Starring Vehicle**

*Set Up and Pitch*—You are approaching the Earth at several thousand miles per hour. Radar is tracking your spaceship, the newspaper presses are already rolling, and real-life media commentators Elmer Davis, H. V. Kaltenborn, and Drew Pearson have taken to the air, remarking on how normal everything appears today and why there is no need to panic. It is, after all, a lovely spring afternoon out there, and people are taking things easy, enjoying the sights in the nation's capital. The war in Korea seems to be taking place a long way away, and William Levitt has just started work on a second Levittown, this time in Bucks County, Pennsylvania. A carefully zoned suburban development of seventeen thousand homes, complete with its own paved streets, electric lighting, off-street water, sewerage system, telephone and power lines, Levittown, PA, also boasts open greens, sites for public schools and recreation areas, together with five Olympic-sized swimming pools.

With West Coast steel tycoon Henry J. Kaiser also constructing prefabricated living units from fiberglass board, aluminum siding, and sheet gypsum throughout Southern California, production-line homesteads are currently being knocked out at a dizzying national rate of one every fifteen minutes. So what can possibly be wrong with this picture? Plenty, if you're Klaatu arriving on Earth for the first time, bringing a flying saucer in to land on the bustling Washington Mall, right by the baseball diamond, directly opposite the White House itself. You come bearing a message of peace to the world and a gift for President Truman, but you don't get very far. In fact, you're barely down the ramp of your spaceship before you've been shot in the arm by some jittery GI with an itchy trigger finger.

In case you hadn't guessed which movie you're in, this is Twentieth Century Fox's *The Day the Earth Stood Still*, and things haven't gotten off to a particularly good start. To begin with, the soldier who just wounded you isn't the only one with the jitters this fine spring afternoon. On April 11, President Truman will announce that General

Douglas MacArthur is no longer Allied Commander of the UN forces in Korea after he threatens to split from the civilian leadership and start attacking Red China. General MacArthur has, in fact, already made his intentions quite plain in the March 24 issue of the *New York Times*, pointing out China's weaknesses "even under inhibitions which now restrict activity of the United Nations forces and the corresponding military advantages which accrue to Red China." The Gravity Research Foundation in New Boston, New Hampshire, notes that MacArthur's dismissal occurs during "a dark phase of the moon," affecting the planet's entire gravitational profile. Founded in 1949 to discover a means of countering the forces of gravity, the foundation has established itself in New Boston for fear that Boston itself will be targeted for major destruction during World War III.

All the same, who'd want to be Klaatu? While recovering from his shooting in a military hospital, he asks the Secretary to the President to convene a meeting of all the world's leaders. No can do, the Secretary replies, the current Cold War climate makes your request impossible. "I'm less cynical about the Earth's politics than you are," Klaatu remarks haughtily in the face of this diplomatic rebuff. Mr. Secretary makes no reply to this, but the look he gives this visitor from another world speaks volumes. "Yeah," it seems to say, "but *I'm* not the one who just got shot."

The Secretary can't take everything away from him, though. Klaatu has at least done one thing that no one else in mainstream popular culture has achieved so far: he's successfully managed to land a flying saucer on American soil. After a frustrating series of flybys, crashes, and near misses, this is still a pretty big deal. The superior technology on Klaatu's home planet also means that he lives longer and is healthier than his terrestrial counterparts.

"He was very nice about it," one Army doctor remarks to another as they prepare to enjoy the rich full flavor you can only get with an unfiltered, high-tar cigarette, "but he made me feel like a third-class witchdoctor."

No wonder Klaatu decides not to bother with the educated ruling elite and goes out among the ordinary people instead. Once again, however, he doesn't seem to get very far. For all its global rhetoric, the entire action of *The Day the Earth Stood Still* takes place within a few city blocks of the Washington Monument. Aside from an occasional taxi ride, Klaatu travels everywhere on foot, dressed in a comfortable lounge suit stolen from the hospital. Who, after all, is going to notice a man in gray flannel on the streets of the nation's capital? Like the film in which he appears, Klaatu is obsessed with power, not people. Everything he says and does makes open reference to it. He didn't set his spaceship down opposite the White House by accident.

Nothing is as it seems in this movie. If power is its main theme, then the hot metal presses, switchboards, radio receivers, and television sets it depicts are the real stars. While newspapers run the headline "Man from Mars Escapes" and the electronic media warn the public that "this is not another flying-saucer scare," Klaatu wanders in off the street only to be confronted by what appears to be the fairly normal sight of a family gathered together around the TV. It's not in the least bit normal, however. Hollywood science fiction does not respond particularly well to the glowing tube, the inhabitants of Earth being more likely to receive their messages from outer space via radio than television. Klaatu isn't in a family home but a rooming house on a busy Washington street. Its occupants are little more than a mismatched set of prejudices and opinions, making jokes about the Democrats at the breakfast table and commenting loudly on the news. In a year when a survey reveals that most married women want an average of four or five children, the nearest thing to a family here is Mrs. Benson, an attractive war widow, and her young son Bobby. Mrs. Benson also happens to work as a secretary in a federal government office and is played by steely Patricia Neal, last seen in King Vidor's overblown adaptation of Ayn Rand's *The Fountainhead*, dropping a sculpted marble head of the Greek god Mercury down an airshaft so she "wouldn't have to love it." Klaatu may not know much about ordinary people, but he can spot power from low Earth orbit.

It is through Bobby and Mrs. Benson that Klaatu gets to meet Professor Bernhardt. A leading physicist with a European accent and close links to the scientific community around the world, is Bernhardt everything he appears to be? To admit to internationalist leanings in 1951 is tantamount to branding yourself a card-carrying member of the Communist Party. Just two years previously, a number of delegates from Europe and Central America were denied visas to attend a Cultural and Scientific Conference for World Peace at New York's Waldorf Astoria while over two thousand red-blooded Americans gathered outside to protest the event. Who, in the end, is Bernhardt working for: the American government or the rest of the world?

That the question of the professor's ultimate allegiance is left open should come as no real surprise at a time when a whole new order of nuclear weapons is being brought into secret being. Known so far only as "the Super," the Hydrogen Bomb promises to change the entire nature of warfare and politics, charting both against a global grid that will inevitably touch everyone on the planet.

James Lipp, having advised the Air Force on how flying saucers might have been attracted to the Earth by its recent atomic detonations, is now asked to join a select group of analysts at RAND determining the strategic implications of the Hydrogen Bomb. These deliberations only take place, however, after the AEC grants the Santa Monica corporation "Q" clearance, allowing access to all its latest research. Lipp and his colleagues are soon laying out great circles on maps of the world, plotting the blast radiuses of explosions that are being calculated for the first time in megatons. Joining RAND at this time is Albert Wohlstetter, whose modernist approach to prefabricated home design has failed to produce any dwellings that come up to California code, forcing him to close his company, despite the current suburban building boom. A better mathematical logician than he is a businessman, Wohlstetter soon becomes deeply involved in calculating the emergent economics of "kill probability" in the nuclear age.

As Klaatu surveys the figures and formulae neatly arranged in chalk across the blackboard in Professor Bernhardt's study, it quickly becomes clear how numbers have come to represent power in the second half of the twentieth century. So far the "Teller-Ulam design" for a Hydrogen Bomb remains nothing more than a complex set of calculations. Its very feasibility, however, prompts only one response from the defense analysts. As the creation of an actual Hydrogen Bomb comes within reach, the game theorists at RAND and the Pentagon must assume that the Russians can also make one. "I think," remarks John von Neumann in November 1951, having helped plot the mathematics of nuclear chain reaction with Stanislaw Ulam at Los Alamos, "that the USA-USSR conflict will very probably lead to an armed 'total' collision, and that a maximum rate of armament is therefore imperative."

Numbers ultimately have loyalty only to themselves: to determine their feasibility is merely to express the range of possible responses to them. "Father of the Atom Bomb" J. Robert Oppenheimer, now head of the AEC's General Advisory Committee, is strongly opposed to Edward Teller's idea of developing weapons as powerful as the H-Bomb. In the autumn of 1951 he becomes involved in a Caltech study codenamed Project VISTA. Its stated aim is to "bring the battle back to the battlefield," thereby avoiding the use of such devices against civilian populations. In a year when Ethel and Julius Rosenberg are found guilty of passing on atomic secrets to the Russians, Oppenheimer's participation in Project VISTA raises some serious questions over where his own true loyalties may lie.

Perhaps a more revealing clue to Professor Bernhardt's character is the photograph of Sigmund Freud hanging on his study wall. Evidently more concerned with psychology than physics, Bernhardt is less interested in the nature of power than in its effects. While readily agreeing to arrange a world symposium of scientists to be held in Washington, he also impresses upon Klaatu the need to make a clear show of strength if he ever hopes to get anybody's attention around here. No problem, replies Klaatu. At noon the following day all the electricity is shut down throughout the world, and Klaatu finally gets his chance to address an international congregation of scientists assembled right outside his flying saucer.

First the good news: developing nuclear weapons gets you noticed. Klaatu, ever alert to the effects of power, is worried that the human race might "apply atomic energy to spaceships" and take its petty political squabbles out into an otherwise peaceful cosmos. Rather than making us feel chastened, however, this is cause for some celebration. The ability to develop a Hydrogen Bomb puts us on the same level, if on a slightly diminished scale, with the rest of the universe. It also means we've arrived: we're now in the future.

The bad news is that we're also subject to the laws of the universe, enforced by a race of giant robots just like the one Klaatu has brought with him. Standing eight feet tall and armed with a highly destructive light beam, Gort can melt tanks, reduce guns to luminescent blobs, and has the power of life and death over everyone around him. In fact, Klaatu's own race is also subject to Gort's iron rule, which suggests they can't be that much more spiritually advanced than we are if they need to have a cop like him around to keep them in line.

"Gort has absolute power over us," confirms Klaatu. "There's nothing he can't do."

Except for one thing: capable only of reacting to the world around him, unable to do anything under his own will or volition, Gort is not an ideal candidate for the Turing Test. Outlined in his essay "Computing Machinery and Intelligence," this is a simple question and answer game designed by Turing as a means to distinguish machine thought processes from human ones.

Gort may not be able to pass for human any time soon, but he is still everything the free market is looking for in a machine right now. UNIVAC I, America's first commercial computer, has recently gone on sale. Built by Remington Rand, the UNIVAC I's first customer is the United States Census Bureau, which takes delivery in March 1951, just as Klaatu is touching down on the Washington Mall. UNIVAC stands for UNIVersal Automatic Computer, a designation that links it directly back to the behavioral formula Turing devised for his Universal Machine, which is to replicate the behavior of any other machine in existence. Having manufactured everything in its long history from typewriters and electric shavers to handguns and rifles, Remington Rand has this pretty much covered. They aren't the only ones to see the computer's potential as a new form of weapons system, however.

"The IBM electronic tube assembly cuts through the unknown like a rocket through the stratosphere," runs ad copy put out in 1951 by one of Remington Rand's biggest rivals. "It probes the mysteries of the atom's core; predicts critical wing flutter of fast aircraft; traces paths of light through a lens system; calculates trajectories of guided missiles; plots the course of planets for the navigator ... IBM Electronic Business Machines are vital defense weapons in the hands of our nation's industrial engineers and scientists...." While Herman Kahn, one of the physicists working at the Lawrence Livermore National Laboratory on developing the H-Bomb under Teller's direction, ties up all twelve of the high-speed computers currently operating in the United States to complete his calculations, John von Neumann designs a new computer to help run such complicated mathematics even more rapidly. He also suggests that his new Mathematical Analyzer Numerical Integrator and Computer be known simply as MANIAC for short. Looks as if Gort really has arrived on Earth after all.

**Second Starring Vehicle**

*Set Up and Pitch*—"It sounds like, well, as if you were describing some form of super carrot," the newsman remarks, suddenly uncertain of his footing. "Nearly right, Mr. Scott," the scientist briskly replies. "This 'carrot' as you call it constructed an aircraft capable of flying some millions of miles through space, propelled by a force as yet unknown to us."

This inspired exchange is from Howard Hawks's *The Thing from Another World*, released the same year as *The Day the Earth Stood Still*. From the Earth to another world is not so great a distance, after all. Both films are based on stories written by editors of *Astounding Science Fiction*, the magazine that brought you L. Ron Hubbard's first declarations on Dianetics. These fictions represent a different order of experience, however. *The Day the Earth Stood Still* is an adaptation of "Farewell to the Master" by former editor Harry Bates and first published in 1940. *The Thing from Another World* is a reworking of "Who Goes There?" written by John Campbell Jr. in 1938, five months before he assumed editorship of the magazine. As such, they refer to a view of the universe and an imagination that has effectively ceased to exist since the events of 1947. The titles alone make this clear: "Farewell to the Master" refers to a power relationship that is in the process of disappearing, while "Who Goes There?" echoes a military challenge originally heard outside the earliest of armed encampments.

As if to make up for this lapse in time and perspective, the scores to both films make heavy use of the Theremin. Its eerie otherworldly tones, as heard on *Music Out of the Moon*, have more recently been featured in Hitchcock's *Spellbound*, *The Fountainhead*, and *Rocketship X-M*. The inclusion of the Theremin on the soundtracks for such films indicates that a specific shift in perceptions has taken place. This is particularly true of *The Day the Earth Stood Still*, where Klaatu's identity is deliberately left open to interpretation. At one specific point in the film we see Klaatu inside his spaceship operating its controls by moving his hands in empty space, just as if he were playing a Theremin. His ability to control the entire planet's power supply by invisible means also links him in the popular imagination to visionary Serbian inventor Nikola Tesla, the originator of AC electricity. Able to interact and converse with it in a language that only he and Gort seem to understand, Klaatu speaks to the invisible new order of the atomic age.

This is not to say that Klaatu's advanced knowledge can't also be interpreted as primarily of a spiritual nature. His emotional continence throughout the film, his death and resurrection toward its conclusion, and his closing message of peace carry strong Christian overtones. He even assumes the name of Carpenter, the original owner of the suit stolen from the Army hospital, in order to walk among humanity. However, it's also worth noting that the garment's original owner was a Major Carpenter, a military man, and that Klaatu's warning to the world's scientists to "live in peace—or else" sounds more like America's current nuclear strategy than the words of a loving god.

Not that you would make that kind of mistake while watching *The Thing from Another World*. There's nothing so ambiguous about this visitor from outer space: an entity so basic it is never even dignified with a name. He may, like Klaatu, be referred to in passing as a "Man from Mars," but that's about as far as it goes. "An intellectual carrot," Scotty the newsman marvels out loud. "The mind boggles."

If man is the measure of all things out here, what scale or domain does that leave for our monsters? And what sense of uniformity is imposed upon us as a consequence?

An entire evolutionary agenda becomes manifest. Once Hollywood finally starts catching up with this newly emergent mythology, versions of it would turn up again and again in the form of remote-controlled slaves, cosmic mutants, brute men, robots, and various assorted space creatures. Between Klaatu and the Thing a whole range of possibilities opens up: from beings of advanced intellect, who quickly become identified with a subtle form of programming, to those of a highly developed instinct, which is essentially a form of programming determined by the environment.

To emphasize this latter possibility, the "intellectual carrot" finds himself trapped at the North Pole, a region not normally conducive to vegetable life, with his flying saucer stuck firmly under the ice. Like many who have gone before him, the Thing has proved to be incapable of successfully landing his spaceship, making Klaatu's achievement all the more remarkable. The human beings he encounters amid the frozen Arctic plains aren't any better: they only manage to blow the spaceship to pieces while trying to recover it, forever stranding him in this bleak inhospitable world.

In Campbell's original novella, the Thing didn't need to develop a specific identity, due to his ability to transform himself into any living being he chose. He was no one precisely because he could become anyone. Little more than a smart predator with a finely honed instinct for survival in Hawks's version, the Thing now has a professional elite ready to do that for him. The scientist quoted earlier, Nobel Laureate Professor Carrington, admires the fact that the creature's development is not handicapped by any emotional or sexual distractions. But as Carrington is also "the fellow who was at Bikini," where the United States carried out its first atomic tests in the Marshall Islands in 1946, it's a pretty safe bet that his enthusiasm is misplaced.

*The Thing from Another World* is first and foremost an Air Force movie, made at a time when more and more pilots admit to seeing UFOs. This includes future Mercury project astronauts Major Gordon Cooper and Donald Slayton. Even the USAF's own newly formed Air Technical Intelligence Centre has had it with UFO reports. "One of these days," an ATIC officer is quoted as saying, "all of those crazy pilots will kill themselves, the crazy people on the ground will be locked up, and there won't be any more flying saucer reports."

The statement has a direct bearing on the crazy pilots of the US aircrew stranded at the North Pole with a bunch of scientists, trying to defend themselves from a rampaging, inarticulate space monster with a taste for human blood. Their only guide on how to proceed is a USAF directive reminding them that all UFO sightings are to be dismissed as "misinterpretation, mild hysteria or a joke." This sideways dig at Project GRUDGE comes at a time when *Life*'s Robert Ginna is discovering, to his mounting frustration, that every question he asks regarding UFOs either sends their representative out of the room to check his files or is met with a blunt and simple "I'm sorry, that's classified."

If you're managing to annoy *Life* magazine, you know you're probably doing something very wrong indeed. "That's the Air Force for you," newsman Scotty remarks. "Smart all the way to the top."

The scientists aren't much help this time either. Their talk of magnetometers, compass spins, and Geiger counter readings leaves Air Force captain Kenneth Tobey and his crew none the wiser. "You lost me," Tobey remarks after another of Professor Carrington's attempts to explain the situation. Establishing a chain of command that goes "all the way to the top" with a space monster on the loose can't be that easy for anyone. "Who will Truman ask when it gets to him?" Scotty remarks in a sarcastic aside. Well, it won't be General MacArthur, that's for sure.

At the same time, there's something strangely familiar about this Arctic terrain. For the glaring, wide-open spaces of the North Pole, read the Nevada Proving Grounds located in a stretch of desert sixty-five miles from Las Vegas, the White Sands rocketry ranges in New Mexico, and the dry lakebeds of Southern California, where air bases and runways proliferate. Whatever the guys at Project VISTA may think, these are the new battlefields of the twentieth century, where the boundaries of physical science are being pushed back in splendid isolation. Taking place during the latter part of 1951, Operation Ranger tests the airborne dropping of atomic devices in the Nevada desert, raising mushroom clouds that are visible one hundred miles away in Las Vegas. Operation Buster Jangle carries out a similar series of tests in the presence of over 6,500 soldiers positioned barely six miles away from ground zero.

These are dangerous, unregulated spaces and represent a scale of thinking so vast that it begins to play havoc with the senses. Ultimately they join with the sky at an invisible horizon, reflecting back its boundless extent. Not surprising then that, at the end of the movie, Scotty doesn't warn the world of what's happening on land, but what lies above it instead. "And now before giving you the details of the battle," he announces to the world once the monster is dead, "I bring you a warning. Every one of you listening to my voice ... tell the world, tell this to everybody wherever they are ... watch the skies, everywhere, keep looking, keep watching the skies!"

Holding a microphone up to his mouth, Scotty is addressing a radio audience, which constitutes Hollywood's conception of the masses in sci-fi movies at this time. This is, after all, an RKO Radio Picture, whose logo features a huge broadcasting antenna located at the very top of the globe: precisely where Scotty is when he issues this famous warning.

But for whom are his words really intended?

Project GRUDGE is currently being staffed by a couple of Air Force Reservists returned to active duty following the outbreak of the Korean War. In an effort to regain credibility with ATIC, they begin to take a keener interest in seriously investigating the unexplained sightings. By the end of 1951 one of the two captains, Edward J. Ruppelt, will start reviewing all previous case histories. It was Captain Ruppelt to whom the ATIC officer was speaking when he made his irate comment about "all of those crazy pilots." Ruppelt will be spending a lot of time watching the skies from now on.

It seems right and proper that Scotty should have the last word. Like the airmen and scientists in this movie, he's just doing his job, after all. Or is he? There's a moment in the film, a brief exchange between Scotty and the airmen, that tends to get overlooked. Initially forbidden from filing a story, he resorts to taking photographs instead. Watching as they prepare to electrocute the Thing from Another World, camera in hand, he is suddenly troubled by a memory from the murky past. "This reminds me of my first execution ...," he murmurs.

"Did you take a picture then?" someone asks.

"No, they didn't allow cameras," Scotty replies, "but there was one guy...." Even though the rest of his sentence remains unspoken, Scotty's line of thought isn't too hard to follow. In 1927 Ruth Mary Snyder and her lover Henry Judd Gray died within minutes of each other in the electric chair at Sing Sing Correctional Facility having both been found guilty of murdering her husband. This particular execution became infamous, thanks to an ingenious newsman who snapped a picture of Ruth Snyder at the moment of her death with a hidden camera strapped to his ankle. The reason Scotty doesn't finish recounting his memory of the incident, however, is that he knows history is about to repeat itself: Ethel and Julius Rosenberg, the atomic spies, are also currently awaiting execution in Sing Sing. Sentenced in April 1951, as Klaatu's flying saucer streaks away from a supposedly united Earth, the couple are scheduled to die at sundown in the same electric chair within minutes of each other. In some unconscious act of clemency, Scotty forgets to photograph the alien's death agonies at the moment the switch is thrown.

**Third Starring Vehicle**

*Set Up and Pitch*—A giant comet, known to despondent astronomers throughout the world as Bellus, is about to smash into Earth, killing everyone upon it. The only way to escape this fate is to load up a rocket with a handful of our brightest and best and blast off for the planet Zyra before it's too late. Stuck with a talky script and an unexceptional cast, George Pal's *When Worlds Collide* is a big and timely concept that ultimately has to rely on its special effects to make a point. Consequently, a tidal wave destroys New York, thereby earning the film an Oscar, while the planet Zyra appears to have been created entirely at the Walt Disney studios.

Following on from Velikovsky's *Worlds in Collision*, published the previous year, *When Worlds Collide* is not really all that concerned with people. To speak of other worlds is to place limits on your own. *When Worlds Collide* extends the suburban exodus out into space: from an overcrowded and imperfect Earth to the wide-open, rural paradise of Zyra. The last surviving members of the human race step out from their rocket ship, half expecting to be greeted by bluebirds. The process by which these survivors are selected, however, points toward some disturbing trends in the prevailing culture. The question of who is allowed into the safety of the suburban bunker and who gets left outside becomes an interesting one at a time when William Levitt has a strict policy of not selling his homes to "Negroes."

A whole universe separates "different" from "alien." In 1951, George Reeves appears on TV for the first time as Superman: the "strange visitor from another planet, who comes to Earth with powers and abilities far beyond those of mortal men." Running contrary to the suburban migration out toward Zyra described in *When Worlds Collide*, Superman comes to Earth as a tiny baby aboard a rocket ship: the sole survivor of the total destruction of planet Krypton.

He couldn't have picked a better time to be going on television, however. In 1951, fans of *Captain Video* are encouraged to join the Video Rangers Club and to buy an increasingly wide range of *Captain Video* merchandise, including helmets, toy rockets, games, and records. Television supplies children with their absolute elsewhere. Life in the suburban home will soon be unthinkable without it. *Captain Video* also attracts large sponsors in the form of Skippy Peanut Butter and Post Cereals, thereby transforming the show into a controlled environment for its young consumers. From the living room, where the first TV remote controls are starting to dominate a progressively open-plan layout, to the endless ranks of supermarket shelves, merchandising exerts an influence as powerful as any Chinese mind control technique. While giving testimony before Senator Estes Kefauver's subcommittee on the connection between television violence and juvenile delinquency, actor Al Hodge, who is currently playing Captain Video on TV, notes that he is never required to use the word "kill" on the show.

There will be plenty of time for that later. Popular culture and scientific endeavor are both shaped by the same forces: it's not so much that one influences the other, but that they are both derived from the same set of social parameters.

"I don't like fooling around with drugs," complains gangster Raymond Burr in the 1951 thriller *His Kind of Woman*. "Something's liable to go wrong."

The German scientist he has hired to pump Robert Mitchum full of an experimental truth serum developed by the Nazis sounds far more ebullient about the prospect.

"He will be unconscious immediately," the doctor confidently declares. "And when he comes to he won't remember a thing. Nothing. His brain will be gone completely."

"Are you positive there is no chance of failure?" Burr persists.

"Absolutely positive."

A CIA memo issued on October 21, 1951, assessing a wide range of potential truth drugs asserts that: "There is no question that drugs are already on hand (and new ones being produced) that can destroy integrity and make indiscreet the most dependable individual." Among the drugs being tested are morphine, ether, mescaline, and, making its first appearance in a Central Intelligence Agency report, LSD.

That same year Project BLUEBIRD is renamed ARTICHOKE, and the agency's new director, General Walter Bedell Smith, approves closer cooperation with the Army, Navy, and Air Force in the development of interrogation techniques.

ARTICHOKE's experimental subjects include suspected double agents, people with "a known reason for deception," American college students, and foreigners. The subjects are hypnotically regressed and made to relive past experiences. Posthypnotic suggestions are then given to erase all memory of their interrogation. "We're now convinced that we can maintain a subject in a controlled state for a much longer period of time than we heretofore had believed possible," asserts an ARTICHOKE memo, dated November 26. "Furthermore, we feel that by use of certain chemicals or combinations, we can, in a very high percentage of cases, produce relevant information."

Turning someone's brain to lard using hypnosis in combination with a wide range of drugs is one thing. Getting them to divulge useful or coherent information under such circumstances is quite another matter. Chemicals that "destroy integrity of personality" also tend to leave test subjects in neither the condition nor the mood to reveal anything they might know. Early experiments reveal that the effects of LSD in particular are unpredictable at best.

"In the LSD test situation," complains Max Rinkel at the 1951 American Psychiatric Association Convention in Cincinnati, "subjects appeared more interested in their own feelings and inner experiences than in interacting with the examiner, confirming behaviorally the test results which indicated increased self-centeredness."

It is possible, of course, that such self-preoccupation serves as a basic defense against the controlled environment, whether it takes the form of a clinical trial in a laboratory, a supervised interrogation in a holding cell, or an average evening spent in a suburban lounge. Increased self-centeredness becomes your final refuge, where few are prepared to follow. The moment they decide to come in after you is when worlds really start to collide. On May 14, L. Ron Hubbard writes a long letter to the Department of Justice in Washington accusing communist infiltrators of derailing his work in Dianetics and undermining his business, thereby ensuring that information vital to the US government is suppressed.

"In August 1950 I found out a method the Russians use on such people as Vogeler, Mindszenty and others to obtain confessions," he confides at one point. "I could undo that method. My second book was to have shown how the Communists used narco-synthesis and physical torture and why it worked as it did. Further, I was working on a technology of psychological warfare to present it to the Defense Department. All that work was interrupted."

A further setback occurs in 1951 when Dr. Joseph A. Winter resigns as medical advisor to the Dianetics Foundation after Hubbard's discovery of GUK, a chemical agent thought to facilitate auditing. The compound's acronymic title suggests it might possibly share some properties with LSD; but its actual content, described by Dr. Winter as "a haphazard mixture of vitamins and glutamic acid" indicates otherwise. Even Hubbard himself has to admit that GUK is "dreadful stuff," comparing it with "what the soldiers used to clean their rifle barrels." As a consequence, GUK's potential remains largely untested. "There were no adequate controls set up for this experiment," Dr. Winter complains following his departure from the Dianetics Foundation, "and it was a dismal, expensive failure."

As if to make up for such lost opportunities, Canada's Defence Research Board hosts a meeting at the Ritz-Carlton Hotel on June 1 with representatives of the CIA and British Intelligence to swap information on mind control and interrogation techniques. Also present is Dr. Donald Hebb, chairman of psychology at McGill University and author of *The Organization of Behavior*. Established in 1947 to coordinate Cold War defense initiatives, the DRB is already funding Hebb's experiments in sensory deprivation.

"All that we can know about another's feelings and awareness," Hebb has remarked on the enigma of human thought, "is an inference from what he does—from his muscular contractions and glandular secretions." Sensory deprivation is a way of turning a subject's increased self-centeredness back on himself by reducing his controlled environment to nothing. To this end, Hebb proposes an experiment "whereby an individual might be placed in a situation ... in which, by means of cutting off all sensory stimulation save some minor propioceptive sensations and by the use of 'white noise,' the individual could be led into a situation whereby ideas etc. might be implanted."

By encasing their limbs in cardboard tubes and with the aid of diffused light and headphones, Hebb hopes to take a number of student volunteers from his department below the level of perception for a twenty-four-hour period. Some start to hallucinate, imagining that they see spaceships. Others can't complete the experiment, giving up after only a few hours. Part of the procedure is to suggest to the test subjects when they are in a susceptible state of sensory withdrawal that they become interested in occult matters. Messages supporting the existence of ghosts, ESP, and psychic phenomena are also piped in to them via their headphones. When a significant proportion of test subjects start checking out books on such subjects from the university library, Hebb has a disturbing moment of realization.

"It is one thing to hear that the Chinese are brainwashing their prisoners on the other side of the world," he later remarks of his experiment. "It is another to find in your own laboratory, that merely taking away the usual sights, sounds and bodily contacts from a healthy university student for a few days can shake him, right down to the base."

At least a world in collision is one that you're suddenly aware of, even when its dimensions are limited to a sense of increased self-centeredness. "I don't care about the rest of the world," Patricia Neal's no-good fiancé replies in *The Day the Earth Stood Still* after she accuses him of acting selfishly at a time when the "rest of the world is involved." No matter what Professor Bernhardt may have to say on the matter, this is a sentiment echoed by Kenneth Tobey in *The Thing from Another World* after he's accused of not comprehending the wider implications of what is happening at the top of the world. "I'm not working for the world," he crisply retorts, inadvertently admitting a little more than he probably intended. "I'm working for the Air Force."

# Moon Farms

MI artist Frank Tinsley has designed this saucer-shaped space farm. Growing tubes are concentrically arranged on the upper deck; drying and collecting equipment, storage bins, living quarters, etc., are in the shallow bowl beneath. A solar power plant (Sept. '53 MI) is set above the saucer, generates current to operate auxiliary mechanisms. Electric eyes coupled to servo gyroscopes keep both reflector and deck continually facing the sun. Air locks give access to a deck for inspection and maintenance. Each plastic trough is maintained as independent unit. Every day a space cargo ship makes contact with the tubular dock in the satellite's belly to milk it of its produce and transport it to earth.

72

FRANK TINSLEY '54

# 1952: RED PLANET

**Flying Saucers over Washington**

*Guides and Messengers*—At any other period in human history this might have seemed the most apocalyptic of times. Whichever way you look at it, 1952 is filled with signs and portents indicating strange beginnings and violent ends: events that wouldn't have looked out of place in some ancient alchemic text. It begins with an unexpected and heavy snowfall in Algeria. There are also reports of freak storms and record-breaking amounts of rainfall throughout the world. Surgeons successfully separate Siamese twins for the first time, while an old king dies and a new queen is named in the United Kingdom. It is also the year in which New York newspapers run headline stories describing how "Ex-GI" George Jorgensen Jr. becomes "Blond Beauty" Christine Jorgensen after undergoing the first sex-change operation in Denmark.

Despite such vast and troubling images out of *Spiritus Mundi*, the world doesn't quite end in 1952, although it won't be for want of trying.

"Disks, cylinders and similar objects of geometrical shape have been and may now be present in the atmosphere of Earth," runs one account written and published during the course of this troubling year. "Globes of green fire also, of a brightness more intense than the full Moon's, have frequently passed through the skies … These objects cannot be explained by present science as natural phenomena—but solely as artificial devices, created and developed by a high intelligence."

This quote isn't from Ray Palmer's *Fate*: it's actually from the April 7 issue of Henry Luce's *Life* magazine. After months of resistance and stalling from the guys at Project GRUDGE, *Life*'s Robert Ginna has finally gotten his story. What makes "Have We Visitors from Space?" so dark and disturbing, however, is not the fact that Ginna has managed to find a few high-ranking Air Force officers in the Pentagon prepared to admit they think flying saucers come from outer space. It's that they are prepared to do so in the pages of *Life* magazine: a publication so established and safe that it recently featured a picture of President

Truman wearing a Hawaiian shirt on its cover. What does this tell us about the American Century, a historically charged concept that Henry Luce himself is responsible for framing and propagating? Never mind that Kenneth Arnold and Ray Palmer are publishing *The Coming of the Saucers* together this year, or that Donald Keyhoe is bringing out his second book, *Flying Saucers from Outer Space*. *Life* has German rocket scientist Dr. Walter Riedel and leading aerodynamicist Dr. Maurice A. Boit both declaring in print their firm conviction that flying saucers are extraterrestrial in origin. "Answers may come in a generation—or tomorrow," the article concludes ominously. "Somewhere in the dark skies there may be those who know."

With Project GRUDGE succumbing to mission creep, unexplained sightings are on the increase again. Now under the sole directorship of Captain Ruppelt, GRUDGE undergoes yet another change of name and direction, becoming Project BLUE BOOK, a designation it will retain for the rest of this decade and beyond. Ruppelt has also requested a change in Air Force regulations in order to speed up the communication of sightings through official channels. This won't in any way alter the fact that all such investigations take place after the fact, but at least the process will no longer involve delays of anything up to two or three months from the time of the initial sighting.

Ruppelt's procedural innovations reflect a concern not so much with what has been seen but with the fact that it has been reported. A cultural mechanism is created in that first moment of contact: a complex arrangement of individual parts and forces that start to work against each other. Ruppelt gives precise form to this contradiction by introducing a standardized questionnaire in which the specific details of each individual sighting can be recorded. Everything from the position of the sun or moon relative to the object seen through to atmospheric conditions and exact geographic location now become objects of an orderly inquiry. "Did the object disappear while you were watching it?" it asks at one point. "If so, how?"

As Alfred Kinsey has demonstrated with *Sexual Behavior in the Human Male*, the virtue of a standardized questionnaire is that quantitative data concerning a wide range of experiences can be processed, compared, and tabulated with greater facility. Furthermore, by unifying this material for the purposes of collation and analysis, it permits such a diversity to be presented as a broad behavioral spectrum. "Have you ever seen this or a similar object before?" Ruppelt's questionnaire also asks. "If so, give date or dates and location."

In adopting this approach, Ruppelt is acknowledging that each sighting is unique, that flying saucers no longer constitute a single phenomenon but a continuous range of objects and impressions that grows over time. The more people you ask, the more accurate a statistical picture of what exactly is going on will emerge. Aided by his questionnaire, Kinsey has amassed case histories running into the tens of thousands for precisely this reason. At the same time, rendering each experience as a collection of statistical tropes ultimately deprives it of its uniqueness. "In order that you can give as clear a picture as possible of what you saw," the BLUE BOOK questionnaire politely requests, "describe in your own words a common object or objects which, when placed up in the sky, would give the same appearance as the object which you saw." The individual declaration that "I know what I saw" is ultimately stripped of its individuality. Thanks to Ruppelt's questionnaire, it becomes a report instead.

The origin of Ruppelt's strategy dates back to the previous spring when he was investigating the "Lubbock Lights," a particularly striking aerial manifestation glimpsed by a large number of eyewitnesses in Texas. Ruppelt found himself confronted by a huge amount of testimony from reliable sources, including ranchers, astronomers, college professors, and amateur cameramen.

"On the way to Dayton," he later recalls, "I figured out a plan of attack on the thousands of notes I'd taken. All of them seemed to be dependent upon each other for importance. If the objects that were reported in several of the incidents could be identified, the rest would merely become average UFO reports."

In this strategic shift from individual declaration to standardized report, a procedural paradox is brought about. The distinction between the lone amateur and the professional organization grows increasingly blurred even as it is formalized. The ultimate truth or reality of the encounter is quickly lost. In the case of the Lubbock Lights, the results of Ruppelt's "plan of attack" remain inconclusive at best.

"Why not just simply believe that most people know what they saw?" an unnamed Air Force colonel asks Ruppelt in June 1952 after reviewing eyewitness accounts of sightings as refracted through the pages of his questionnaire. Ruppelt fails to make an adequate reply to the colonel's question. As a consequence, astronomer Donald H. Menzel can argue that flying saucers are the result of atmospheric anomalies in the June 17 issue of *Look* under the title "The Truth about Flying Saucers," while the personal testimony of Dr. Clyde Tombaugh, the man responsible for finally discovering Pluto lurking on the outer reaches of our solar system, is announced on the cover of *Fate* as "World-Famed Astronomer Sees Flying Saucer." At the same time Ruppelt institutionalizes Project GRUDGE's practice of referring to flying saucers as "Unidentified Flying Objects," as the former term "seems to represent weird stories, hoaxes, etc."

The problem with the truly unidentified, however, is that it tends to remain unidentified. Just before midnight on July 19, 1952, after a hot and humid day in Washington, radar screens at Air Route Traffic Control start picking up a series of fast-moving unidentified objects. Pilots and members of the public also begin calling in reports of weird lights and fireballs in the sky. Sightings will continue throughout the following week, resulting in a monthly total for July twice that for each of the years since 1947, flooding telephone switchboards and dominating the newspaper headlines. The 1952 "flap," as it quickly becomes known, catches the Air Force institutionally prepared but procedurally unaware. "In Air Force terminology," Ruppelt explains, "a 'flap' is a condition, or situation, or state of being of a group of people characterized by an advanced degree of confusion that has not quite yet reached panic proportions."

The CIA is secretly called in to study the Washington sightings, the main concern being that Ruppelt's "average UFO reports" are now in danger of clogging up communication channels, flooding the media, and alarming the public. During the first few weeks of August a number of classified memos go into circulation, and a whole new set of questions starts to emerge. Why aren't there any records of UFO sightings in the USSR? Do the Soviets already have a saucer of their own? Or is this a communist plot to drive the American public insane and distract official attention?

"With worldwide sightings reported," comments a secret CIA paper for August 19, "we have found not one report or comment, even satirical, in the Russian press. This could result only from an official policy decision and of course raises the question of why and whether or not these sightings can be used from a psychological warfare point of view either offensively or defensively."

This point is further developed in a memo dated September 24 to new CIA Director Walter Bedell Smith: "Other intelligence problems which require determination," it states, "are a) The present level of Soviet knowledge regarding these phenomena. b) Possible Soviet intentions and capabilities to utilize these phenomena to the detriment of the United States security interests. c) The reasons for silence in the Soviet Press regarding flying saucers."

Here's one: United Artists film release *Red Planet Mars* shows Peter Graves picking up TV transmissions from Mars and subsequently learning that an advanced utopia based upon Christian values already exists there. His discovery demoralizes the entire United States, causing a stock-market collapse. The Soviets aren't laughing for long, though. It turns out that the Supreme Authority ruling Mars is none other than God Himself. This in turn provokes a global religious revival, with the forces of righteousness overthrowing the Soviet regime, restoring the monarchy, and making a humble orthodox priest the new Tsar. In a year of marvels and portents such as this, adopting a new religion makes quite a lot of sense. *Kiss Me Deadly* author Mickey Spillane, creator of brutal private eye Mike Hammer, becomes a Jehovah's Witness and temporarily forswears writing lurid crime fiction, while L. Ron Hubbard starts spreading the good word about Scientology having "come across incontrovertible, scientifically-validated evidence of the existence of the human soul."

As president-elect Dwight D. Eisenhower has declared in a moment of freewheeling spiritual fervor: "Our government makes no sense unless it is founded on a deeply felt religious faith—and I don't care what it is!"

### Electronic Brains

*A New Creature Is Born*—"Never heard of Hofmann," William S. Burroughs writes from Mexico City in March 1952, replying to a letter from Allen Ginsberg on Dr. Albert Hofmann's discovery of LSD. Burroughs is far more interested at the moment in the telepathic properties of the Yagé vine, which is to be found growing deep in the Amazonian rain forest. "Did not score for Yagé," he continues. "I think the deal is top secret. I know the Russians are working on it, and I think, in the US as well. Russians trying to produce 'automatic obedience' have imported vast quantities of Yagé for experiments on slave labor. I will score next trip." Three weeks later Burroughs is reporting to his friend Ginsberg that he still has "not found anyone who knew Hofmann." Maybe he just isn't asking the right people.

By 1952, the CIA's Project ARTICHOKE is funding research into just about anything that could make the mind do things it isn't normally predisposed toward doing. Promising areas of interest include hypnosis, electroshock therapy, psychosurgical procedures such as frontal lobotomies, the use of UHF sound waves to alter brain patterns, and the development of an "amnesia ray." One extensive program even involves "the search for and development of exceptionally gifted individuals who can approximate perfect success in ESP performance": agents are encouraged to follow "all leads on individuals reported to have true clairvoyant powers" and subject them to "rigorous scientific investigation."

Once again the main justification for such research is a fear of what the Russians and the Chinese might be up to. A CIA memo dated March 3, 1952, stipulates that although "the USSR and its satellites are capable of any conceivable atrocity against human beings to attain what they think are their ends, we should not—with our high regard for human life—use these techniques unless by using them we save the lives of our own people and the situation is highly critical to the nation's safety."

Meanwhile the CIA collaborates with the Navy on Project CASTIGATE to test a "secret potion" consisting of a depressant, a stimulant, and the active ingredient in marijuana. The drugs are administered over a three-day period at a secure location in Germany.

Experimental subjects include a known double agent, a suspected double agent, and three defectors. It's also around this time that CIA reports start referring to their human test subjects as "unique research material."

By now the agency is testing an increasing number of drugs sourced from around the world, including heroin, cocaine, various barbiturates, and the hallucinatory effects of psychotropic plants, such as Burroughs's Yagé vine. A new and pressing concern is consequently that the Soviets and the Red Chinese may be stockpiling natural rye ergot, the substance from which LSD is derived. Although grown commercially in a number of Eastern Bloc countries, none of it has ever appeared on the international market. As the absence of any mention in the Soviet media of flying saucers has led to fevered agency speculation, so the lack of rye ergot exports from the East raises a number of similarly compelling questions. What are they doing with it? Have the USSR and its satellites already developed an effective mind control drug? One that can scramble consciousness in the case of interrogation? Make a false personality seem real? Make the real personality seem false? Make the subject forget something? Recall something? Recall and then forget something? What if, in other words, the Reds know how to work the switches on the human tape recorder better than we do?

This is certainly the year to take a fresh look at the mind and how it works. Seconal, "the secret of sleep in a capsule" and the first of a new range of barbiturates, goes on the market; and Mr. Potato Head becomes the first kids' toy to be the subject of a televised advertising campaign. Not to be outdone, EC comics launches a new type of periodical in the autumn of 1952: one that will make a point of savagely parodying all the other comic books, cartoons, TV shows, and magazines that are currently fighting for the reader's attention. Appropriately enough, this wildly successful satire goes by the name of *Mad*.

Less immediately popular than *Mad*, but equally influential in its own sphere, "A New Approach to Schizophrenia," coauthored by psychiatrists Humphrey Osmond and John Smythies, starts to gain a readership after it appears in the *Hibbert Journal*. Noticing strong structural similarities between the formulas for adrenaline and mescaline, they initially hypothesized that a condition of stress might transform the former into the latter, thereby allowing the brain to sever all perceptual connections with the outside world and withdraw into madness. In an attempt to test this hypothesis Osmond ingested 400 milligrams of mescaline one afternoon. One of the first things he noticed was that the tape recorder he and Smythies had borrowed to keep track of his mental processes started to glow a deep menacing purple. Then it turned bright red and seemed to become incredibly hot to the touch.

Who now is working the switches? Confronted with a tape recorder that, by glowing, changing color, and altering its physical properties, apparently chose to behave like a UFO, a thought struck Osmond: the schizophrenic mind expressed itself in literal not figurative terms.

No mediating language of metaphor or simile lies between the delusional and the real. Like someone filling in Ruppelt's questionnaire, schizophrenics are not seeking to describe common objects "which, when placed up in the sky, would give the same appearance as the object which you saw." They know what they saw.

In "A New Approach to Schizophrenia" Osmond and Smythies extend this into a more nondeterministic approach to how the mind works, proposing an unorthodox methodology that would have to take into account electronic computers, ESP as "a scientific fact," and the psychobiological effects of mescaline as a therapeutic tool.

The glowing tape recorder does have a metaphorical presence in this story, however. Freud mistrusted the phonographically registered text of his patients, claiming that his own written "record" of a hysteric's speech had a "high degree of trustworthiness," higher certainly than any mechanically reproduced version. With the introduction of the Turing Test for machine intelligence, in which questions are posed to, and answers received from, an unseen entity by means of a typewriter keyboard, the notion arises that technology can deliberately mislead and confuse the human exchange of information. The behavioral intelligence of machines is read as human, while human mental activity is increasingly interpreted in mechanistic terms. With such aberrant behavior now a distinct possibility, the psychiatric process is slowly becoming a dialogue in which two machines, trapped within their own individual time tracks, find themselves trading data with each other.

The glowing tape recorder, like the glowing UFO, presupposes a radical break with this new technological order. Understood from this perspective, Osmond and Smythies have picked exactly the right time to include the study of "electronic computers" in their new methodology. Consider the following scenario. On the night of the first Tuesday in November 1952, CBS borrows a UNIVAC computer belonging to the Atomic Energy Commission to predict the outcome of the national election. Who will it be: Stevenson or Eisenhower? With a sample of just 1 percent of the voting population to go on, the UNIVAC predicts that Eisenhower will win by a landslide. Walter Cronkite, sitting next to the computer, starts to look distinctly uncomfortable. Everyone who has been following the polls agrees that the electoral math is a lot tighter than this. The result should be way too close to call, nothing like the 438 electoral votes UNIVAC is giving Eisenhower against Stevenson's 93. CBS decides not to broadcast the first on-air computer forecast, assuming it must be an error.

Media intervention, the distance afforded by keyboards and printers, is what permits a machine to pass for human in the Turing Test; its behavior is accepted as a technological illusion. The truth is that the computer Cronkite is sitting next to in the studio is a fake: a display panel fitted with twinkling Christmas lights, hooked up via teletype to the real UNIVAC, which, weighing over sixteen thousand pounds, is actually still at home in Philadelphia. CBS correspondent Charles Collingwood, sitting with the real UNIVAC, is the one who calls in the computer's alarming prediction, the program for which was written by University of Philadelphia statistician Max Woodbury in collaboration with one of the computer's creators, John Mauchly. Blacklisted as a communist, Mauchly is no longer allowed onto Remington Rand property, so Woodbury has had to work on the algorithms with him at his home.

With CBS refusing to take UNIVAC's prediction to the nation and thinking he has made a mistake, Woodbury reworks the program to reflect a much closer electoral race, giving Eisenhower 8–7 odds over Stevenson, which Cronkite duly reports on air at 9:15 that evening. Meanwhile Woodbury checks his figures again, finding that UNIVAC made the right call the first time around. In fact, with the official count ending up being 442 electoral votes for Eisenhower and 89 for

Stevenson, UNIVAC had been off by less than 1 percent. Embarrassed, Charles Collingwood confesses to millions of television viewers that UNIVAC predicted the right result hours earlier.

The real loser, however, will turn out to be IBM, which is poised to launch its new 701 range of computers in January 1953 with a massive publicity campaign. UNIVAC may not have passed the Turing Test on the night of November 4, but thanks to a complex interplay of lies and illusions, its name becomes synonymous in the public mind with the "electronic brain," much to IBM's annoyance.

A much simpler way of discovering the voters' choice before election night, however, is to go see *Red Planet Mars*. Not only does the actor cast to play the President of the United States in the movie look alarmingly like Dwight D. Eisenhower but the story line also indicates that he's a former Army general. Anyone struck by this strange similarity should probably think of it as just another sign of what is to come.

## Planetary Engineering

*Damaged Gods*—"The time is coming when we will have to reconstruct the solar system," *Popular Mechanics* announces in August 1952. Based on an interview with noted Caltech astrophysicist Professor Fritz Zwicky, "Shall We Move to Another Planet?" is an early take on the logistics of colonizing the universe at a time when US industry is in the process of consuming half the world's oil and steel. "We may have to rearrange the planets," the article boldly continues, "and in some cases rebuild them to fulfill our future requirements for living space." Harnessing the power of the atom, we will soon be able to move Mars out of its orbit, sending it "off on a tangent past some other planet to draw off an atmosphere," while our outermost worlds can be "broken apart and shrunk" so that they can be brought "closer to the sun."

Too bad Professor Zwicky isn't the only one to come up with this idea. "The orbit of our planet Mars is so far from the sun that climatic and atmospheric conditions are much inferior to those on Earth," explains the Martian ringleader in the 1952 Republic movie serial *Zombies of the Stratosphere*. "But in spite of these physical handicaps, my people have developed a means of correcting the situation."

"You mean you can change the orbit of the planet?" an awestruck nuclear scientist asks as he learns of the Martians' plan to knock Earth off its current course and have Mars take its place as third planet from the sun. "The conquest of the outskirts of the atmosphere and eventually space," according to an unnamed expert in space medicine quoted in the same *Popular Mechanics* article, "is a revolutionary event comparable only to the transition of aquatic animals to the land in geological times." A lot depends on who's doing the conquering, however. What may appear as the inevitable outcome of an evolutionary process when we contemplate it for ourselves suddenly becomes an act of dangerous expansionism when pursued by others. "Trips to the Moon, Mars and Venus will be commonplace by 1977," rocket scientist Willy Ley writes in an article examining what life will be like twenty-five years into the future.

Will they be commonplace for us, however? Eyes other than ours may already be fixed upon the stars. The design for the flag of the newly established People's Republic of China, approved at the First Plenary of Chinese People's Political Consultative Conference in 1949, contains a cosmic arrangement of five-pointed stars. The Soviet Union has prominently featured stars in its national emblems since the First Congress of Soviets in 1922. It's worth recalling in this context that the sun is the biggest star in our sky and that the word "disaster" is derived from a Latinate tag meaning "from the stars."

Not that there aren't a few stars on Old Glory already. Caught somewhere between manifest destiny and impending doom, American households prepare themselves for the challenge of tomorrow. After being prototyped in 1947, the first microwave ovens go on sale in 1952, transforming the act of cooking into a deep scientific mystery. Fire, our constant companion, will no longer play a direct part in the preparation of food. As if to compensate in some way for this radical intrusion of the future, the Weber Kettle charcoal grill barbeque unit goes on sale. Pretty soon its glossy metallic form, strongly reminiscent of a successfully landed flying saucer, is gracing backyards and patios throughout Suburbia.

As an unprecedented post-war economic boom starts to kick in, promising a seemingly endless supply of consumer goods, America seems to be enjoying the benefits of Marx's "classless society" without the need for any five-year plan. Wealth is not so much redistributed from this point on as allowed to overflow its bounds, filling the consumer with a new sense of self. The means of consumption are becoming more important than those of production in defining who you are. The differences between capitalism and communism, as a consequence, increasingly appear psychological rather than ideological. It's a question of what you have come to expect as commonplace: what you regard as staple to your existence. Instead of worrying over where the Reds may be hiding their UFOs and their LSD supplies, perhaps the question the CIA should be asking itself is: where is Russia's Mr. Potato Head? Where is its *Mad* magazine? Its Christine Jorgensen? Aren't these the things that will take us out from under the stars and move us closer to the sun?

It will require huge quantities of power to bring about this colonization of the other planets, this transformation of the solar system into one vast Levittown. As President Truman approaches the end of his period in office, Operation Ivy begins at the Pacific Testing Grounds in the Marshall Islands. Halloween sees the first full test of the "Teller-Ulam design" for a staged fusion bomb. Codenamed "Ivy Mike," the multimegaton thermonuclear device is the first Hydrogen Bomb to be detonated on Earth, yielding an explosive power 650 times greater than the bomb dropped on Nagasaki. The blast obliterates the island of Elugelab, leaving an underwater crater 6,240 feet wide and 164 feet deep in its place. "My mission here," declares the Martian ringleader in *Zombies of the Stratosphere*, "is to plant an H-Bomb explosion sufficiently strong to send Earth spinning out into space and leave room for my own planet."

As James Lipp quits RAND's H-Bomb study team, sickened by the prospect of calculating body counts running into the tens of millions, it looks as though we may well be doing the Martians' job for them.

Ivy Mike is followed on November 16 by Ivy King, which involves detonating the largest pure fission bomb ever tested by the United States. Dropped from a B-36H bomber over the Enewetak atoll, it produces a five hundred–kiloton explosion, sending a clear signal to Moscow and Peking about the current state of American nuclear capability. Just as visible and a good deal nearer to home are the atomic tests still being carried out in the Nevada desert, so close to Las Vegas that they are now becoming a tourist attraction in their own right. "There's always something going on in Las Vegas," boasts one 1952 magazine advertisement featuring images of glittering casinos illuminated by the violent crimson glare of an atomic fireball.

Referring to itself now as the "streamlined City of the West," Vegas is nothing if not precisely that. Unrelated in any way to functional aerodynamic principles, streamlining is a purely visual phenomenon left over from the late 1930s. Instead of helping things go faster, it simply makes them look as though they do—which is why its presence can still be detected in the sharply angled contours of Chuck Yeager's Bell X-1, the plane that took him through the sound barrier, now being incorporated into the lines of the latest model automobiles. The gap between everyday life and the promise of the future grows smaller by the day. It all becomes a matter of scale. The December 1952 issue of *Popular Mechanics* runs an article on "Selecting Your Christmas Tree" right after one on "Playing Safe with Atomic Rays."

Atomic materials, according to the author of the latter, are a lot like psychotics: dangerous when handled carelessly. "If not put under control, an unstable man can be dangerous," he argues. "Same with unstable isotopes ... Both humans and isotopes sometimes 'blow their tops.'" Having failed to create a Moon Child with L. Ron Hubbard back in 1946, Caltech rocket scientist Jack Parsons manages to blow himself to bloody chunks while handling explosive chemicals in his Pasadena garage on the afternoon of June 17. This event occurs just as the first biography of his spiritual mentor, Aleister Crowley, appears in print. "It is madness," declares *The Holy Book of Adolf Hitler*, also published in 1952, "to think that suddenly a majority can take the place of a man of genius." Meanwhile five million children become Junior Forest Rangers, and the CIA approaches Caltech physicist H. P. Robertson to head a scientific inquiry into UFOs at the start of 1953. Robertson is particularly well qualified for the job. In 1943, he was asked to determine whether the German V1 rocket was a hoax or not: he decided that it wasn't.

It is the CIA's hope that the Robertson Panel will deliver the final word on the subject of UFOs, taking them out of the sky and removing them once and for all from the Air Force call sheet. The agency is no longer concerned with mass panics or Soviet saucer scares but with what US citizens are now prepared to believe in. In this new "classless" society of consumer plenty, where the ideological has been replaced by the pathological, UFOs are rapidly providing an outlet for extremists to vent private grievances and frustrations. Are these now to be the subject of legitimate study? Professor Fritz Zwicky has a habit of referring to humanity in general and other astronomers in particular as "spherical bastards" because that's how they appear whichever way he looks at them.

According to one secret CIA paper circulated during August, the Air Force has already "investigated a number of civilian groups that have sprung up to follow the subject. One—the Civilian Saucer Committee in California—has substantial funds, strongly influences the editorial policy of a number of newspapers and has leaders whose connections may be questionable."

Apocalyptic saucer cults have started to spring up all over America. One small group, which has been receiving messages from outer space via Lake City housewife Mrs. Marian Keech, becomes the subject of a research team led by psychologist Leon Festinger. According to an alien entity named Sananda, the end of the world is due any day and under the most cataclysmic of circumstances. The group meets regularly to discuss the latest predictions from Sananda and the rest of the Space Brothers, as relayed to them by Mrs. Keech. Some members bake cakes in the shape of flying saucers to be consumed during their gatherings while local college football scores are closely debated. Suburbia has finally come to meet Lemuria.

Then one afternoon Sananda casually lets slip that the apocalypse will be taking place on December 21, 1952, but not to worry: a fleet of flying saucers will be on hand to rescue the true believers. Those who want to be saved, however, must be prepared for this great moment. They must sell everything they own and, discarding all metal objects, be gathered together in the open air at the appointed hour to be whisked away to safety. Ever wondered what happens when the world ends and the Space Brothers don't even bother to show up? You find yourself standing on the front lawn of a member's house, singing Christmas carols in the rain, and being jeered at by a whole crowd of spherical bastards who have turned up to see what's going on. Despite all the signs and portents to the contrary, it looks as if the apocalypse may have to be postponed for another year.

# 1953: OTHER TONGUES, OTHER FLESH

## Creating a Desert and Calling It Peace

*"Welcome to California"*—These are to be the first words of greeting addressed to a visitor from another planet in George Pal's film adaptation of the classic H. G. Wells novel, *The War of the Worlds*. Unfortunately the mouths that are meant to speak them will be reduced to radioactive ash before they barely get a chance to open. The first three men to meet the Martian invaders are blasted to powder by a devastating heat ray within seconds of making their presence known. The fourth human to welcome the Martians, a devout pastor with a Bible in his hand and a psalm on his lips, will meet exactly the same fate.

Initial encounters never go well in this movie. Despite having written "a thesis on modern scientists" and teaching "library science over at USC," Sylvia Van Buren fails to recognize the stranger she's just met. "Clayton Forrester—ever hear of him?" she enthuses to a bearded and bespectacled Clayton Forrester, who does nothing to stop or correct her. "Forrester's the one behind the new atomic engine," she gushes. "They had him on the cover of *Time*. You know, you've got to rate to get that."

She's not alone in her ignorance. "I think they're scientists," a park ranger remarks of Clayton and his associates in a movie where beards and glasses aren't automatically signs you're an absolute whiz with atoms. Even this, however, does not stop the bearded and bespectacled Norbert Wiener from becoming the subject of an intensive FBI investigation after MIT agrees to undertake a new top-secret Air Force project developing the SAGE automated radar system for tracking incoming Soviet bombers. In fact, the only one who isn't fooled by appearances in this movie is General Mann, sent out to sunny California by the White House to find out what the Martians are up to.

"Clayton Forrester," he confidently announces. "I haven't seen you since Oak Ridge."

"Good to see you, General," Forrester replies with equal confidence, divested now of both beard and spectacles.

Having last met at the Oak Ridge facility in Tennessee, home away from home for technicians working on the Manhattan Project, it makes sense that they'd recognize one another with such ease. It also makes sense that they'd meet again on the very edge of the devastation created by the Martian invaders with their atomic heat rays.

According to its own preamble, George Pal's *War of the Worlds* is pitched as nothing less than World War III: "fought with the terrible weapons of super-science, menacing all mankind and every creature on earth." An apocalyptic event in the making, the arrival of the Martians seems like a portent left over from the previous year. Initially mistaken for fireballs or meteors, their spaceships choose neither to land on earth nor to crash into it. Instead they slam down upon the rural terrain, quickly transforming the California countryside into an arid wasteland that even the animals are soon fleeing. Not that the US Army can do much about it. Despite an unprecedented $52.8 billion being spent on defense during 1953, the Martian invaders still have to be fought off with outdated weaponry. The screen bristles with equipment left over from the Korean War, including bazookas, tanks, mortars, and rocket launchers. None of it is effective, however. The Martians continue to widen their area of devastation, as if trying to transform the whole of Earth into one vast desert.

They aren't alone in this.

"There's only one thing that will stop the Martians," a grim-faced Secretary of Defense announces back in Washington. "We've held back because of the danger of radiation to civilians. Now there's no choice."

So desiccated and battered is the terrain, and so closely packed are the lines of troops preparing to witness the explosion, that the atomic strike against the Martians looks remarkably like an AEC test being carried out in the Nevada desert. "It's the latest thing in nuclear fission," a newsman says of the bomb they're about to detonate. "Nothing like this has ever been exploded before, and we're going to be pretty darned close. But there are observers down in the valley in a forward bunker who will be a lot nearer than us."

This might be another Operation Ranger or Buster Jangle but evidently no Ivy Mike. The newsman is still talking fission here, not fusion.

As if to emphasize this drift toward obsolescence, the nuclear device is delivered to its target by the Northrup Flying Wing: a futuristic bomber that is all wing and no fuselage but that has already ceased production by 1953 due to stability problems. Stock footage of the Flying Wing undergoing trials over Nevada is inserted into the attack on the Martians, giving the impression that the action is dragging behind current events, caught in the wake of actual military-industrial progress.

This represents a grim lapse of vision, coming as it does in a year when the Douglas F-4D Skyray, one of the fastest fighter jets on the planet, is influencing the shape and look of the modern automobile. The visual effect of streamlining continues to grow sharper and more swept back in emulation of the Skyray, whose name alone speaks volumes in 1953. Meanwhile, the *Toronto Star* prints an early report on the "Avro-Car": a disc-shaped flying craft designed by British engineer John Frost and being developed by Avro Canada at its Ontario plant. Originally known as "Project Y," the Avro-Car is taken over by the US Air Force and renamed "Project 606," giving an indication of where some of that $52.8 billion is now heading.

Back on the edge of the Martian desert, however, things are getting tense. "Two minutes to bomb time," warns a voice relayed over a loudspeaker. "Prepare to take shelter. If you have no goggles, turn away. Remember that the heat flash and the concussion that follows are dangerous."

The Martians survive the blast, however, as do most of the humans, despite the rather questionable advice they've been given. In a year when the US Army has sprayed highly toxic quantities of zinc cadmium sulfide over Winnipeg as part of a biochemical warfare exercise, it's no big surprise to see soldiers brushing powdery white fallout off their shoulders as if it were a bad attack of dandruff. The Pentagon had informed authorities in Winnipeg that it was testing a new chemical fog that would "protect" the city in the event of nuclear attack.

General Mann grimly surveys the desert landscape, his face thickly speckled with radioactive dust. "Washington issued orders," he reveals. "In the event the A-Bomb failed … our best hope lies in what you people can develop to help us." In this particular case, "you people" refers to Clayton Forrester and his colleagues at "Pacific Tech," otherwise known as the Pacific Institute of Science and Technology: a thinly veiled allusion to Caltech, where they've been having problems of their own with alien invaders.

At the CIA's request, H. P. Robertson of the California Institute of Technology has drawn up his panel of distinguished scientists, who spend four consecutive days in January watching films of UFOs and assessing eyewitness reports. They find little to be excited about. It's all mass hysteria. A public relations initiative should be established, they suggest, to debunk UFO sightings and to give old-fashioned science projects a boost in high school. This should involve contributions from psychiatrists and scientists, as well as from popular forms of entertainment such as Disney cartoons, and will take at least one or two years to have an effect. "At the end of this time," the panel declares, "the dangers related to flying saucers should have been greatly reduced if not eliminated."

In an echo of the internal reports circulating within the CIA over the previous year, the Robertson Panel also views civilian saucer clubs and related societies as a potential threat. "It was believed," the panel states, "that such organizations should be watched because of their potentially great influence on mass thinking if widespread sightings should occur. The apparent irresponsibility and possible use of such groups for subversive purposes should be kept in mind."

These last two considerations should certainly be kept in mind at a time when millionaire oilman Silas M. Newton and Leo "Dr. Gee" GeBauer of the Western Radio and Engineering Company are standing trial for fraud, having attempted to sell a device for discovering oil that supposedly operates on the same electromagnetic principles as a flying saucer. "My chief witnesses," Frank Scully emphatically declares after they are found guilty, "have not repudiated one sentence of *Behind the Flying Saucers*. Dr. Gee was a composite of eight different scientists, whose stories were tape recorded and then synthesized by me where they were in substantial agreement."

This is not a good year to be a scientist, however. While the chairman and vice-chairman of MIT's mathematics department mount a querulous and pathetic defense of their political beliefs before the House Un-American Activities Committee in Washington, Robert Oppenheimer is labeled "a hardened Communist" and a suspected "espionage agent." In New York the Josiah Macy Foundation Conference on Cybernetics holds its final session, having lost all direction and dissolved into what Chairman Warren McCulloch describes as "a babel of laboratory slangs and technical jargons." Behind this proliferation of languages is a number of deep personal schisms and misunderstandings, the main outcome of which is that Norbert Wiener and John von Neumann are no longer talking to each other and Wiener has severed all personal contact with both the conference in general and Warren McCulloch in particular. "For all our sakes I wish Wiener were still with us," McCulloch mournfully concludes. On June 19, in upstate New York, Julius and Ethel Rosenberg are executed one after the other in Sing Sing's electric chair, just as Scotty the newsman always knew they would be. Perhaps Clayton Forrester was right to make it so hard for people to recognize him in public.

Home to the crashed saucer and beloved of the Martian invader, the desert continues to exert its powerful hold over the popular imagination, becoming a favored location in which to meet representatives from other worlds. As these encounters tend to occur on the outside edges of human society, it often takes a while for reports of such events to become common knowledge, blurring the moment of first contact and robbing it of any real historical significance. Such is the case with George Adamski, who now reports meeting a man from Venus in a ravine near Desert Center, to the east of Caltech's Hale Observatory at Mount Palomar, on November 10, 1952.

It remains an incident high in drama, especially in the retelling. "Someone take me down the road—quick!" Adamski announces to his party after watching a spaceship circling high over the desert. "That ship has come looking for me and I don't want to keep them waiting! Maybe the saucer is already up there somewhere—afraid to come down here where too many people would see them."

Not long after that, Adamski is gazing into the smiling face of a beautiful, longhaired youth. "Now for the first time I fully realized that I was in the presence of a man from space—A HUMAN BEING FROM ANOTHER WORLD!" Adamski's account of their meeting constitutes the concluding chapters to *Flying Saucers Have Landed*, being readied for publication in 1953. Its author is the Irish aristocrat Desmond Leslie, who would soon be creating space music using magnetic tape. The latest in a lengthening line of books that seem to have spaces at the end of their titles to accommodate a missing exclamation point, *Flying Saucers Have Landed* lists Don Keyhoe's *The Flying Saucers Are Real*, Gerald Heard's *The Riddle of the Flying Saucers*, Frank Scully's *Behind the Flying Saucers*, and Velikovsky's *Worlds in Collision* in its bibliography, alongside more established works by Annie Besant, Madame Blavatsky, Rudolf Steiner, and Plato.

In the main body of his text, Desmond Leslie takes a mythological overview of flying saucers dating back to prehistoric times, noting significant points of intersection between spacecraft and human history. Adamski's testimony, however, offers something that breaks with that history, both transcending and leaping far beyond it. Having managed to land on Earth without colliding with it, Adamski's man from space establishes a new evolutionary agenda simply by confirming what people have suspected all along: that space is filled with higher minds and nobler spirits than our own. "Let's face it, neighbors," radio talk-show host Long John Nebel will later remark, "the sad truth is that all space people are always superior."

Having "made a number of trips to desert areas," however, Adamski knows exactly what to do: instead of welcoming the young stranger to California, he asks where he has come from. Through a mixture of sign language and telepathy, the human being from another world reveals that he comes from Venus. He also brings a message of peace, expressing a concern for the "radiations going out from Earth" as a result of the nuclear weapons being detonated on this planet.

Occurring at roughly the same time in 1952 that Sananda is warning Mrs. Keech and her circle in Lake City of the impending end of the world, there is little about Adamski's encounter that appears new.

We've been out in this particular desert before. The actual substance of his assertions isn't as important as the extent to which it fits the prevailing mood of the period. What makes Adamski's account so attractive, however, is the way in which he surrounds himself with technicians, government agencies, and military officers. He begins, for example, by qualifying his relationship with "the big Hale Observatory" at Mount Palomar. "I am friendly with some of the staff members but I do not work at the Observatory," he states flatly. He has his own telescopes set up near the lunch counter where he works nearby: two Newtonian reflectors, one mounted under a dome, the other "out in the open." Pretty soon he's using them to photograph flying saucers, an activity that attracts visits from representatives of the Point Loma Navy Electronics Laboratory of San Diego; "six military officers" subsequently engage him in conversation on the subject at his lunch counter. The military then requests his "cooperation in trying to photograph strange objects from space"—and this is before he's even met anyone from another world.

Going by previous experiences, it is hard not to detect an underlying eroticism to Adamski's account of meeting the beguiling young Venusian with the "beautiful white teeth that shone when he smiled or spoke." However, the real sexual charge comes from Adamski's direct contact with more professional bodies. "All saucer researchers," he pants, "are looking forward to the time when the bulging files of the Air Force may be opened." The "government agencies" Adamski mentions in his contribution to *Flying Saucers Have Landed* are the ones who ultimately provide the elusive truth of his encounter in the desert, even when they subsequently deny knowing anything about him.

In 1953 Adamski prefaces a talk he is giving at the Lions Club of Corona in California with a statement that its content "has all been cleared with the Federal Bureau of Investigation and Air Force Intelligence." After J. Edgar Hoover's office instructs agents to "read the riot act in no uncertain terms" to him about making such claims, Adamski will tell interviewers that he has been "warned to keep quiet ... not to mention the government or any of its services."

Encounters with beings from other worlds tend to isolate the individuals involved, stranding them in a cultural desert. Adamski creates a personal narrative out of this isolation: one that connects him to the secret here and now of an increasingly paranoid age. The authorities consequently spend so much time denying any connection with him that the truth of his meeting with a man from Venus in the California desert goes largely unchallenged. "Everything Adamski wrote about us was fiction," a representative from the Point Loma Navy Electronics Laboratory will later assert. The true meaning of that fiction is to be found elsewhere.

### Am I Going to Get My Coffee?

*Sandrock, Arizona*—Adamski's Venusian feels close enough to the desert to leave a message inscribed on its surface, the soles of his shoes imprinting the soft sand with strange hieroglyphics. The Martian invaders in *The War of the Worlds* love the dry wilderness so much that they bring it with them, as if attempting to re-create conditions on their home planet wherever they go. John Putnam, the central character in Jack Arnold's *It Came from Outer Space*, is content merely to build his house there. "To think of the time I wasted living in the city," he marvels to his fiancée Ellen one starlit night, echoing a sentiment expressed by over 30 percent of the country's middle classes who have made the move out into the suburbs by 1953. In fact, Putnam's relocation is so recent that his spacious, ranch-style dwelling isn't even finished yet. Housing in Suburbia is getting bigger, more expensive, and now comes in a much wider variety of styles than ever before, with William Levitt and Sons currently completing over 150 new homes per day.

"It's nice out here," Ellen placidly concedes in a statement that has important ramifications not just for this movie but also for the rest of the decade. Thanks to Suburbia's relentless expansion, "out there" is rapidly becoming "out here": a shift in perception that implies a very different metaphysics altogether. Colonization is revealed as a form of domesticated alienation: the experience of a displaced population building a home for itself in the Martians' dry wilderness.

Like Adamski, John Putnam has a reflector telescope set up in his backyard and is on good terms with the staff of the nearby Wayne Observatory, a name in close phonemic proximity to Caltech's Hale

Observatory at Mount Palomar. He also goes out into the desert where he meets with an extraterrestrial and converses alone with him. His written account of their encounter is entitled "Report on the Arrival of Strangers from Outer Space," which can be read as a somewhat long-winded reworking of *Flying Saucers Have Landed*. More importantly, Putnam's experience confirms what Adamski has also demonstrated: meeting creatures from space is an isolating experience, carried out by men without families. Unencumbered by wives, fiancées, parents, or children, the isolated male is free to meet his alien counterpart in a brief moment of pop-culture transcendence. Not surprising then that the conversation quickly focuses on God.

Adamski's Venusian professes his belief in the "Creator of All," while Putnam's alien affirms that he has a soul and a moral sense. "If they are more advanced than us," the devout pastor argues in *The War of the Worlds* before going out alone to meet the Martians in their wilderness, "they must be nearer the Creator for that reason."

He's right in theory, of course, but wrong in this particular case. The Martians turn out to be butt-ugly, and so too are the aliens Putnam has discovered lurking among the Joshua trees. The desert, after all, is a treacherous place: "ready to kill you if you go too far" claims Putnam. Even the aliens aren't supposed to be there. "Only an error dragged us toward Earth," the chief alien lamely admits as they set about trying to extricate their crashed spaceship from the desert sand. Putnam consequently spends the rest of the movie trying to mediate between the spaceship's occupants and the jittery townspeople who don't want them around. "Give us time," the chief alien pleads, "or terrible things will happen … things so terrible you have yet to dream of them." The underlying message here is that we aren't ready to meet with each other yet: which also explains why so many stories of flying saucers and occupants involve crashes rather than controlled landings. Any and all choice in the matter is kept to an absolute minimum.

"You will have a greater chance to be yourself than any people in the history of civilization," *House Beautiful* informs its readers without the slightest hint of irony in 1953. Being yourself is a difficult business in the suburbs, especially at a time when the standard codes of social conduct are still being drawn up. The first issue of *Playboy* hits the newsstands at the end of the year, along with Alfred Kinsey's *Sexual Behavior in the Human Female*, suggesting that there clearly aren't clean sheets on every bed in America. Just what are mom and dad up to? "It's all right, Mary, I'll put the coffee on," George McLean assures his wife in the darkness of their bedroom as he fumbles for his robe at the start of *Invaders from Mars*.

There's trouble at the breakfast table the next morning, however, when George suddenly appears in the kitchen doorway, still in his night attire. "Any chance for a cup of coffee?" he growls by way of a greeting. George has been out all night checking out "the sand pit": an endless expanse of desert that lies beyond the white picket fence marking off the end of the McLeans's backyard. David, their son, reported seeing a spaceship coming to earth there and then disappearing beneath it. "It didn't fall," David insists. "It landed." He's certain of this because he watched it going to ground through his telescope.

So has Dad found anything out there? "Am I going to get my coffee?" George McLean brusquely replies, indicating that he doesn't want to talk about it anymore.

As consumption and personal well-being usually go together in TV commercials, a grouchy dad asking for his morning coffee would be the customary start to a pitch for a new blend of aroma-rich beans. Here it means he's been taken over. "Out there" has become "out here" once again, but the dynamic has changed this time. Back in *It Came from Outer Space*, John Putnam finds it harder to mediate between the aliens and the townspeople the more the aliens pretend to be the townspeople.

"Look at him," the local sheriff fumes as an alien saunters down the street in the guise of a telephone repairman, "walking around like he belongs here."

Like he belongs where precisely?

"I have come to know," asserts William Levitt in an attempt to explain why you rarely ever see a black face in Levittown, "that if we sell one house to a Negro family, then ninety to ninety-five percent of our white customers will not buy into the community. That is their attitude, not ours."

It is very easy to "be yourself," easier still to take a transcended view of humanity, when we all look and act the same. Adamski's Venusian is "human" to the extent that he is also fair-haired and white. It is perhaps no coincidence that George Hunt Williamson, who accompanied Adamski out into the desert for his meeting with a human being from another world, had connections with the Silver Shirts, a prewar fascist movement.

By now the aliens are even tracking dust from the desert through John Putnam's new home. Seething away at his desk in Sandrock, Arizona, the sheriff is less concerned with the notion that creatures from outer space can repair their disabled spaceship using the contents of a telephone repair truck or a nearby hardware store than by their ability to pass for human while they do so. "How do we know they're not taking over?" he angrily demands. "They could be all around us, and I wouldn't know it!"

The only thing harder than being yourself is being under the control of someone else. It marks the point at which "out here" and "out there" meet and coexist.

Shot mostly from a child's point of view, *Invaders from Mars* follows young David McLean's attempts to persuade the authorities that there really are Martians at the bottom of the garden and that they've taken control of people's minds. Family life enters a nightmarish dimension; the process of colonization, by which alienation is domesticated, becomes inverted and nothing is now what it seems. First Dad gets tetchy about his morning coffee, and then Mom starts acting weird. A little girl down the street picks flowers for her mother before burning their house down. Next thing anyone knows David is behind bars in the local jail. "He's been reading those trashy science-fiction magazines again," his own mother informs the desk sergeant. "He's completely out of control."

There's that word again. "Do you mean those Martians out there could be giving instructions right now to people they've operated on, and they do exactly as they were told?" a horrified doctor asks in *Invaders from Mars*. It would appear that some form of control device has been surgically implanted in their brains. "We've made white mice follow directional impulses with high frequency oscillation," a fellow scientist admits, but that's about as far as it goes in this particular movie.

All the same, "out there" still threatens to become "out here." Allen Dulles, General Walter Bedell Smith's successor and the CIA's first civilian director, rails against Russian "brain perversion techniques ... so subtle and abhorrent to our way of life that we have recoiled from facing up to them" while addressing the Princeton alumni conference on April 10, 1953. "The minds of selected individuals who are subjected to such treatment," he continues, "are deprived of the ability to state their own thoughts ... the individuals so conditioned can merely repeat the thoughts which have been implanted in their minds by suggestion from outside. In effect, the brain becomes ... a phonograph playing a disc put on its spindle by an outside genius over which it had no control." At the express urging of Richard Helms, however, Allen Dulles is about to change the record.

Agency memos circulating at the start of 1953 suggest that the Russians don't enjoy any particular technical advantage over the West when it comes to mind control. "Apparently," reads one from January 14, "their major emphasis is on the development of specially trained teams for obtaining information without the use of narcotics, hypnosis or special mechanical devices."

Which means that they are just not trying.

Within three days of delivering his speech to the Princeton alums, Dulles sets aside $300,000 to fund MK-ULTRA: one of the most infamous covert mind experiments in modern history. An offshoot of Project ARTICHOKE, MK-ULTRA is run by a relatively small unit, the Technical Services Division, but the implications of its various researches are enormous. If, as Helms enthusiastically claimed back in 1950, LSD really is "dynamite," then MK-ULTRA constitutes the CIA's attempt to get it combat-ready.

At the head of this new initiative is one Dr. Sidney Gottlieb, a man whose very presence transforms even the most rational account of this project into the synopsis for a low-budget movie serial. Born with a clubfoot and a stammer, Gottlieb seems to have stepped out of the shadows of prewar Mittel-Europa, the living embodiment of Dr. Eberhard Schleppfus, "your humble servant," poisoning the mind and spirit of the young Adrian Leverkühn in Thomas Mann's novel *Doctor Faustus*, first published in 1947. As if to complete this picture, his twin passions are folk dancing and goat husbandry.

In reality, however, Sid Gottlieb hails from the Bronx and is a Caltech graduate with a special interest in chemical warfare. Like Helms, he can also see the potential of LSD as a weapon and starts setting up numerous field trials and laboratory experiments to study its effects. These range from basic tests in which two operatives take LSD and monitor each other closely for any changes in behavior to surreptitiously dosing certain targeted individuals without their knowledge or consent. The inmates of prisons and asylums, the terminally ill, blacks, foreigners, sexual deviants, and drug addicts are unwittingly encouraged to no longer "be themselves," thanks to LSD supplied by Dr. Gottlieb.

The Agency, meanwhile, is making every effort to ensure that there will be plenty to go around. Despite an internal memo dated November 16 warning that the enterprise may prove "too risky," two CIA agents go to Switzerland bearing $240,000 in cash to buy ten kilos of Delysid—enough for one hundred million doses—from Sandoz, its proprietors. They soon discover that Sandoz has produced less than two ounces of the drug in the past ten years, obliging them to come up with another plan: Sandoz agrees to supply the CIA with 100 grams a week, plus it will inform the agency if anyone else shows an interest in the drug.

Three days later, on November 19, another internal memo reveals that the Project ARTICHOKE committee has "verbally concurred" with the proposal that all CIA operatives should be required to try LSD. Intended to both widen their experience and weed out the mental weaklings, their tacit agreement effectively means that even accepting a cup of coffee from anyone attached to MK-ULTRA is now a dangerous undertaking. That very same evening Dr. Frank Olson of the Army Chemical Corps is informed that someone has slipped some LSD into the glass of after-dinner Cointreau he's just been enjoying.

Dr. Olson has been participating in a working session with representatives from the CIA's Technical Services Division at Fort Detrick, the Army's biological warfare center in Maryland, and as such, would normally be considered "fair game" for this kind of prank. Pretty soon, however, Olson is in New York urgently seeking the counsel of

Dr. Harold Abramson, one of the CIA's principal LSD researchers and a part-time consultant to the Army Chemical Corps. In the grip of a prolonged psychotic episode, Olson confides to Abramson that the Army is out to get him, that he is receiving telepathic messages to throw his wallet away, and that the CIA is putting something in his coffee to make him stay awake at night. A few weeks later Olson checks into New York's Statler Hilton, where he commits suicide by throwing himself out of his tenth-floor bedroom window. The NYPD subsequently writes up the death as the unfortunate result of a homosexual lovers' quarrel between Olson and his partner, Richard Lashbrook, who was in the room with him at the time.

What the police report doesn't reveal is that Lashbrook is actually Sidney Gottlieb's deputy at Project MK-ULTRA and that he is now busily engaged in trying to cover up the whole incident. Why? Because Dr. Gottlieb is the one who spiked Olson's after-dinner drink with LSD in the first place: a frat-house stunt that already has the Technical Services Division wondering whether they shouldn't shut down the entire MK-ULTRA program. Allen Dulles also seems to be reviewing his position on mind control, commissioning Dr. Harold Wolf of Cornell University, where he is treating Dulles's son for brain damage following a head wound sustained in Korea, to conduct an official study of communist brainwashing techniques.

Olson killing himself so publicly in New York also places him a little too close to another MK-ULTRA project taking place at this time. Gottlieb has hired drug enforcement officer George Hunter White to set up a Greenwich Village pad where bohemians, artists, sailors, and drifters can hang out. A martini-drinking, white-collar berserker of the old school, White is charged with secretly testing LSD on his unsuspecting guests. Their reactions are often so extreme that White's own codename for the drug is "Stormy." Undisturbed by Olson's death, White will continue to operate his behavioral laboratory in New York until he is eventually called away to bigger and better things on the West Coast. In the meantime, Sid Gottlieb continues to rise at dawn every morning to milk his goats before heading back in to work at CIA headquarters in Langley, Virginia. It's nice out here....

## Calculating the Spectrum Dust

*Enriched Environments*—A family is grouped around the mouth of a cave in the desert trying to persuade a little boy that everything he's just experienced has all been a dream. There is no Robot Monster and the human race has not been destroyed. *Invaders from Mars* has already been released in two different versions: one in which David McLean is shown sleeping at the end of the movie having helped defeat the Martians, the other where he is shown waking up, discovering it was all a dream, and then witnessing the Martian spacecraft disappearing into the sandpit once again. "Really, Johnny," the boy's big sister exclaims at the end of *Robot Monster*, "you're overdoing the spaceman act. There really are no such things as monsters." After the family leaves the cave entrance, however, the Robot Monster emerges from its dark depths, raising his arms threateningly toward the audience. Because it has been shot in 3D and is the first sci-fi movie to come out with a stereophonic soundtrack, this closing shot is repeated until we see it three times altogether, just so we won't miss the point.

Things have started to change inside the cave.

The introduction of television into the suburban lounge, along with other gadgets such as improved high-fidelity sound systems, remote controls, and dimmer switches, means that the range of effects available in the home is widening considerably. An enriched environment is now becoming accessible to everyone, making the division between actuality and illusion, reality and dream appreciably narrower. That's what Johnny's family, standing in a concerned huddle around the cave's entrance, are about to find out. The paintings on its walls are taking on a life of their own.

George Pal's *The War of the Worlds* is concerned with more than just an invasion from outer space. "All radio is dead," a radio newsman announces into a microphone, "which means that these tape recordings I am making are for the sake of future history … if any."

In a film that still depicts groups of people huddled in public around radio sets in bars, factory workshops, general stores, and diners, it is significant that the first thing the Martians do is disrupt the electromagnetic field in the areas they take over. "Well, sir, radio's out," a trooper explains to General Mann as the Martians continue their attack, "but field phones are OK. They'll go the minute there's another heat ray."

The future may still be received rather than transmitted, but the means of reception is now under serious review. In his book *Other Tongues, Other Flesh*, published in 1953, Adamski's sidekick George Hunt Williamson describes using radios and telepathy to get in touch with the Space Brothers. However, in transferring his commentary from radio to magnetic tape, the newsman in *The War of the Worlds* is responding to the new overheated forms of media that are beginning to saturate the suburban lounge.

"I will calculate the spectrum dust in the Calcinator Death Ray to counteract this antibiotic," the Robot Monster announces from his cave in the desert, where he is able to keep in touch with his home planet by means of a radio transmitter that blows a steady stream of bubbles whenever he uses it.

In short, the Martians are the new media: or at least the possibility of them. Their heat ray tends to isolate people and objects, making them stand out in relief against a two-dimensional background, as if transforming traditional 2D cinema into 3D. Since the release of *Bwana Devil*, promising "a lion in your lap" the previous year, 3D movies have offered the chance of creating a more lifelike set of paintings on the cave wall. However, unlike *Robot Monster* or *It Came from Outer Space*, both genuine 3D movies released in black and white, *War of the Worlds* is a Technicolor movie that enthusiastically embraces the new technology without actually using it. The structural anatomy of the Martian eyes is even based upon a similar color separation to the one used in the special glasses handed out in cinemas to watch 3D movies, substituting a red/green/blue division for the standard red/green one. Their eyes have three distinct pupils, it transpires, and strong light also shocks them, making them excellent cinemagoers. "That's how the Martians see us," remarks a Pacific Tech scientist of an image captured through a Martian eye. And how we see them.

"I don't remember ever seeing blood crystals as anemic as these," comments another of his colleagues at Pacific Tech, having examined a specimen of Martian blood. "They may be mental giants, but by our standards physically they must be very primitive." They also prove to be no match for the enriched environment of Earth, teeming with unseen strains of bacteria that finally corrupt and destroy the Martians' bodies, which have no resistance to them. Similarly, the Martians in *Invaders from Mars* are all brain and very little else: simply a head attached to a set of atrophied tentacles, dependent upon human slaves and their own mindless "mutants" to get around in this material world. By comparison, the strapping "Ro-Man," as he calls himself in *Robot Monster*, is an impressive amalgam of cold logic and a powerful physique, perhaps not so impressively represented by a costume that is four parts gorilla suit to one part deep-sea diver's helmet. "How Can Science Meet the Menace of Astral Assassins?" runs part of the poster copy for this movie. "New Science Fiction Thrills! Adventures into the Future in new Tru-3 Dimension!"

To give a little context to such cut-rate hyperbole, this is also the year in which audiences are free to enjoy *Canadian Mounties vs. Atomic Invaders, The Lost Planet, Magnetic Monster, Phantom from Space, Rod Brown of the Rocket Rangers, Project Moonbase, Cat Women of the Moon*, and a prospect less welcome than it is inevitable, *Abbott and Costello Go to Mars*.

There is little in the evolutionary scheme of things to separate "Ro-Man" from the Martians or any of the other freaks, mutants, or monsters that flash across the screen in 1953. Each represents some crisis point out of which the future unfolds. As such, they also constitute that which must in due course disappear through a systematic historical process more commonly known as progress.

In the interests of low-budget entertainment, *Robot Monster* flings everything at its audience in 3D and stereophonic sound; this includes stock footage of dinosaurs fighting, newsreels showing cities in ruins at the end of World War II, and outdoor scenes shot extensively in Bronson Canyon, the abandoned gravel quarry in Los Angeles where the Lone Ranger first emerged blinking into the sunlight back in 1949. In fact, the cave where Ro-Man sets up his bubble-blowing transmitter, and where little Johnny is persuaded by his family that the whole experience has been nothing but a dream, is the very same cave in which Tonto assisted the Lone Ranger in his spiritual rebirth. But then, Los Angeles always has been a great place for that kind of thing.

At exactly the same time as Allen Dulles is setting funding aside for MK-ULTRA in April 1953, Gerald Heard's old friend Aldous Huxley is writing a short note to Humphrey Osmond from his home in Los Angeles. Huxley has just finished reading Osmond's "A New Approach to Schizophrenia" in the *Hibbert Journal* and likes the way the young scientist's mind works. Pretty soon they're arranging to meet. The American Psychiatric Association is holding its convention in LA this May, and Osmond is planning to fly down and will bring with him some mescaline for Huxley to try.

"But Aldous," his wife Maria worries when she hears that Osmond will be staying with them, "what if we don't like him? What if he wears a beard?" She's evidently just been to see George Pal's *War of the Worlds* and knows how that can work out. At the same time Osmond is worried that in giving Aldous Huxley mescaline he will go down in history as the man who drove one of the finest minds of his generation round the bend and then left it there.

As it is, they get on famously, Osmond taking Huxley to the American Psychiatric Association Convention, where the famous writer makes a show of genuflecting every time Sigmund Freud's name is mentioned. It's not until May 5 that Osmond dissolves some mescaline crystals into a glass of water and gives it to Huxley to drink. Huxley in the meantime has obtained a tape recorder to preserve a record of the experience, although this is perhaps unnecessary.

In an age of 3D movies with stereophonic sound, Huxley finds himself stepping through a screen into another world in which he will later recall seeing "what Adam had seen on that first morning of creation." This isn't madness. This is the bigger picture: an experience in which you can lose yourself. "This is how one ought to see" is actually the phrase Huxley keeps murmuring to himself. What exists on the other side of the screen has only ever been hinted at from this side. Here, Aldous can see, is a vaster, more colorful world of heightened senses: an enriched environment in which to immerse oneself fully. Wait until Gerald hears about this....

The cave in the desert appears to have given up some of its secrets. Enriching the environment turns out to be a complex two-way psychic process. In 1953 the RAND Corporation moves into its new purpose-built headquarters. Located right next to the beach in Santa Monica, the facility appears to be nothing more than a gaunt office block designed to keep out the California sun. Once past security, however, you find yourself inside a precisely organized maze of small courtyards and interconnecting corridors specifically designed by chief RAND mathematician John Williams to maximize the possibility of random encounters between members of the Corporation's increasingly diverse personnel. Pretty soon RAND employees from different specialist divisions are dropping by each other's offices, informally swapping ideas and passing on information, following an established pattern of behavior that will persist to the end of the century and beyond.

Meanwhile, thanks to the use of certain drugs, subjective responses to the environment can also be heightened to the level of unpredictability. Reality becomes an experiential blip: a random concurrence of events. No wonder psychiatrists and technicians working away in impoverished environments from Montreal to Langley, Virginia, are having such a hard time studying the effects of LSD under laboratory conditions. A slippage tends to occur from statistical data to the purely anecdotal. A hallucination, it turns out, is a narrative that doesn't fit a standardized questionnaire. What if you have answers for questions that aren't even on the form? Despite his fondness for "government agencies," Adamski doesn't bother with the BLUE BOOK questionnaire when documenting his encounter with a Venusian, preferring instead to ask that those who accompanied him sign sworn affidavits affirming that they know what they saw.

By the same token, Aldous Huxley doesn't need a tape recorder to tell him what he already sees. Nor is it likely, knowing what he now does, that he will wish to stay on at the APA convention long enough to hear outgoing president Dr. Ewen Cameron make his closing address.

"Nothing that has thus far transpired," Cameron asserts in a speech that can be read as the complete antithesis of Allen Dulles's remarks to the Princeton alumni, "is likely to be more serious than for humanity to learn how to control the development of personality and how to master the forces of group dynamics before we have developed a value system capable of dealing with such a situation … Our knowledge of human behavior, our techniques for the exploration of motive and memory, if torn from their framework of professional integrity and proper concern for the individual and the community may, their use perverted, become the most deadly weapons yet directed against the dignity and serenity of human life."

That the CIA will end up financing his experiments with tape recorders, LSD, and sensory deprivation in search of a possible cure for schizophrenia constitutes the grimmest of historical ironies, especially when Cameron goes to such great lengths to ensure that Humphrey Osmond never receives funding for his own LSD research. In the meantime it's enough to wonder whether Allen Dulles is aware of Dr. Cameron's remarks, or what Sidney Gottlieb, Richard Lashbrook, and George Hunter White might make of them.

# 1954: MEET THE MONSTERS

**Pledge of Allegiance**

*Coming to Earth*—We expect a great deal from a little word like "never." It has to cover everything that hasn't happened, isn't happening, and remains unlikely to happen. The word cancels out events for all eternity: consigns them to nonbeing. That's an awful lot of work for a handful of letters to do, even in a year when Ann Elizabeth Hodges becomes the first human in history to be hit by an extraterrestrial object when a meteorite crashes through the roof of her Alabama home, bruising her arm and leg and demolishing her radiogram, which happens to be on at the time.

This incident takes place in the wake of Edwin Armstrong, the inventor of FM radio, jumping to his death from the window of his thirteenth-floor apartment in New York's River House. In despair at the prospect of his continuing legal dispute with RCA over the rights to his invention, Armstrong decides to take his own life in what will be the future home of the Marconi Society, just as the final episode of the original *Lone Ranger* radio serial is being prepared for broadcast. At a time of such rapidly lengthening odds, Congress votes heavily in favor of including the words "under God" in the pledge of allegiance. With President Eisenhower having already declared that he doesn't care what faith a government follows, just so long as it has one to follow, the time has come for the household God, the corporate Lord of the military-industrial machine, to start moving across the face of the Earth.

Somehow the world seems safer "under God," even as it edges its way slowly toward obliteration. Viewed from above, the traditional battlefield has all but disappeared from its surface, taking the military caste system with it. Conducted at a distance by a professional elite of academics, scientists, mathematicians, planners, and strategists, global conflict increasingly takes on the form and substance of a media event. After the recent Korean fiasco, leaving the country's pro-Western South irrevocably divided from its communist North, the Cold War

has become a series of feints and simulations, transforming itself into a campaign fought almost exclusively with beliefs and perceptions. The distinction between military strategy and a commercial one is also beginning to disappear: something reflected in advertisements of the period. "The Bomb's brilliant glow," proclaims a newspaper advertisement in 1954, "reminds me of the brilliant gleam Beacon Wax gives to floors. It's a science marvel."

That the conventional prosecution of war is considered a thing of the past is reflected in the Domino Theory, given expression for the first time by the Eisenhower Administration in 1954. This argues that communist infiltration in Southeast Asia, if left unchecked, will lead to the collapse of individual countries, all of which will fall like a line of dominoes, each knocking the other over. The emergence of this new global theory also marks a creeping awareness that the doctrine of Massive Retaliation may no longer be workable in a world where the Soviets now possess a nuclear arsenal of their own.

This does not prevent Secretary of State John Foster Dulles from starting the year with a speech to the Council of Foreign Relations in New York enthusiastically extolling the nation's "massive retaliatory power" as a "further deterrent" to the spread of world communism. "Soviet communists are planning for what they call 'an entire historical era,'" he announces, giving his argument the kind of evolutionary sweep that can be understood from Lemuria to Levittown, "and we should do the same."

It soon becomes clear, however, that the prospect of America's "historical era" is looking surprisingly shaky when RAND Report R-266, *Selection and Use of Strategic Air Bases*, comes out in April 1954. Over the course of its 424 pages, this massive, top-secret document spells out the message that RAND analyst Albert Wohlstetter has taken over ninety separate briefings to hammer home to Washington's defense establishment: the closer Strategic Air Command's nuclear bomber bases are to their intended targets, the more vulnerable they are to a Soviet first strike.

Even with the introduction of in-flight fueling in 1954 to keep at least a handful of its nuclear bombers in the air at all times, Wohlstetter's calculations reveal that the vast majority of Strategic Air Command's B-47s will never leave the ground in the event of a Soviet surprise attack. The chance of a retaliatory second strike from the United States would, as a consequence, be statistically out of the question. One possible solution to the problem, R-266 goes on to suggest, is to house the bombers in blast-proof bunkers. Wohlstetter has already brought in Paul Weidlinger, a civil engineer who worked with him at the National Housing Agency, to design a reinforced suburban homestead for SAC's nuclear wing. Helping him to devise a hardened concrete shell capable of withstanding a blast of two hundred pounds per square inch is Herman Kahn, who has left the Lawrence Livermore National Laboratory to work in the Physics Division at RAND and is now happily wandering the corridors, involving himself in one interesting project after another.

As commercial and military considerations continue to merge with each other, this quantitative approach of SAC vulnerability leads Wohlstetter and his colleagues at RAND to develop an economics of "kill probability." Putting together a proposal for a new national defense package, they estimate that it will cost the United States $10 billion to destroy the Soviet Union's nuclear capability as compared to SAC's more conservative and spendthrift $35 billion. Head of Strategic Air Command Major General Curtis "Bombs Away" LeMay, having helped set up RAND in the first place, is beginning to wonder what kind of monster has been brought forth in the Santa Monica sun. A brusque and decisive man of action who once famously declared that "on some Mondays I don't even trust myself," LeMay looks upon RAND's army of social scientists, logicians, and economists with mounting suspicion.

A more alarming truth for him to contemplate, however, is that the H-Bomb's "brilliant glow" is getting just a little too big to be deployed in any useful way. Which is why RAND strategist Bruno Augenstein has now come up with memorandum RM: 1191: *A Revised Development Program for Ballistic Missiles of Intercontinental Range* and starts briefing the Defense Department on how the new Intercontinental Ballistic Missile will soon be capable of delivering an atomic payload to its target with greater accuracy than LeMay's beloved B-47s, meaning that smaller and less devastating warheads will be required. Or to use the words of former president Harry S. Truman, if you can't stand the heat, don't set fire to the kitchen.

Capitalism is the real permanent revolution, taking place "under God" here on Earth. Communism is merely a psychological aberration. Who would want to live that way, given the choice? "Can one say today," writes former director of policy planning Paul Nitze, refuting Dulles's assertion that reliance upon conventional weapons will eventually bankrupt the nation, "when our population is living better than any people on earth have ever lived, when our steel plants are only being used to 75% of their capacity, when we feel threatened by the magnitude of our agricultural surpluses, that we are even closer to the economic limits of what we could do if we were called upon with clarity of purpose and nobility of vision to do it? Are we facing 'practical bankruptcy' with average consumer expenditures five times those of the average Soviet citizen, while the Russians are not?"

As Nitze fully appreciates, a new spirit has been let loose upon the land, offering material progress, the blessings of the Lord, and the possibility of enjoying both in the comfort of your own home. It can already be seen at work in the recent development of the Swanson TV dinner, created at the end of 1953 in response to the massive logistical problems involved in disposing of an uneaten excess of Thanksgiving turkey that year. The answer is to repackage it with cornbread dressing and gravy, alongside some precooked buttered peas and sweet potato in one of those little aluminum compartmentalized trays used on commercial airlines. Stick a picture of a TV set on the front of the box, and you're away.

After all, television holds up a mirror to the true nature of family life today. For the first time people see themselves reflected and refracted within its curved glass screen: helping them to define who they are and how they should behave. The introduction of the TV dinner and the TV tray means that families can now watch themselves while they eat. Behavior patterns start to undergo a radical alteration even as they are being affirmed; a rescheduling of life in the suburban living room has taken place. Eating in front of the television set means that household furniture has to be not only portable but washable too. Surfaces become lighter and shinier. Metal and plastic reflect the "brilliant glow" of modern life. "Con-Tact" self-adhesive vinyl sheeting is introduced into the home, covering walls and countertops with photographically reproduced expanses of marble, sandstone, and crumbling brickwork: a two-dimensional illusion that can be wiped clean.

Even so, the word "never" still has a lot to do in 1954.

"Never before," *Life* magazine proclaims, "so much for so few," referring to the fact that postwar production is now far outstripping consumption. Even though 1954 is proving to be a great year for Big Business, with profits soaring to an all-time high at General Electric and Westinghouse, the existing generations of adult consumers just don't have the numbers to cope with this unprecedented economic expansion. For a system that still requires scarcity in order to regulate itself, help is already at hand. "Never underestimate the buying power of a child under seven," Miss Francis of television's *Ding Dong School* tells a conference of advertisers in Chicago, referring to the generation of consumers born after 1947, that *annus mirabilis.* "He has brand loyalty and the determination to see that his parents purchase the product of his choice." But in whom or what does his loyalty lie?

"Our American children are, for the most part, normal children. They are bright children. But those who want to prohibit comic magazines seem to see instead dirty, twisted, sneaky, vicious perverted little monsters who use the comics as blueprints for action." Thus speaks Bill Gaines, publisher of Entertaining Comics, addressing the Senate Subcommittee to Investigate Juvenile Delinquency on April 21, 1954. Unfortunately, he has chosen to make his spirited defense of the nation's youth at exactly the wrong time and to precisely the wrong set of people. Featuring presidential hopeful Estes Kefauver, fresh from tackling mobsters and racketeers as head of the 1950 Senate Special Committee to Investigate Crime in Interstate Commerce, this particular body has an overriding interest in identifying "vicious perverted little monsters" and how they got that way. Its members are also not feeling particularly well disposed toward a man responsible for such unsettling publications as *Tales from the Crypt, The Haunt of Fear,* and *The Vault of Horror.*

Narrated by ancient mottled entities known affectionately as the Crypt Keeper, the Old Witch, and the Vault Keeper, EC horror comics have an unenviable reputation for thrilling kids with creepy yarns of bloodily poetic justice, madness, and revenge. Mr. Gaines has consequently come to Washington in order to defend both his comics and, more importantly, their readership. He soon finds, however, that his work is cut out for him. During the course of the previous day, the subcommittee has had its blood frozen and its flesh set crawling by the testimony of psychiatrist Dr. Fredric Wertham, who has made a special study of what he calls "crime comics" and who has come to some pretty alarming conclusions. Author of last year's shock best seller *Seduction of the Innocent*, Dr. Wertham's findings have already sent countless parents rummaging through their kids' bedrooms, hunting down and destroying every comic book they come across.

"By and large much younger children read crime comics than is commonly and conveniently assumed," his book warns. "Crime comic books are available almost anywhere. Any child who meets other children has access to them. They are in kindergartens, pediatric clinics, pediatric wards in hospitals. They are in playgrounds and schools, at church functions and, of course, in the homes of the child or his friends."

Comic-book circulation has reached over sixty million copies a month by 1954, with more than a hundred individual horror titles coming into print since 1950. So far as Dr. Wertham is concerned, however, all comics are by definition "crime comics." Unable to share the same idealistic vision of youth enjoyed by the publisher of *Tales from the Crypt*, he considers every title to be an active incitement to its readers to commit acts of violent delinquency. Crime, however, is what sells. Crime is what gives crime-fighting superheroes something to do: as such it helps bring a visceral poetry to society's notions of justice. Crime also grabs the attention of the concerned citizen, as Dr. Wertham must have discovered with the success of his two previous books, *Dark Legend: A Study in Murder* and *Show of Violence*. However staid or sober their contents, both these titles might easily have been lifted from the garish front covers of the very comics he most despises.

Examined through Dr. Wertham's eyes, comics and psychiatry have a lot in common. Comic books give immediate access to the voices running inside people's heads. Their most intimate memories, undeclared motives, and unconscious urges are graphically displayed across the grid-like page in the form of thought bubbles and speech balloons. Conflicts often exist between the two within the same panel:

what is said is not always what is actually on a character's mind. Only the reader is in the privileged position of having access not only to all the objective facts of a scene but also to the violent, unspoken currents that are running just beneath its surface.

Dr. Wertham first became aware of the pernicious effects of horror comics after watching a child on the subway completely absorbed in one. The boy's trance-like passive condition, open-mouthed, and oblivious to everything else around him as he continued his reading, is that of a psychiatrist's patient waiting to be probed. This scenario is enough for Dr. Wertham to see dark influences hard at work.

"Only someone ignorant of the fundamentals of psychiatry and the psychopathology of sex," he declares in *Seduction of the Innocent*, "can fail to realize a subtle homoeroticism which pervades the adventures of the mature Batman and his young friend Robin."

In one of the most infamous chapters of his book, provocatively entitled "I Want to Be a Sex Maniac" in reference to the body-building advertisements usually found in comic books, Dr. Wertham goes after two of the most famous crime-fighters in popular culture in no uncertain terms. "The atmosphere is homosexual and anti-feminine," he writes. "If the girl is good looking she is undoubtedly the villainess. If she is after Bruce Wayne, she will have no chance against Dick." Only someone ignorant of the fundamentals of psychiatry and the psychopathology of sex can fail to nod their heads knowingly at the sentiments hidden behind that last sentence.

However, instead of taking the Fifth or standing on the First Amendment in the face of such barely suppressed hysteria, EC's Bill Gaines makes the huge mistake of suggesting that his conduct as a publisher is bounded by the canons of good taste. Big mistake. Suddenly Gaines finds himself confronted by Senator Kefauver of Tennessee brandishing the May 1954 issue of EC's *Crime SuspenStories*. Its cover depicts the aftermath of a particularly gory beheading: a man holds a woman's severed head in one hand and a dripping axe in the other.

And does Mr. Gaines consider this to be in "good taste"?

"Yes, sir, I do, for the cover of a horror comic," replies Mr. Gaines, causing every red-blooded American child and free-speech advocate to run screaming from the room. "A cover in bad taste, for example, might be defined as holding the head a little higher so that the neck could be seen dripping blood from it and moving the body over a little further so that the neck of the body could be seen to be bloody."

Mr. Gaines has just said a mouthful. While this marks one of the few occasions when a body is described as having two necks, neither of which is actually depicted on the cover in question, it is also the last hurrah for the American horror comic. From this point on, the comics industry will regulate itself, which means that shows of extreme violence and excessive criminality are banned from superhero adventures. The newly formed Comics Magazine Association of America will also see to it that words like "weird," "strange," and "uncanny" are no longer featured on any of its members' covers. Batman will also start fighting beings from outer space, unaware that Superman represents the most successful alien take-over ever attempted on Earth.

Struggling to keep up with an industry hell-bent upon reforming itself into a state of blandness, Bill Gaines tries to change EC's image, even to the extent of coming up with a new comic called *Psychoanalysis*, but news vendors start receiving death threats for stocking his titles, the police scrutinize each publication for further abuses, and his comics come back to the warehouse in unsold bales.

The only EC publication to rise above the madness is *Mad* itself. Having started out as a parody of the horror-comic genre, promising "humor in a jugular vein," *Mad* retains brand loyalty among its readers precisely because it is now free to parody everything: from television shows, movies, and advertisements to the latest fads and fancies, including the most recent findings of "Dr. Frederick Werthless" that baseball is corrupting the minds and morals of the nation's youth. "The evidence was overwhelming," declares Dr. Werthless. "Almost every delinquent child brought into court had a past record of either playing or watching baseball!"

Sales of *Mad* continue their steady rise throughout the rest of the decade. The children of America have spoken once again.

**Contact**

*Weird Science*—As the home becomes linked to the outside world through increasingly powerful and sophisticated communications media, the peaceful comings and goings of everyday domestic existence are being influenced in ways never seen before. The view we have of ourselves is no longer limited to earthly dimensions. Dr. William Marston, inventor of the lie detector test who went on to create Wonder Woman, gives an interview in which he states that the scenes of panic greeting the Orson Welles radio adaptation of *The War of the Worlds* were the result of a credulous public brought up on comic books.

Meanwhile Robert S. Richardson of the Hale Observatory at Mount Palomar announces that the twin moons orbiting Mars, which suddenly appeared to astronomers in 1877, may well be artificial satellites launched that very year. They are called Phobos and Deimos: "Fear" and "Terror" respectively. Noted rocketry pioneer and former technical advisor on *Destination Moon* Hermann Oberth offers an equally disturbing perspective on the bigger picture. His article "Flying Saucers Come from a Distant World," published in the October 24 issue of *American Weekly*, asserts that spaceships from other planets "have been sent out to conduct systematic, long-range investigations, first of men, animals and vegetation, and more recently of atomic centers, armaments and centers of armament production."

In *The White Sands Incident*, a slim volume from the New Age Publishing Company of Los Angeles, Aerojet employee Daniel Fry gives a detailed account of his journey to New York and back aboard a flying saucer. Lasting about thirty minutes, the flight takes place on the night of July 4, 1950, starting at the US Army's proving ground near Las Cruces in the New Mexico desert, where Fry has been installing instruments "for the testing of some very large rocket motors."

Fry first goes public with his story at the Giant Rock Spacecraft Convention, an event recently hosted in the Mojave Desert by George Van Tassel. An aviation engineer formerly employed in Southern California's booming aerospace industry, Van Tassel is the author of *I Rode a Flying Saucer*, in which he describes his encounter during the night of August 24, 1953, with a Venusian named Solganda. Contact occurred after a period of meditation in one of the chambers beneath Giant Rock, a sixty-foot-high, freestanding boulder out in the desert where Van Tassel has built a home, a café, and a small airstrip. The visiting extraterrestrial passes on to him a technique for rejuvenating living tissue, and in 1954 Van Tassel and his family start work at Giant Rock on the Integratron: a giant structure designed to "supply a broad range of frequencies to recharge the cell structure."

Also in 1954, contactee Truman Bethurum publishes *Aboard a Flying Saucer*, an account of his encounter in the Arizona desert outside Mormon Mesa with Aura Rhanes, the female captain of a flying saucer from the planet Clarion. "She was a real swinging chick," Bethurum later tells Long John Nebel, and spoke colloquial English. Unlike the twin moons orbiting Mars, the planet Clarion has remained undetected by astronomers because its orbital path keeps it constantly hidden from sight behind our own Moon.

The desert locations and aerospace references in the above accounts must seem strangely comforting by now. We have been out here before: in a deepening nuclear winter, the blue skies stretching over Southern California are transformed into some of the most important military airspace in the western hemisphere, attracting huge amounts of government funding and a unique concentration of scientists, academics, and technicians. What's becoming increasingly noticeable about these new encounters, however, is the extent to which they take place in Revealed Time: that is, in the hiatus between the actual incident and its eventual disclosure to the media. There is a distinct chronological blurring in the presentation of each narrative. Contact with Aura Rhanes, for example, occurs on the night of July 7, 1952, but is not reported until this year. Revealed Time has a strong psychological dimension to it, confirming the contactee's own sense of uniqueness as a chosen representative of humanity. Meanwhile the public, in an advanced state of evolutionary obsolescence, lags far behind him in his splendid isolation. Revealed Time also marks the reclassification of information previously kept hidden. As such, it plays with concealment in the same way the US Air Force currently does.

Having been commissioned by Captain Ruppelt to create the BLUE BOOK standardized questionnaire for classifying UFO reports, the Battelle Memorial Institute, a privately owned research company based in Columbus, Ohio, is also charged with computerizing the results. After two years' study, their massive statistical survey of Air Force sightings, entitled *Project Blue Book Special Report No. 14*, is now ready. Among its findings is the observation that too many UFOs are still being explained away on the flimsiest of evidence just so the Air Force can formally designate them as "identified." The more complete the facts of a case are, the report concludes, the more likely the sighting will remain unidentified.

Too bad Ed Ruppelt is no longer around to read it. He applied for reassignment from BLUE BOOK in August 1953, just as the Korean War was winding down; and the contents of *Special Report No. 14* will not be made available to the public until 1955. In the meantime the USAF, following recommendations laid down by the Robertson Panel, whose findings will also remain a secret, reverts to its former policy of denying and debunking in order to stem what the CIA considers to be a rising tide of UFO hysteria.

Secrecy is the new medium of communication: one whose presence can only be detected through its effects. Where secrecy prevails, contact becomes an article of faith. With Van Tassel's Giant Rock Spacecraft Convention set to become an annual event, the contactees start to move in from the desert, slouching toward Los Angeles in search of bigger audiences. Daniel Fry appears at a convention organized by the Saucer Research Foundation at the Carthay Circle Theatre in Hollywood, where he publicly agrees to undergo a polygraph test. "Fry's story appears to be one of the many incredible narratives cropping up on the West Coast which seem quite fantastic and unbelievable but almost convince you when you talk to the tellers of them," comments issue five of *The Saucerian* magazine. "Almost" doesn't quite make the bit, however. The press has a field day when his retelling of the White Sands Incident fails to impress Dr. Marston's lie detector.

The president of the newly formed Saucer Research Foundation turns out to be one William Gilroy, who also happens to be press agent for television psychic and "saucer columnist" Jerome Criswell. The Amazing Criswell has in the meantime been attending weekly meetings of Flying Saucers International, eventually suggesting that the group hold its own convention in the music room of the Hollywood Hotel. Speakers at the event include Frank Scully, George Van Tassel,

George Adamski, Truman Bethurum, and Orfeo Angelucci, a former Lockheed employee who claims to have ridden a flying saucer back to its mother ship in 1953. Angelucci's more earthly encounters are often the most intriguing, however. He remarks, for example, on the presence at the convention of a mysterious "Dr. X," who speaks "long and eloquently on the saucers" then promptly leaves.

By its very nature, contact is temporary, often fleeting: a glancing moment between bodies impervious to intimacy and yet capable of leaving a mark. Con-Tact vinyl sheeting could not have been introduced to the market at a more appropriate time. A habitué of the Los Angeles suburbs rather than the empty desert, Angelucci spends his time hanging out with science-fiction writers, attending their monthly meetings, and listening to their discussions. He observes with some sadness that they no longer care to write about flying saucers or their occupants as such imagery has become cheapened in the eyes of the public. Even Batman and Robin get to beat up people from outer space these days, for crying out loud.

Angelucci is sitting in on a convention of science-fiction writers at the Hotel Commodore in Los Angeles one evening, growing impatient with such talk, when Gerald Heard rises to address the room. The author of *The Riddle of the Flying Saucers* begins by berating his audience for turning out material of "an inferior grade." Angelucci notes how the writers start squirming in their chairs while Heard continues his harangue. Then a moment of contact occurs. "As our eyes met and held," Angelucci later recalls, "a kind of mutual understanding passed between us in ever widening circles."

Their circumference seems to reach far beyond the limited confines of the pulp imagination in 1954. On February 18, the first Church of Scientology is established in Los Angeles, "to accept and adopt the aims, purposes, principles and creed of the Church of American Science, as founded by L. Ron Hubbard," while Heard's old friend Aldous Huxley is preparing to publish *The Doors of Perception*, a short account of his mescaline experiences the previous Easter.

Contact remains the first principle of belief; not enough for proof, it often requires positive assertion when confronted by the paucity, or even lack, of physical evidence.

"There is one in this room tonight—I do not know who he is, but he's going to upset the whole apple cart," Gerald Heard announces to the sci-fi writers gathered for their convention at LA's Hotel Commodore. "He is the Awakener—he has not yet appeared, but he well may be here in this room tonight."

And with that, the moment of contact ends. Angelucci feels the "mystic wheels between us set in motion by the controlled magnetic vortices" slowly recede and vanish. By the end of 1954, he will have left Los Angeles and moved out to the high desert, near Twenty Nine Palms, just north of Van Tassel's Giant Rock.

## I, Nautilus

*Awakenings*—Without seeming to realize it, Commander Pete Mathews of the United States Navy has suddenly found himself at the center of a modern suburban home. Practically the first words we hear him utter form a list of everything he has just had for breakfast. "Orange juice, bacon, eggs, coffee," he announces contentedly. "How are we doing?" Pretty good, we'd have to say, considering we're stuck inside the conning tower of the nation's first "atom-powered submarine" returning from its shakedown cruise in the Pacific. Given the circumstances, confusing a nuclear submarine with a modern suburban home is an easy thing to do. There's Hawaiian music playing throughout the ship in a year when the September issue of *Popular Mechanics* is breathlessly reporting from its front cover that "Hi-Fi Is Sweeping the Country"; and the easygoing crew has little else to do than "push a button when there's work to be done," according to Mathews's second-in-command, Lieutenant Griff.

Begun in 1953, when President Eisenhower initially announced his "Atoms for Peace" program, production on Columbia Pictures' *It Came from Beneath the Sea* is now nearing completion, just as the USS *Nautilus*, America's first nuclear-class submarine, is being readied for active service under the command of Eugene P. Wilkinson, USN. Although Commander Mathews is played by Kenneth Tobey, last seen as the Air Force captain in RKO's *The Thing from Another World*, much of the onboard footage has been filmed on location at San Francisco Naval Yard and features actual service personnel in some of the supporting roles. This includes Lieutenant Chuck Griffiths in the part of Mathews's second, Griff. Even so, the dialogue has a distinctly suburban feel to it. Lieutenant Griffiths, in particular, manages to sound as though he were actually in a television commercial. "Roomy? My gosh!" he gushes when Mathews asks what he thinks of their new ship. "This conning tower is just like a ballroom." This is more than any commanding officer can stand to hear. "Take it easy, Griff," Mathews replies. "It's still a submarine." Not anymore it isn't. "All we need is champagne and dancing girls," Griff continues. "Shall I have the Chief change the record, sir?"

Having spent some real time in the silent service, Lieutenant Griffiths is much more keenly aware of how little separates nuclear subs from the suburbs. Both provide rich, carefully controlled environments in which the simple act of pushing a button or changing a record can radically alter mood and behavior. Both are equally capable of transforming themselves into ballrooms at the flick of a switch, if only because the technology they use is derived from precisely the same source. The atomic engines that power the USS *Nautilus* are manufactured by Westinghouse: a company best known for producing such humble domestic appliances as the toaster, juicer, and coffeemaker without which Commander Mathews's breakfast would have been unthinkable. In either case, the sales slogan remains comfortingly the same: "You can be sure if it's Westinghouse."

Although unnamed, the atomic submarine featured in *It Came from Beneath the Sea* also has a reassuringly familiar history: having started out on "a Navy drawing board," according to an unseen narrator, the vessel was then put "through months of secret experiments out in the western desert." An unusual location to test a submarine, it may be argued, except by those who have paid any attention to what the contactees have been saying recently. Strange and mysterious things have been known to stir themselves in such remote locations these days. This is perhaps why Commander Mathews issues an order for the Chief to change the record: "before we all start chasing mermaids." Lieutenant Griffiths is in complete agreement.

"Let's get off this Hawaiian kick," he urges the Chief. "It's even demoralizing the captain."

Pretty soon an unidentified blip on the sonar is attracting attention. The crew are quickly roused from their indolent torpor by a sudden change in the music. Something's moving out there, but no one can verify what it is. Meanwhile the sonar still picks up a solid reading.

Shot on black-and-white stock aboard a real-life submarine in a documentary style, the entire sequence plays out like an aquatic version of a US Air Force encounter with a flying saucer, right down to details of the target's range, velocity, location, and course. A series of high Geiger-counter readings on the submarine's hull adds further confirmation that the unidentified blip is real. In a world increasingly mediated by screens, vectored by electronic instruments, and calibrated in radiation levels, a blip can mean anything and everything. An unidentified presence, no longer capable of being accurately read by the senses, it plugs the action of *It Came from Beneath the Sea* straight into the new strategic order of things.

The sea, like the open sky and the wide-open expanse of the empty desert, is the perfect battlefield, especially once you start establishing your nuclear test sites there.

Hydrogen Bomb detonations continue throughout 1954 at the US Pacific Test Site in the Marshall Islands, where many of the inhabitants have been forced to leave their former homes in order to make way for the H-Bomb's "brilliant glow." On March 1, Bikini Atoll bears the brunt of Operation Castle Bravo, the largest atomic accident to hit the atmosphere so far. A nuclear device with an estimated yield of six megatons suddenly turns out to be the Little Bomb That Could, producing an unprecedented fifteen-megaton explosion that covers over 1 percent of the entire Earth's surface with radioactive fallout. The electromagnetic pulse generated by this mighty detonation causes traffic lights to malfunction and other electrical blackouts as far away as Honolulu. No wonder the sound of Hawaiian music demoralizes Commander Mathews so.

Meanwhile off-camera sources in the movie report that "part of the Japanese fishing fleet" has disappeared without a trace; and an

American merchant ship is shown being dragged into the deep by a giant tentacle. Hydrogen Bombs detonated in the Pacific Ocean have been responsible for raising a gigantic octopus from its customary habitat in the Mindanao Trench: "a chasm in the floor of the ocean so vast that it has never been explored." Now intensely radioactive from the fallout, the unhappy creature has taken to haunting the sea-lanes in search of food. "We checked our answer with Professor Emoto in Tokyo," a scientist back in San Francisco declares, "and he concurs."

Professor Emoto is the right person to ask at the moment: the crew of the Japanese fishing boat *Lucky Dragon No. 5* is caught in the fallout from Operation Castle Bravo, causing the death of one crewmember and the hospitalization of several others. Their entire catch is so radioactive that it has to be buried on land. It looks as if the movie's off-camera sources may have been right, after all. "Accidentally an experiment was performed on twenty-three unfortunate men," declares a Navy report on the *Lucky Dragon No. 5* incident, voicing some of the difficulties US doctors encountered in examining the victims. "Compassion must always be present, but for the advancement of man which occurs whenever a truly new segment of data is obtained, the loss of an expert evaluation in this experiment may well outweigh all other reasons for seeing those patients."

"Since the atomic age," runs part of the title sequence at the start of *It Came from Beneath the Sea*, "man's knowledge has so increased that any upheaval of Nature would not be beyond belief." Confronted with the prospect of a giant radioactive octopus attacking the world's shipping lanes, a visiting State Department official remains shrilly dismissive, however. "H-Bombs have been blamed for every freak accident that has happened since, up to and including marine monsters being disturbed," he complains. America's request for access to the crew of the *Lucky Dragon No. 5*, made by the Atomic Bomb Casualty Commission, is turned down because its surviving members fear that visiting scientists will use them for further tests.

Meanwhile the blip on the screen is growing to alarming proportions.

Following the successful 1952 reissue of *King Kong*, giant monster movies have become a major box-office draw. Also released in

1954 is *Them!*, in which gigantic ants, the mutant offspring of atomic testing, sweep in from the desert to threaten Los Angeles. Nature itself has become a vast hallucination of unbearable intensity. Not surprising then that Thorazine, the first tranquilizer, goes on sale. Then comes Miltown, followed by Stellazine, Mellaril, Valium, Librium, Elavil, and Tofranil. The mass production of LSD is also made possible when Eli Lilly manages, in secret and with CIA funding, to synthesize the drug from readily available chemicals. No longer dependent on Sandoz to dole out the drug to them on a weekly basis, the CIA quickly becomes Eli Lilly's biggest customer. With the hallucinogen available in vast quantities, Allen Dulles notes that LSD can now be treated as a weapon of mass destruction. The discovery that Thorazine can control the effects of LSD in the treatment of schizophrenics seems almost negligible by comparison. An internal CIA memo circulated at the start of the 1954 Christmas season warns all staff against sampling the contents of the punchbowls at departmental parties this year.

One unfortunate CIA operative is already rumored to have fled across Washington in a fine frenzy after discovering his morning coffee had been dosed with LSD. His colleagues eventually find him cowering behind a street sign. "He reported afterwards," a Technical Services Staff member later reveals, "that every automobile that came by was a terrible monster with fantastic eyes, out to get him personally. Each time a car passed he would huddle down against a parapet, terribly frightened. It was a real horror for him."

Nothing is what it seems anymore. There are monsters wherever you look. The 1950s complete themselves in the shadow of the apocalypse: "under God." The addition of these two simple words to the pledge of allegiance places a limit on humanity's evolutionary trajectory. Up to now the prevailing cultural fantasy has concentrated itself upon those high above us in the cosmic scale: invaders coming down from the skies. As we approach the middle of the decade, however, our attention is drawn toward the creatures that dwell beneath us: the monsters coming up from the primordial slime, the bottom of the sea, or the ground beneath our feet.

Or perhaps they even come from somewhere deep within the unconscious mind, as the CIA agent cowering before the oncoming traffic has come to realize. Sailors who have witnessed the giant octopus attacking their ship won't admit to what they have seen for fear that the doctors at the naval hospital will think they're "sick in the head" or have "read too many comic books," which in 1954 amounts to the same thing. Finally it is up to actress Faith Domergue, playing a marine biologist, to cajole one of them into revealing precisely what he saw. Her interview with the reluctant sailor is conducted in a manner remarkably similar to the interrogation technique favored by MK-ULTRA operative George Hunter White when testing the loyalty of US servicemen during World War II. Just like Faith, he would put his subjects at their ease and then offer them a cigarette, the only difference being that his pack of Luckies had been liberally laced with liquid marijuana. Caught up in such a scenario, both of which are shadowed by the hint of madness, the subject is lured into divulging secret information to an unseen third party—in Faith's case, a clutch of naval intelligence officers listening in at the other end of an office intercom.

A Howard Hughes discovery best known for playing a dangerously insane temptress in the 1950 psychological thriller *Where Danger Lives*, Faith Domergue is a little different from the kind of actresses we're used to seeing in such movies. For one thing, she has a face to suit the age: severely disfigured in a car accident, her features have been reconstructed through extensive bouts of plastic surgery, giving her a sultry, alien look. No one, it must also be said, screams quite like Faith. She brings a full-throated terror to her role as a scientist, particularly when the giant octopus attacks San Francisco's Bay Area and finally has to be destroyed by a jet-propelled torpedo "triggered by electronics."

On the other side of the world, another giant monster chooses this precise moment to come ashore in Tokyo, another city by a bay but on the opposite side of the Pacific this time.

"Why has this monster appeared in Japan?" noted paleontologist Dr. Yamane asks the crowd of politicians gathered in the Diet Building in an early scene from *Gojira*, the first *Godzilla* movie, released by Toho films in 1954.

Good question. Whereas *It Came from Beneath the Sea* hints only indirectly at the *Lucky Dragon No. 5* incident, *Gojira* places it front and center as the reason for the monster's very existence, re-creating the event at the start of the movie in a terrifying play of light and shadow. As such, the two films essentially offer different perspectives on the same tragedy.

The giant octopus seen in *It Came from Beneath the Sea* relies upon the same stop-motion technique used twenty years previously in *King Kong* to sustain the illusion that a living creature now fills the screen. Time-consuming and expensive, its days are already numbered; budgetary constraints have ensured that the octopus has only six legs instead of the customary eight. Meanwhile, the makers of *Gojira* utilize a number of different animation techniques, from puppetry and stop motion to an actor in a specially designed costume, to maintain their monstrous illusion. This, however, has less to do with notions of realism than with specific shifts in perspective.

A tale of human evolution run backward, *Gojira* poses a riddle and answers it at the same time. Born out of an atomic explosion, the monster enters the city, before finally dissolving into the sea at the end of the movie, thanks to the "oxygen destroyer," an invention that renders the waters of Tokyo Bay uninhabitable. In this sense, Godzilla is quite literally what he appears to be on the screen: a man in a rubber suit. The release in 1954 of Universal's *The Creature from the Black Lagoon*, also played by a man in a rubber suit, confirms where the focus now lies. Anything else is just an expensive distraction.

When it comes to sea creatures and distractions, however, scale is no longer an issue. Both are present, for example, in the tune "Cockles and Mussels," played on the violin by Alan Turing before being questioned by police about his sexual orientation. Still considered a security risk in a year when Oppenheimer is forced to resign from the AEC even after his name has officially been cleared, Turing dies from taking a bite out of a poisoned apple—just as Snow White appears to do in a scene from his favorite Disney movie. Like Edwin Armstrong, the inventor of FM radio, the verdict is suicide. Evidently having read the chapter in Fredric Wertham's *Seduction of the Innocent* entitled "I Want to Be a Sex Maniac," the breaker of codes and creator of the first test for machine intelligence has answered his own riddle.

# 1955: POPULAR MECHANICS

## Your Future Is Great

*Disneyland*—"Do you know there are fifteen thousand babies born in the SAC every month?" James Stewart asks in the movie *Strategic Air Command*: a tense domestic drama about national defense initiatives in which references to nuclear strike capabilities are lightly folded into scenes of family life on an American airbase. He's picked a really good time to keep score. "Your future is great in a growing America," runs a public service notice appearing on the New York subway system. "Every day 11,000 babies are born. This means new business, new jobs, new opportunities." In *Strategic Air Command*, there's even talk of "a new family of nuclear weapons" and a newborn baby called "Hope."

It soon becomes clear, however, that devising nuclear bombing strategies can seriously affect your home life. Despite Albert Wohlstetter's grim mathematics, SAC has become one of the main players out on the test ranges and proving grounds of the New Mexico desert, responsible for deploying the latest B-52 "Stratofortress" as well as coordinating attack plans for an eventual showdown with the Soviets or the Red Chinese. By 1955, SAC pilots are even being recruited by the CIA for a top-secret operation running high-altitude reconnaissance flights over the Soviet Union in a new experimental plane currently undergoing trials in the Nevada desert. Resigning their Air Force commissions and assuming false identities, the former SAC officers are taken to a secluded airbase located on a flat expanse of empty desert out by Nellis, right next to the Atomic Energy Commission's main test site. Built in only a few months by the CIA, operating through a nonexistent construction company, Groom Lake is now the home of Lockheed's U2 spy plane.

Thanks to a new generation of high-resolution lenses and ultrasensitive films created by Edwin Land, inventor of the Polaroid camera, the U2 is capable of taking detailed photographs of Soviet military installations from as high up as eighty thousand feet in the stratosphere. With both plane and target separated by distance and kept at the extreme

ends of visibility, the politics of deterrence is beginning to concern itself with remote locations, unseen presences, and barely perceptible outlines. Caught in the dark optics of the U2's spy cameras, military and civilian targets are transformed into spaces waiting to be haunted: vast communities of ghosts in the making. "We've been bombing cities every day and every night all over the US, only people never know it," one of Jimmy Stewart's SAC colleagues excitedly remarks during a training exercise in which real targets are hit from above with imaginary ordnance.

Seen from the skies, from the edge of space itself, the family is beginning to look increasingly like one uniform entity, formless and indistinct, constantly repeating itself across the country. Called "the world's most perfect community" by its backers and "tomorrow's marketing target" by *Tide* magazine, Miramar is a vast planned development of ready-furnished homes that has just opened in Florida. "Anyone can move into one of the homes with nothing but their personal possessions and start living as a part of the community five minutes later," boasts Robert Gordon, Miramar's founder and first mayor. Each housing unit comes completely furnished, including bed linen, towels, china, and cutlery, together with a fully stocked refrigerator. "The trend to 'packaged' homes in 'packaged' communities," *Tide* enthuses, "may indicate where and how tomorrow's consumer will live." Everything in the Miramar home of tomorrow is available on the installment plan, right down to the food in the icebox. "To make Miramar as homey and congenial as possible," continues *Tide*, "the builders have established what might be called 'regimented recreation'. As soon as a family moves in the lady of the house will get an invitation to join any number of activities ranging from bridge games to literary teas. Her husband will be introduced, by Miramar, to local groups interested in anything from fish breeding to water skiing." With only each other for company in their own little packaged community, the former SAC pilots at Groom Lake enjoy access to an excellent cafeteria, a steady supply of booze, plus pool tables and a 16 mm projector on movie nights. Nuclear fallout and radioactive matter from hundreds of kilotons of AEC explosions sweep in over the mountains, helping to keep unwanted visitors to an absolute minimum.

The suburban household is increasingly adept at re-creating itself in tiny low-cost installments: in magazines, newspapers and comic books, in TV dinners and other heavily processed, brightly packaged food items. Reality is slowly being reconfigured, one fifteen-cent item at a time. This is the current asking price for a McDonald's hamburger in a year when its first franchise is opened for business in Illinois. The yellow parabolic arches supporting each end of the roadside stand assume the form of incomplete elliptical orbits, arcing up from the ground into space and then falling quickly back to earth again, like the trajectory of an ICBM. At the same time the Atomic Energy Commission poses a smiling housewife atop a pushbutton electric range within sight of its first operational nuclear plant, flipping "atomburgers" in a stainless steel skillet. Intended to celebrate the commercial introduction of atomic energy to the national grid, the demonstration also seeks to underline just how easily the mighty atom can be tamed and domesticated. Or can it be that the nature of family life is becoming stranger, more dangerous? Certainly the sight of the reactor's spherical core and cooling towers rising up behind her seems to suggest some new order of domestic reality never really glimpsed before.

As if in response to this development, the Portland Cement Association, also based in Illinois, markets a ranch-style "blast-resistant house," made out of solid concrete to provide "comfortable living— PLUS a refuge for your family in this atomic age." "Interiors of a blast-resistant house," their ad copy proudly boasts, "have all the charm and livability of conventional houses." However, any potential purchaser of this remarkable new design for living may wish to consider just how much protection a twenty-foot-wide picture window is likely to afford in the event of a nuclear attack.

To this end, some of the more adventurous-minded analysts at RAND can be found following the winding hillside roads of Laurel Canyon up to Albert Wohlstetter's elegant modernist home, the latest landmark of the atomic age. Its rooms, starkly decorated in the International Style, provide the setting for relaxed evenings devoted to gourmet cooking, fine wine, and informed conversation. Dressed casually in sports jackets, the guests either sit on the floor or lean against the stark minimalist furniture, conversing easily on everything from philosophy and art to music and politics. Outside, the lush California vegetation glows in the warm night air while the conversation inside turns toward how to reconstruct the US economy following an all-out thermonuclear war. Meanwhile *Better Homes and Gardens* publishes an article in 1955 suggesting that housewives rotate the stocks of canned foods in the family bomb shelter in order to prevent their contents from building up any unpleasant metallic aftertaste. "Livability," it seems, is where you find it.

When it comes to modern family life, however, the magic is still in the big numbers. "In the next twelve months 1,000,000 boys and girls under the age of 21 will commit crimes serious enough to cause them to be picked up by police," warns Benjamin Fine, education editor of the *New York Times*, in his best-selling study of teenage nonconformity, *1,000,000 Delinquents*. In a society of mass media and mass consumption, uniformity is ultimately what raises us up: the fifteen-cent item that everybody shares is where the big changes are now happening.

On July 17, the day before the AEC makes atomic energy commercially available for the first time, one of the darkest and strangest events in recent history takes place. After "Black Sunday," as it comes to be known, human consciousness will never be the same again. Having sold his home and cashed in his life insurance, Walt Disney has staked everything on establishing Disneyland where formerly only orange trees grew in Anaheim, California, and very nearly loses it all on the first day. Far more people turn up than anticipated, causing massive traffic jams. Their numbers also mean that the concession stands run out of food and drink very early on. Furthermore, most of the rides don't work; the asphalt hasn't set properly, causing the heels of women's shoes to sink into it; and a plumbers' strike means that none of the drinking fountains are working on that hot July afternoon. Within a month, however, Disneyland will be welcoming its millionth customer.

A suburban conurbation that pretends not to be one, the Happiest Place on Earth has only a single entrance, ensuring that everyone who visits Disneyland can have the same experience, enjoying the same view of

Sleeping Beauty's Castle, going on the same ride, and taking part in the same adventure. It also takes you straight out onto Main Street USA, an idealized evocation of small-town life in the days before television and the suburbs came along and spoiled everything. Then it leads you smartly away to one of four separately themed realms: Frontierland, Tomorrowland, Fantasyland, and Adventureland. Here the suburban experience is reconfigured as living cinema: the picture window, which threatens to violate the safety of the blast-resistant house, suddenly offers up a series of dream-like perspectives instead. Frames of reference are expanded to the point where they are no longer relevant. Pulled in deeper through a sequence of carefully staged establishing shots and close-ups, visitors are dazed by the sense of distance involved. There is just so much to see: exactly one week after Disneyland opens to the public, the first U2 spy plane takes off from Groom Lake on a test flight.

What prevents complete sensory overload from setting in, however, is the care with which Disney has already prepared his audience in advance by presenting each of the four realms in the form of hour-long segments on prime-time television. In order to finance the Disneyland project, Walt has created an anthology series for the ABC network entitled *Disneyland* and themed around Frontierland, Tomorrowland, Fantasyland, and Adventureland. For Tomorrowland he enlists the help of Wernher von Braun, who has been kicking his heels down at the Redstone Armory in Huntsville, Alabama, having been forced out of White Sands after SAC had taken over the vast tracts of desert around Fort Bliss. With the US Navy and the Air Force already running their own missile programs, the man who once had the ear of Adolf Hitler is now advising Walt Disney on how to sell space exploration to the American public. The resulting presentations, *Man in Space* and *Man and the Moon*, mix animation with live action and scale models, introduced by von Braun himself in a crisp white shirt talking straight to the camera in his distinctive German accent. An eager student of Hermann Oberth's treatise *Die Rakete zu den Planetenräumen* in his youth, von Braun never really adjusts to using the English word "rocket," his pronunciation maintaining a vestigial echo of his native "rakete."

"Tomorrow can be a wonderful age," Disney says of Tomorrowland, actually the last realm in Disneyland to be completed. "Our scientists today are opening the doors of the Space Age to achievements that will benefit our children and generations to come. The Tomorrowland attractions have been designed to give you an opportunity to participate in adventures that are a living blueprint of our future."

The narrator at the beginning of George Pal's *Conquest of Space* tries to sound even more confident than Walt about the prospect but doesn't quite manage it. "This is a story of tomorrow," he booms before lamely adding "or the day after tomorrow." The movie never really recovers from this faltering step, presenting its audiences with what one critic subsequently describes as "a series of impressive funerals." Based on a book of the same name by Willy Ley and artist Chesley Bonestell but also incorporating material from von Braun's *Das Marsprojekt*, published in German in 1953, *Conquest of Space* offers a glimpse of life in the year 1980, where a space station is shown wheeling around the Earth and work is nearing completion on the first rocket to the Moon. A crew has already been selected, its members given to the kind of griping and joshing usually associated with servicemen in Hollywood war dramas. They sound as if they'd be more at home in a Navy submarine than an orbiting space station. The math and the rocket design may both have been correct, and the astronomical art as accurate as it can be, but the overheated dialogue, plus the tension developing between mission commander Samuel Merritt and his son Barney at the heart of the movie, make *Conquest of Space* a particularly turgid viewing experience.

If we're never far from space in these stories, we're never that removed from family life either. Ranked as general and captain, respectively, father and son are caught in a chain of Oedipal command that permits Merritt Senior to keep the newly married Merritt Junior from his young wife and then go quietly nuts after the mission's true destination is revealed to be not the Earth's moon at all, but the planet Mars instead. Cue more joshing and griping from the crew, followed by General Merritt's slow spiral into madness, finally obliging the son to kill the father when his increasingly erratic behavior threatens the safety of the mission. Despite the technical attention to detail, *Conquest of Space* presents such an inaccurate vision of tomorrow that we don't even accept it as a convincing portrait of today. It does, however, offer further evidence of von Braun, Ley, and Bonestell working the crowd, fully aware that it's the fifteen-cent things that are going to take the American people into the future. For the price of a cinema ticket or a copy of *Collier's* magazine, it seems that everyone can find themselves in outer space, taking in a world they'd scarcely imagined before.

**Plug It In, Joe....**

*Planetary Generator*—The main reason General Merritt goes bughouse is that he believes God never intended humanity to venture out into space in the first place. It's not covered in the Bible, for one thing. A more likely truth, however, might be that God was never meant to be part of the Early American Space Age. Even the term "God" itself is starting to look a little fusty and old-fashioned. Klaatu in his one-piece silver spacesuit spoke of "The Creator of All Things" in *The Day the Earth Stood Still*, and the designation seems to have stuck. The benign Venusian who contacted George Adamski in the desert also spoke of how his people "live according to the Will of the Creator, not by their own personal will, as we do here on Earth." Continued exchanges between the various contactees and the Space Brothers who visit them pointedly emphasize the value of spiritual evolution over material progress.

The theme is a simple one, subject to endless variation. In *The Secret of the Saucers*, edited and published by Ray Palmer, Orfeo Angelucci speaks of the Space Brothers' world as one of "eternal youth, eternal youth, eternal day." In a series of return appearances during 1955, Clarionite saucer captain Aura Rhanes instructs Truman Bethurum to establish a "Sanctuary of Thought" dedicated to "brotherly love." Meanwhile in *Alan's Message to Men of Earth*, telepathically communicated to him by the extraterrestrial known simply as "A-lan," Daniel Fry warns that Lemuria was destroyed in a major war with Atlantis leaving only a few survivors to escape to Mars.

Bland and interchangeable, this succession of higher beings with their even loftier messages constitutes a communications medium in itself. Making countless appearances on radio and TV, the contactees are careful to keep this channel open by never openly contradicting or questioning each other in public.

The medium and the message form a seamless whole together. Acting as Mae West's personal psychic, Jerome Criswell predicts that she will be elected President of the United States next year, at which time she, accompanied by Criswell himself and Liberace's brother George, will ride a rocket ship to the Moon. As a tribute to television's Man of Prophecy, the buxom movie star records the song "Criswell Predicts," named after his syndicated show on KCOP Channel 13 in Los Angeles, for her 1955 album, *The Fabulous Mae West*.

Also due out this year is *Project Blue Book Special Report No. 14*, finally made public by the Air Force, just as Edward Ruppelt attends George Van Tassel's 1955 Giant Rock Spacecraft Convention, sharing the stage with George Adamski, who is less than impressed by the proceedings. Still hard at work on his Integratron, Van Tassel chooses this moment to give a practical demonstration of his latest invention: the "adaphone" with which he is able to communicate directly with the Space Brothers. In a rare breach of media etiquette Adamski tells Ruppelt that he is greatly irritated by Van Tassel's "channeling" antics, a form of cosmic ventriloquist's act during which he speaks in a bewildering array of otherworldly voices.

Adamski finds himself engaging with the Space Brothers on a completely different level these days. "At our work and in our leisure time we mingle with people here on Earth, never betraying the secret that we are inhabitants of other worlds," a man from Saturn confides in him during a drive through the outskirts of Los Angeles. "That would be dangerous, as you well know. We understand you people better than most of you know yourselves and can plainly see the reasons for the many unhappy conditions that surround you."

This admission comes at the start of *Inside the Space Ships*, Adamski's sequel to the best-selling *Flying Saucers Have Landed* and soon to be hailed by his followers as "the most important book since the Bible." This time around Adamski briefly shifts his personal narrative away from the desert, focusing instead on the hotel lobbies, garages, and bars of LA. It is here that he encounters a separate and private universe of extraterrestrials living and working among us, represented in Adamski's narrative by the Saturnian, a Martian, and the Venusian Adamski claims to have met back in 1952. They appear to have no names of their own so Adamski refers to them as "Ramu," "Firkon," and "Orthon," respectively. As *Inside the Space Ships* begins, all four of them are heading down a highway late at night to rendezvous with a Venusian scout ship that has just landed out in the desert. However, it is the world they are leaving behind them that now seems the most interesting and the least familiar.

"We are permitted to make brief visits to our home planets," Ramu the Saturnian also reveals. "Just as you long for a change of scene or to see old friends, so it is with us. It is necessary, of course, to arrange such absences during official holidays, or even over a weekend, so that we will not be missed by our associates here on earth."

Adamski's reaction to this particular revelation is worth noting. "I did not ask whether my companions were married and had families here on our planet," he writes, "but I had the impression this was not the case."

From Tomorrowland to Mars and beyond, the family in outer space has become a recurring theme. It is interesting to note in this context that Adamski is the first to use the term "Mother Ship" to describe the large craft orbiting unseen around the Earth, sending down scout ships to explore our world.

Commuting in from their homes on other planets to work in the cities of Earth, the Space Brothers are the apotheosis of the suburban ideal. To live "according to the Will of the Creator" means to lead a life unblemished: one in which alcoholism and despair, adultery and divorce, fear and emotional breakdown no longer have a place. According to some of the lurid sociological accounts appearing in print at this time, however, these are the very things affecting life in Suburbia. Titles such as *The Crack in the Picture Window* and *The Split Level Trap* make a big show of pulling back the curtains on the scenes of emotional isolation and psychological decay to be found within. No wonder Ramu and the rest of the Space Brothers would seem to constitute a secret public, an alienated lonely crowd existing far beyond the reach of the social anthropologist's probe. "Man in space is free," Van Tassel proclaims in a written appeal to his followers for a further $45,000 to make the Integratron a reality. Even so, Truman Bethurum is heard making frequent remarks during public lectures in 1955 that his second wife divorced him because she was jealous of Captain Rhanes.

It can also get very lonely in space, as astronomer Morris K. Jessup is about to find out the hard way. With the paperback edition of his successful study, *The Case for the UFO*, being readied for publication, a strange sequence of incidents has already been set in motion. Like Desmond Leslie, coauthor with George Adamski of *Flying Saucers Have Landed*, Jessup takes a broad view of the phenomenon, looking back over human history for examples of saucer activity. His researches concentrate upon breaks with the accepted rules of physics, anomalous events that defy rational explanation. The brutal chemical pushing and pulling of today's rocketry, he concludes, will not have the necessary power to take us into space. "If, on the contrary," he argues, "we shift our concentration to the intensive study of gravity, and put on that problem brains and education comparable to those which have solved the problems of fission and atomic structure, it is my honest belief that we can whip the problem of space travel within a decade."

He is not alone in this conviction. "The current efforts to understand gravity and universal gravitation both at the sub-atomic level and at the level of the Universe have the positive backing today of many of America's outstanding physicists," writes Ansel E. Talbert, military and aviation editor for the *New York Herald Tribune*, during the course of a series of articles in 1955. "These include Dr. Edward Teller of the University of California, who received prime credit for developing the hydrogen bomb; Dr. J. Robert Oppenheimer, director of the Institute for Advanced Study at Princeton; Dr. Freeman J. Dyson, theoretical physicist at the Institute; and Dr. John A. Wheeler, professor of physics at Princeton University, who made important contributions to America's first nuclear fission project."

Around this time Jessup starts to receive a number of strange rambling letters from one Carlos Miguel Allende, who claims to know about secret government experiments along the lines advocated in *The Case for the UFO*. Jessup is much closer to the truth than his researches might suggest, the letters warn. He will soon discover that for himself.

A copy of Jessup's book is mailed anonymously to Admiral N. Furth, head of the Office of Naval Research in Washington, DC. Each of its pages has been covered with strange annotations in different colored inks, giving every indication of having been read and commented upon by highly intelligent beings with access to detailed information on the subject of alien technology. The package is postmarked "Seminole, Texas, 1955," with the words "Happy Easter" scrawled in ink across the front.

Ramu and the boys have evidently been busy. In Universal International's *This Island Earth* a mysterious catalog is mailed anonymously to Professor Cal Meacham of the Ryberg Electronics Corporation in Los Angeles, California. Each of its pages is filled with references to unfamiliar parts and components, giving every indication of having been written and compiled by highly intelligent beings with access to detailed information on the subject of alien technology. "This isn't paper," Professor Meacham remarks as he flips through the entries. "It's some kind of metal."

Cal has just returned from a conference in Washington on the industrial applications of atomic energy. "Electronics is your specialty," he is asked at a hastily convened press conference on an airport runway just prior to his departure from the nation's capital. "How does this fit in with atomic energy?" Commercial reactors are hardly news to these reporters, who are used to covering the Washington science beat and were undoubtedly on hand when the AEC's housewife first served up her "atomburgers."

"You boys like to call this the 'Pushbutton Age,'" Cal retorts, his chiseled features caught in dramatic profile against the skyline. "It isn't. Not yet. Not until we can team up electronics with atomic energy."

In fact, the connection between atomic fission and the domestic environment has never been closer. Formica countertops, alloy containers, and stainless-steel utensils, plus a glowing array of electrical goods complete with dials, lights, and readouts, mean that the typical suburban kitchen is beginning to look more like a modern laboratory: a place of experimentation rather than household chores. Similarly, being able to build your own uranium detector or a low-cost fallout shelter connects you with Big Science at a time when it is becoming the domain of Big Business and Big Government. *Popular Mechanics* even runs "Detroit Listening Post" and "Sidelights from the Pentagon" as regular columns to stop its readers from feeling left out. This does not prevent Cal from flying back to California in a military jet with Air Force markings. "One of the boys at Lockheed handed me this," he smirks, indicating just where his position lies within the military-industrial complex.

"Hope you taxpayers don't mind." Never have nuclear physicists led such adventurous and glamorous lives.

It also helps that Professor Meacham has no family to speak of. As he flicks through the pages of the mysterious catalog with his assistant Joe, Cal's true feelings about life in the Pushbutton Age start to reveal themselves. While he breathlessly grapples with such technological marvels as an "Interossiter incorporating planetary generator," an "Interossiter with voltarator," and an "Astroscope," Joe is far more phlegmatic. "Here's something my wife could use in the house," he dryly interjects, "an Interossiter incorporating an electron sorter." Preoccupied by figuring out exactly what an Interossiter is, Cal doesn't appear to appreciate the connection. "Oh, she'd probably gain twenty pounds while it did all the work for her," is his only comment. As he pointed out to the newsmen in Washington, the course of the Pushbutton Age will be determined by whoever creates the devices rather than those who use them. It is an attitude that blinds him to the complex and contradictory relationship developing between advanced technology and the modern suburban home.

"You know what my kids would say," Joe remarks as they both survey the finished Interossiter they have successfully built out of parts ordered from the mysterious catalog. "Dig this crazy mixed-up plumbing."

Once again, Cal manages to miss the point. Instead of pausing to note how even Joe's children are getting hip to what's happening in their own domestic environment, Professor Meacham goes on to deliver what is undoubtedly the giddiest line to be heard in a sci-fi movie so far.

"Plug it in, Joe," he gamely instructs his assistant. "We'll see what happens."

As if the entire universe were wired into the North American grid. All the same, there is no limit to what an Interossiter can do. In attempting to gauge its power, electronics expert Cal Meacham can only see the bizarre gizmo in terms of the culture that produced it, not the one that will now use it. The future still being something that is received rather than transmitted, it shouldn't surprise us that the Interossiter connects Cal to a colony of aliens existing here on Earth or that the device is used to transport him aboard an otherwise empty plane to their secret base of operations. Nor should we be too shocked to discover that Joe, Professor Meacham's able assistant, is left behind with his family in California, never to be seen again. Without anything to connect him directly to a home environment, Cal Meacham is constantly moving on from one location to the next without ever being required to go back and revisit any of them.

So where will this one-way trajectory take him now?

South Georgia, according to the woman in the wood-paneled station wagon who has come to meet his plane; but Cal still has trouble telling the strange from the familiar, the domestic from the alien.

"I kind of expected Neptune or Mars," he counters cheerily.

The good news is that the woman behind the wheel turns out to be Dr. Ruth Adams: a fellow scientist played once again by Faith Domergue. The bad news is that they are both to be part of a team of nuclear physicists busily engaged in coming up with new ways of supplying a race of extraterrestrial aliens with vast amounts of cheap atomic energy. The chief alien, known simply as "Exeter," runs this tight little scientific community as if it were a cross between the RAND Corporation and an exclusive country club, right down to the black maid serving coffee after dinner. Like Cal, Exeter readily confuses the strange with the familiar.

"What do you think of Mr. Mozart, Exeter?" Professor Meacham asks him, referring to the music playing over an unseen speaker system in the community's main dining room.

"I'm afraid I don't know the gentleman," Exeter begins before rapidly correcting himself. "Your composer of course."

"Our composer?" Cal Meacham blithely retorts in a spirit of generosity that any American will appreciate but an Austrian might properly question. "He belongs to the world."

The world will soon be left far behind, however. Cal's restless forward trajectory takes him and Dr. Ruth Adams to Metaluna: a world, according to Exeter, that "lies far beyond your solar system—in outer space." Things on Metaluna are tough all over at the moment. A disastrous war with the neighboring planet of Zaygon means that their stocks of uranium are almost exhausted. There is no longer enough power to shield Metaluna from Zaygon's renewed attacks. "Our edu-

cational complexes now rubble ... over there was a recreation center,"
Exeter mourns, as if surveying the last remains of some suburban re-
development program. Suing for peace is not an option: relocation to
Earth now seems to be the only recourse. Forget it, Cal says. There's
only room for one race on Earth, and we're it. "Our true size," he concludes, tellingly reverting to outmoded terminology in order to make
his point, "is the size of our God." Maybe George Van Tassel, laboring
patiently away on his Integratron, has been right all along. Man in
space is free.

**Inside the Exposed Brain**

*Mutants*—On the whole, the characters in *This Island Earth* seem remarkably comfortable with the technology of the future. Cal Meacham
takes a reading off a Geiger counter without even bothering to refer
to the device by name. Exeter controls some of the Interossiter's functions merely by waving his hand in space, and no one appears to register any surprise at this. Similarly, Meacham and Adams take in the
smooth seamless lines of Exeter's spaceship and the gray one-piece
spacesuits worn for their journey to Metaluna without comment,
while the neat "atomic" motif, repeated throughout the extraterrestrial decor, depicting three electrons tracing elliptical orbits around a
central neutron, barely raises an eyebrow. These are already part of
what is by now a familiar iconography, the atomic logo in particular
having established itself as a design feature in the modern suburban
home, adorning everything from clocks and coat racks to electric ra-
zors and refrigerators.

A more striking aspect of *This Island Earth* is the misshapen creature that comes slouching along the ruined walkways of Metaluna's
suburbs to confront the startled earthlings. "I'd hoped to have prepared you somewhat beforehand," Exeter apologetically confesses to
Meacham and Adams. "This is a Mutant. We've been breeding them
for ages to do menial work. Well, actually they're similar to some of
the insect life on your own planet, larger of course and with a higher
degree of intelligence."

Which possibly helps to explain why the creature appears to have
most of its brain on the outside of his head. Advanced and backward at

the same time, this monstrous drone stands out in a year characterized by its onscreen chimeras, not the least of which are *The Creature with the Atom Brain*, *The Beast with a Million Eyes*, *Devil Girl from Mars*, *Revenge of the Creature*, *King Dinosaur*, *Tarantula*, and *The Cult of the Cobra*, starring Faith Domergue yet again, this time able to transform herself into a giant snake.

The same year that Einstein's brain will be surgically removed seven hours after his death and preserved for further study, the Mutant's artificially trained mind remains on public view, drawing graphic attention to another piece of future technology that is never actually seen in the movie and only rarely mentioned. Nevertheless, its effects are there for all to see. Described by Ruth as a "sunray lamp," the Transformer is designed to control people's minds. "Only instead of a suntan, you get your brain cells rearranged," she helpfully adds, it being her turn to confuse the domestic with the strange. "It's similar to lobotomy," another scientist concurs. "Renders useless certain areas of the brain, those areas controlling the power of the will."

Tell that to Donald Hebb. Having received Rockefeller funding for his sensory deprivation experiments to brainwash students into developing an interest in occult matters, the author of *The Organization of Behavior* is currently in Washington briefing a couple of scientists at the National Institutes of Health. This is prior to both candidates being approached by the CIA with an offer to underwrite their work on mind control.

The first possible recipient of agency funding is Dr. Maitland Baldwin. A former student of both Hebb and Wilder Penfield, Dr. Baldwin's researches into sensory deprivation have taken the form of an "isolation box" for which he now requires "an antagonistic subject" he can take "to termination." Baldwin knows how to play scientific hardball, having previously performed lobotomies on laboratory monkeys, even going so far as to transplant the brain from one unfortunate ape into the skull of another. So when the good doctor says "termination," you know he means it. The "antagonistic subject" is to be stuck inside a padded box, deprived of all light and sound, being fed tasteless pap through a tube until his ego collapses. "Anyone going through a complete breakdown," Dr. Baldwin observes in his proposal, "would come out with somewhat lowered mental faculties."

Confronted with the prospect of having a Mutant of their very own loping around the corridors at Langley, Virginia, as a result of Baldwin's proposed experiment, even the CIA holds back. "Does [the] Project officer approve of these immoral and inhuman tests?" a shocked internal memo asks. "I suggest that all who are in favor of the above-mentioned operation volunteer their heads for use in Dr. Baldwin's 'noble' project."

The second and more likely candidate is John C. Lilly, who is currently conducting sensory-deprivation experiments upon himself, suspended in the lukewarm water of a "float tank" located within a darkened soundproofed room. Lilly preferred to test the float tank's effectiveness upon himself, having grown uncomfortable over his own research with apes, which involved surgically implanting electrodes in their brains. Such scruples will mean that Lilly ultimately turns down the offer of CIA assistance, just as his experiences floating in warm dark silence will lead him to start studying the therapeutic effects of LSD by testing it upon himself.

Of course not everyone gets to have a choice in the matter. In 1955 George Hunter White is transferred from his Greenwich Village pad to run a new operation from a safe house on San Francisco's Telegraph Hill. The change of location also indicates a change in test subject. Instead of dosing drifters and bohemians, White will now be entertaining a different type of clientele. A specially trained squad of hookers have been hired to lure visiting businessmen back to what, at first glance, appears to be the gaudy splendors of a whorehouse, unaware that they are actually entering a behavioral field laboratory set up, financed, and run by the CIA. Here they will be served drinks laced with LSD while White sits on a portable toilet behind a two-way mirror, sipping a martini and watching the results. The main aim of Operation Midnight Climax, as it has been so thoughtfully named, is to conduct further research into the drug's effectiveness as a mind-control agent. Pretty soon, any powerful new hallucinogen that comes to the attention of the boys at MK-ULTRA or the Army Chemical Corps is routinely dispatched to Telegraph Hill for further testing.

One of the many possible side effects of Operation Midnight Climax is the indirect influence the program exerts upon the gradual gentrification of the hallucinatory experience. Its clientele represents the first of a new generation of white-collar drug fiends, bent upon discreet pleasures. Who, after all, is going to admit to their family and friends that they have just seen God in a San Francisco whorehouse? It's not as if the experience is deductible, after all. At the same time, the important role pleasure now plays in the furtherance of this kind of experimentation is worth noting. The electrodes inserted by John C. Lilly into the exposed brains of his laboratory apes allowed them to reward themselves by directly stimulating the pleasure centers in their cerebral cortex. Thus empowered, Dr. Lilly observes, the apes are capable of maintaining themselves in a state of continuous orgasm for hours at a time. Not surprisingly, Midnight Climax is one of the few CIA research projects to turn an appreciable profit.

For those wired directly into their own experience, the reward is in and of itself enough. The smart monkey understands that beyond and behind therapy lies the pleasure principle. What John C. Lilly and George Hunter White have so far only hinted at, another voice is now ready to proclaim.

If Al "Cappy" Hubbard did not already exist, some painstaking historian of the future might well feel the need to invent him. A former officer in the OSS, wartime precursor to today's CIA, Al Hubbard later struck it rich as a uranium prospector and is now dedicating his considerable resources as President of the Vancouver Uranium Company to spreading the word on LSD. More than simply connecting the split atom with the split mind, Al Hubbard brings a profoundly spiritual dimension to the relationship. A devout Catholic, Hubbard's approach to science favors the visionary Age of Tesla over the pragmatic Era of Edison. He even claims to have invented, as a child, his own "atmospheric power generator," capable of drawing energy from the air, and a form of radar based on Tesla's ideas.

Hubbard is consequently concerned with the more spiritual aspects of the LSD experience. He has already used the drug in the treatment of alcoholics with "miraculous" results, impressed by its power to shatter the old habits of the self, rendering the mind more susceptible to being reintegrated through exposure to religious symbols and imagery. He has even persuaded Humphrey Osmond of the superiority of this therapeutic response over the old psychotomimetic model and is found taking mescaline in the company of Aldous Huxley and Gerald Heard in 1955. By Christmas he will have accompanied Huxley on his first LSD trip. But then Al Hubbard can afford it, having put in a bulk order for thirty-four cases of LSD earlier in the year. Despite dismissing the CIA as "lousy deceivers," Hubbard operates in a remarkably similar manner, checking out everyone's research and stockpiling massive amounts of the drug, which he distributes freely to anyone who asks for it. And therein lies the big difference between Hubbard and the lousy deceivers at MK-ULTRA: those who try LSD thanks to his benign agency are at least aware that they are taking it.

Leaving behind the old mechanistic view of how the mind functions, which has so far manifested itself in a reduction of laboratory conditions to degree zero of sensory deprivation, Hubbard is one of the first to grasp how important environment is to mental abreaction. This emphasis on setting directly correlates with the enriched domestic environment of the suburban home, where the living room has become a departure lounge to a heightened world of gracious living, informed by color, light, fabrics, textures, sound, and vision. In the same way, Hubbard has started using carefully selected music and pictures, religious iconography, and encouraging words to take you through the experience; and just as the domestic environment has the capacity to transform itself into your own personal theme park, so too does LSD. One of Hubbard's grander plans is to design a whole LSD experience to take place in Death Valley, which he considers to be an "extraordinary power spot." Although this transcendental Tomorrowland will never be realized, it does indicate the extent to which drugs in general, and LSD in particular, are becoming new forms of media: tentative environments of brief connections, interactions, breaches of meaning, fleeting perceptions of reality that hitherto have only existed in electronic terms. Some, however, will simply feel their entire personalities coming apart or find themselves being pursued by unspeakable horrors. LSD's effectiveness in treating mental disorders remains open to question, the results being patchy and inconclusive, to say the least.

No two subjects react to it in the same way, and what often appears to be a "miracle cure" can vanish overnight. "So far as I'm concerned,"

George Hunter White says of his experience running Operation Midnight Climax, "'clear thinking' was non-existent while under the influence of any of these drugs. I did feel at times like I was having a 'mind-expanding experience,' but this vanished like a dream immediately after the session." Although it should also be noted that the decor in his Telegraph Hill bordello is a staggeringly garish mix of African fabrics, Toulouse Lautrec reproductions, black velvet tablecloths, plaid drapes, and candy-stripes.

"Canadian Scientists Develop Beneficial Brainwashing" runs a headline in an October issue of *Weekend* magazine. Having been investigated by the Rockefeller Foundation over his Cold War remarks at the APA convention in Los Angeles, Dr. Ewen Cameron continues to receive funding for his "psychic driving" experiments at Allan Memorial Hospital, where he has stepped up the repetition of tape instructions and augmented their effect with massive doses of LSD. Seen from the perspective of Al Hubbard's experience, psychic driving takes the shattering of the self to a mechanistic extreme. Over the past two years, Cameron has been using recordings of his sessions with patients to confront them directly with their own words. You can't argue with a revelation, however inadvertent, that has been captured on magnetic tape. Responses tend to be violent and uncontrollable, obliging the patient to be sent into prolonged periods of chemical sleep dosed on a cocktail of barbiturates mixed with chlorpromazine, a new drug used in the treatment of schizophrenics. This period of artificially suspended animation is now being "driven," thanks to the introduction of tape loops playing back positive messages, reinforcing the need to get well. As well as LSD, Cameron has also been breaking up his patients' sleep patterns with the introduction of powerful amphetamines and ECT sessions, augmented by periods of sensory deprivation, much to Donald Hebb's chagrin and disgust.

No big surprise then that Cameron should select a family publication like *Weekend* to present his findings to the world rather than having them first appear in a professional journal for review by his peers.

Psychic driving, the article argues, is really a beneficial form of brainwashing, encountering similar forms of resistance in its subjects. "The Doctors at the Allen of course are doing the exact opposite of mental murder," it continues reassuringly, "they are making sick minds well again. But they face many of the same problems as the professional brainwashers. Prisoners of war resist attempts to indoctrinate them— and almost every patient tries to defend himself against the unpleasant impact of his own recorded voice by deliberately not listening to it, or by thinking of something else."

Even the extraterrestrial Exeter in *This Island Earth* knows this to be the case.

"The Transformer is morally abhorrent to the subjects," he objects when ordered to use the mind-control device on Meacham and Adams. "It sets up subconscious blocks which defeat our very purpose."

Meanwhile Cameron keeps tinkering with different combinations of effects, hoping for an automated breakthrough into sanity. For him, psychic driving remains the perfect model for mental health in an age of parkways and interstates, when human contact is diminishing due to the growing presence of the automobile.

With car sales for 1955 hitting $6.5 billion, automobile registration is now twice what it was in 1945; and General Motors has just become the first corporation in history to make over $1 billion in a single financial year. Over at GM's main rival Ford, "whiz kid" Robert McNamara, a former Air Force lieutenant, initiates a test program at Cornell in which students drop padded human skulls down a campus stairwell in order to study the fractures and breakage caused by automobile collisions. Never has the human brain been exposed to such a beating.

"It was fun, fun, fun," George Hunter White later reveals about his time on Operation Midnight Climax. "Where else could a red-blooded American boy lie, kill, cheat, steal, rape and pillage with the sanction and blessing of the All-Highest?" Let's just hope he isn't talking about the Creator of All Things. In a year when the annual sales of tranquilizers hit $2.2 million, J. Robert Oppenheimer manages to express this same sentiment in a slightly more palatable form. "In a very profound sense, and in a way that cannot be lightly dismissed," declares the former director of the AEC, "we scientists have sinned."

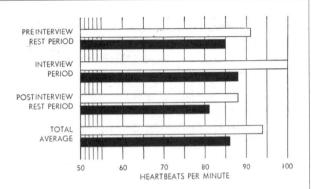

**HEART RATE increases under LSD.** The open bars indicate the heart rate of subjects to whom LSD has been administered; the black bars, subjects to whom no LSD has been given.

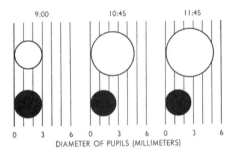

**PUPIL SIZE gradually increases under LSD.** The open circles indicate, over two hours and 45 minutes, the pupil diameter of a subject to whom LSD had been given. The black circles show at the same intervals and the same light the pupil diameter of the subject without LSD.

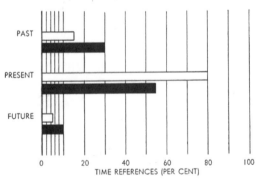

**TIME SENSE is also affected by LSD.** Here this is plotted on the basis of references to time in the Thematic Apperception Test, in which the subject is shown a dramatic picture and asked to tell a story about it. The open bars represent time references by 29 subjects to whom LSD had been given. The black bars represent time references by the subjects without LSD.

# 1956: "GREETINGS, MY FRIEND!"

## Criswell Predicts

*Los Angeles*—The lights come up inside the darkened shell of Merle Connell's Quality Studios, and the Amazing Criswell, his hands arranged neatly on the desk in front of him, stares confidently into the lens of a whirring movie camera. "Greetings, my friend!" he cheerfully proclaims. "We are all interested in the future—for that is where you and I are going to spend the rest of our lives."

It is late November; and Criswell, with his blond spit curl and natty bowties, can sense that the future is on the other side of now. As a television psychic, he has long been dispensing the kind of information that would cause mass panic if it weren't presented with such a confident smile. Only a few weeks ago, in the October 22 edition of the *New York Enquirer*, he has already started speculating about what kind of treatment humanity can expect at the hands of visiting aliens. "Will they perform cruel experiments, to see what makes us tick?" he wondered. "This may sound frightening, terrifying and unbelievable, but it may be part of your Incredible Future."

It is also Criswell who announced that an interplanetary convention of visiting aliens will be held in Las Vegas and that someday soon the laws of gravity will stop functioning altogether.

"And remember, my friend," he admonishes, as the camera closes in on his face. "Future events such as these will affect you in the future."

And who understands his age better than the man who looks into its future? While the American Century continues to gather pace, the Amazing Criswell is coming to the end of his opening speech in one of the cheapest sci-fi flicks of all time. "We cannot keep this a secret any longer," he confides to the impassively turning camera, nodding his head for emphasis. "My friend, can your heart stand the shocking facts of ... *Grave Robbers from Outer Space?*"

Made with financial backing from the Baptist Church of Beverly Hills, *Grave Robbers from Outer Space* is the latest offering from enthused filmmaker Edward D. Wood Jr. Operating on the outer fringes

161

of Hollywood as producer, director, writer, and occasional actor, Ed Wood is responsible for such inspired cinematic misfires as *Glen or Glenda* (a.k.a. *I Changed My Sex*) and *Bride of the Monster* (a.k.a. *Bride of the Atom*). Like an alien contactee, he also works best in Revealed Time, making movies whose titles and final release dates are constantly shifting, their casts and themes reflecting a fragmented, disparate galaxy of faded movie stars and pinup girls, established pulp conventions and tabloid headlines.

And now he brings you a terrifying tale of beings from another world attempting to avert the destruction of the entire universe by proving to mankind that flying saucers really do exist. Joining Criswell in its telling are TV horror show hostess Vampira, retired professional wrestler Tor Johnson, radio announcer Dudley Manlove, and Hollywood's original Vampire Count, Bela Lugosi, making his last ever appearance on celluloid. Assisting Ed Wood Jr. in the editing of his latest blockbuster is Phil Tucker, the man responsible for bringing *Robot Monster* to the screen.

What even Criswell cannot predict, however, is that Ed Wood's latest film is destined to remain on the laboratory shelf, languishing in Revealed Time for another three years before finally being released as *Plan 9 from Outer Space* at decade's end.

This is perhaps not the best year in which to make wild predictions. Leon Festinger and his research team have finally published an account of their experiences with Mrs. Marian Keech and her Lake City circle back in 1952. Thanks to *When Prophecy Fails*, the public is introduced for the first time to the concept of "cognitive dissonance": a term adopted by Festinger to describe the internal conflicts between "opinions, beliefs, knowledge of the environment, and knowledge of one's own actions and feelings" that can occur in an individual, especially when a fervently prophesied event fails to materialize. Festinger's surprising discovery is that such a failure actually serves to strengthen belief rather than dispel it.

"The individual will frequently emerge, not only unshaken, but even more convinced of the truth of his beliefs than ever before," Festinger remarks, thinking of Mrs. Keech and her followers standing out in the rain in the run-up to Christmas, waiting for the Space Brothers to make their final appearance. "Indeed, he may even show a new fervor about convincing and converting other people to his view." Out of the flying-saucer group's original eleven members, only two have left the circle; the rest have become more committed than ever to the truth of Mrs. Keech's revelations. In other words, cognitive dissonance is the affirmation of belief expressed in Revealed Time.

"The future seems so strange," chirps Thelma Tadlock in the General Motors short, *Design for Dreaming*. "But not as strange as it's going to be...." Produced for Motorama '56, this promotional film shows the young performer singing and dancing her way through a glittering universe of cars and fridges until she is finally whisked away in a futuristic car onto the highways of tomorrow.

What's good for General Motors, after all, is good for the whole nation.

As the Suez Canal crisis threatens to put the squeeze on the importation of crude oil into the West, government scientists at the University of California Radiation Laboratory, established in 1952 to tend America's nuclear stockpile, propose using atomic weapons to excavate a brand new canal through Israel. What's good for the whole nation turns out to be good for General Motors as well.

Other schemes being kicked around as part of what is optimistically designated "Project Plowshare" include the use of thermonuclear bombs to mine for oil, locate natural gas, create an "instant harbor" on the northern Alaskan coastline, dig a "Panatomic Canal" in Nicaragua, and lay a multilane highway through the Southern Californian mountains. Father of the H-Bomb Edward Teller becomes one of Plowshare's most enthusiastic supporters.

Ed Wood's vision of brain-dead zombies marching on Washington in order to convince the world to give up its atomic weapons may not be to everyone's taste, but the antinuclear message contained in *Grave Robbers from Outer Space* is expressed in a far more overt fashion than audiences have come to expect from Hollywood at this time. The US version of *Gojira*, released in 1956 as *Godzilla: King of Monsters!*, has had all explicit references to Nagasaki, Bikini Atoll, and the effects of radioactive fallout carefully removed.

"I wonder how we would re-shoot the atomic bomb dropping?" remarks Ed Wood, a man used to courting disappointment. Unlike the scientists at Project Plowshare, however, he is well aware of the dangers involved in trying to get everything right in one take.

Under a title that links past with future, *Grave Robbers from Outer Space* is a contradiction in terms, successfully inhabiting Revealed Time by covertly reflecting very real public concerns. "Saucers seen over Hollywood!" Criswell grimly intones as martial music swells to a climax beneath his voice on the soundtrack. "Flying saucers seen over Washington, DC!"

Except that Air Force figures for 1956 indicate a dramatic decline in the number of unsolved sightings, constituting a mere 0.4 percent of all reported incidents as opposed to nearly 25 percent during Captain Ed Ruppelt's time as head of Project BLUE BOOK. As luck will have it, and as the Robertson Panel's findings continue to eat into the statistical evidence, this is also the year in which Ruppelt publishes *The Report on Unidentified Flying Objects*, detailing his experiences at BLUE BOOK.

There is enough internal evidence to suggest that *Grave Robbers from Outer Space* is partly based on his account. The bemused and fair-minded Colonel Tom Edwards, shown reluctantly ordering an armed attack on flying saucers seen dangling over Washington on invisible wires in Ed Wood's film, bears more than a passing resemblance to the bemused and fair-minded Edward Ruppelt to be found in the pages of *The Report on Unidentified Flying Objects*. Frustrated references to the Defense Department's "upper echelons" and to commercial pilots being "muzzled by Army brass" also find distinct echoes in Ruppelt's book, whose title combines official Air Force rhetoric with an apparent sympathy for those members of the public bold enough to have reported what they have seen in the skies over America.

That same year Ed Ruppelt also appears in the theatrically released documentary, *UFO*, which offers a dramatic recap of major saucer activity to date, including the Thomas Mantell incident of 1948. "See it all as it actually happened—and is still happening!" the poster copy claims. And it is. John Kraus, an astronomer at Ohio University, claims to have detected weird signals emanating from Venus.

But how will the public ever get to hear the truth about this? Gray Barker's *They Knew Too Much about Flying Saucers*, also published in

1956, offers one of the first accounts of people reporting UFO sightings and then being visited by the mysterious Men in Black, who wear outdated clothes and drive cars with fake license plates. "One by one," Barker remarks of the Men in Black's intimidation technique, "the leading figures among flying saucer researchers, who have challenged the government denial that saucers come from outer space, have been silenced."

The growing suspicion that the government is actively colluding with the Pentagon in keeping Americans unaware of what is happening in the skies above them remains a predominant theme in the writings of Major Don Keyhoe. His ability to interpret the thinking behind the Air Force's impassive policy of denial reaches dramatic new heights with his latest book, *Flying Saucer Conspiracy*, originally published in 1955. In it he has begun to describe the inner workings of a "silence group," embedded deep within the government and dedicated to keeping a tight lid on saucer sightings, charting in pulp-magazine prose the group's mercurial mood swings from "cold determination" to "desperate decision." The silence group, it seems, has the power to keep everyone quiet—except of course for Major Don himself.

Where they have failed, however, perhaps Hollywood will succeed. *Earth vs. the Flying Saucers*, a gripping tale of invaders from outer space "suggested" by Keyhoe's *The Flying Saucers Are Real*, finally hits the screens in 1956. Shot in a semi-documentary style, the film relies upon an uneven mix of stop-motion animation and old newsreel footage to tell a tale that bears very little relation to anything that appears in Don Keyhoe's first book.

Dr. Russell Marvin, played by Hugh Marlow, last seen in *The Day the Earth Stood Still* as Patricia Neal's shifty fiancé, is about to spend his honeymoon sealed away with his new bride inside a bunker located deep beneath a rocket silo in the New Mexico desert. "Today I've got a hot date with a three-stage rocket," he pants at a time when TV and the movies still portray most husbands and wives as sleeping in separate beds.

Dr. Marvin is head of Operation Skyhook, an ambitious attempt to establish a network of satellites in orbit around the Earth. Unfortunately, things haven't been going too well lately. For one thing, the satellites keep crashing back down to earth. For another, Dr. and Mrs. Marvin have just been buzzed by a flying saucer while driving to their honeymoon bunker. Next thing they know, the whole of humanity is under attack from alien invaders. The flying saucers are eventually defeated but not before Washington's administrative buildings are left in smoldering ruins, thanks primarily to special-effects virtuoso Ray Harryhausen, the man responsible for the giant six-legged octopus menacing San Francisco in *It Came from Beneath the Sea*. One wonders with what satisfaction Keyhoe must have watched the demolition of Washington and the routing of the Pentagon's massed forces.

It is interesting to note, however, that during the course of the entire film neither the Air Force nor the US government officially confirms the existence of flying saucers, even while their occupants are busily abducting citizens and blowing up major landmarks in the nation's capital.

In an attempt to challenge such institutionalized complacency, former Navy physicist T. Townsend Brown and Clara L. John, a close friend of George Adamski, establish NICAP: the National Investigations Committee on Aerial Phenomena. Its aim, according to T. Townsend Brown, is to coordinate the activities of individual saucer groups "into a pattern that will prepare humanity for this startling new event in human existence." Those assisting at its early meetings include Donald Keyhoe and Morris K. Jessup, still troubled by the revelation that the Office of Naval Research has received a copy of his book on UFOs apparently annotated by individuals possessing knowledge of alien propulsion systems.

As well he might be. In "How I Control Gravity," a 1929 article for *Science and Invention*, T. Townsend Brown expounded on his observation that a high-voltage electric current passing through a capacitor causes a tiny force to move it toward its positive pole. Postulating that there might be a connection between gravity and electromagnetic fields, Brown foresaw a radical new means of transportation. "Perhaps even the fantastic 'space cars' and the promised visit to Mars may be the final outcome," he mused. "Who can tell?"

**"In God We Trust"**

*Secrets of the Krell*—Just as the cheapest sci-fi movie of all time goes into production, one of the most well-appointed film fantasies ever made is being readied for release at MGM. *Forbidden Planet* is set, somewhat reassuringly for the human race, in the twenty-third century; and technological progress appears to have been relatively smooth up to this point. By the final decade of the twenty-first century men and women in rocket ships will have landed on the Moon; and by 2200 they will have reached the other planets of the solar system. And now, some four hundred years into the future, United Planets Cruiser C57-D is in deep space rapidly approaching the planet Altair IV. "The Lord sure makes some beautiful worlds," ship's physician "Doc" Ostrow murmurs reverently to himself as he gazes down at its surface.

Little does he know.

Altair IV was once home to the Krell, a mighty race of highly evolved, intellectually advanced creatures who were mysteriously wiped out in a single night, leaving their world a barren desert with a gigantic nuclear reactor at its core. With its surface devoid of all civilization and its suburbs hidden far below ground, Altair IV is another Metaluna. Maybe Doc Ostrow is wrong about the beauty of this world. Just as Metaluna turned into a distant supernova exploding in the dark depths of space at the end of *This Island Earth*, so too does Altair in the final scene of *Forbidden Planet*. Doc's reference to the Lord should also be taken under advisement. This is pretty much the only mention the Great Creator is going to get until the closing message in a movie that effectively outlines the dangers inherent in transforming ourselves into gods.

One early indicator of how far humanity has already advanced over the intervening centuries is that the United Planets Cruiser C57-D is quite evidently a flying saucer. Seamless and without discernible joins, its interior could easily pass for a busier version of those described by Adamski and his fellow contactees. According to *Forbidden Planet*'s generous vision of things to come, it would seem that we ourselves are now the Space Brothers—or at least have the potential to become them, which is as much as popular culture might decently allow at the moment. Back on Earth, Title 36, Subtitle I, Part A, Chapter 3, Section

302 of the United States Code replaces the secular sentiments of "*e pluribus unum*" with the more pious "In God We Trust" as the nation's official motto.

The crew of the C57-D are considerably less advanced than the craft they are flying, however. Formerly a symbol of technological superiority, and a challenge to all who encounter one to change their lives, this particular flying saucer seems to have had little effect upon its occupants. Careful attention to the soundtrack reveals that the first exchange between Skipper John Adams and his "Astrogator" Lieutenant Jerry Farman is an angry expostulation. A test edit of *Forbidden Planet* has proved so successful with audiences that the preview version has been rushed into general release with parts of the dialogue either missing or incomplete. Consequently, the exchange in which the Skipper chews out Lieutenant Farman for steering them too close to the sun remains largely obscured.

Nor is Lieutenant Farman so very different from his fellow crewmembers, all of whom talk and behave as if they last saw action fighting the Imperial Japanese Navy, right down to the Southern-fried ship's cook, seen swigging "genuine Ancient Rocket bourbon" straight from the bottle. Looking at them, not so very far removed from the spacestation crew in *Conquest of Space*, we share the same sense of panic that must have run through the American psychiatric community when it first discovered that, out of fourteen million service personnel tested during World War II, a staggering 14 percent were unfit for active duty due to psychological disorders.

Did the therapeutic strategies, personality tests, and psychological screening devised in the wake of World War II help to guarantee the future of the human race or is it still a question of plain, old-fashioned discipline?

"I will have less dreaming aboard this ship!" the Skipper thunders at one point, clearly not a man for mental aberrations.

Fortunately, the advanced design of the C57-D doesn't leave its crew with much to do beyond lifting heavy objects, moving them around, and then putting them down again. Throughout the film, they continue their sweaty labors as if still patrolling the Pacific. The lotus-eaters glimpsed at the start of *It Came from Beneath the Sea*, sealed inside their pushbutton world aboard America's first atomic submarine, seem indolent to the point of unconsciousness by comparison. "Keep them busy," the Skipper commands the ship's bos'un at one point. "Right," the bos'un replies, evidently knowing his shipmates well. "The busier the better." The secret of Altair IV is not meant for them, in any case.

The only individual to have glimpsed even a part of that secret is Dr. Morbius, sole survivor of the only other expedition ever to reach the planet. "Prepare your minds for a new scale of physical scientific values, gentlemen," he announces before taking Doc and the Skipper on an underground tour of Krell Suburbia. As they move from laboratories packed with mind-expanding educational equipment to the gigantic atomic piles that still power the entire complex, it quickly becomes apparent that Morbius isn't kidding. A seemingly endless arrangement of flashing lights, glowing switches, sparking electrodes, and flickering meters, the Krell suburbs glitter and pulse like a gigantic brain. Highly evolved both spiritually and intellectually, the Krell may have vanished overnight, like the inhabitants of ancient Lemuria, but there is more to their mysterious disappearance than that. Morbius has also discovered that the Krell were on the verge of developing a radical new form of technology capable of harnessing the collective power of thought, sending it anywhere in the universe they chose in any shape or form they wished. "A civilization without instrumentality," marvels Doc Ostrow, sensing how close invisibility and divinity are to each other. "Incredible," Morbius replies, finishing the thought for him. Doomed to dematerialize one way or another, the Krell faced only two options at the end of their evolutionary trajectory: become gods or die trying.

Living in idyllic isolation on Altair IV, Morbius is also on the verge of becoming a god. Having experimented with the Krell "plastic educator," his intellect has been expanded to twice its original capacity, effectively rendering him an intermediary between the two races. Able to control the workings of his home by the simple wave of a hand in space—a sure sign of technological advancement since Klaatu first demonstrated the trick back in 1951—Morbius commands all that he sees around him, not least his attractive teenage daughter Altaira and his robot servant, Robby, both of whom hang on his every word. Nor do the correspondences end there.

The same mysterious force that destroyed the Krell was also responsible for tearing his colleagues apart and is now busily working its way through the crew of the C57-D. Part of the problem is that Robby and Altaira are just too obliging. The robot will do anything short of killing people on command while Altaira runs around dressed like an intergalactic cocktail waitress, kissing the first guy who asks her. In no time at all, Jerry the hotshot Astrogator is putting the make on Altaira, while Cookie talks Robby into secretly running off sixty gallons of his favorite booze. No wonder Morbius is constantly urging the Skipper and his crew to go back where they came from. It is pretty clear by now to whom this particular planet is forbidden.

The one exception is Doc Ostrow, for whom Morbius develops quite a liking. The two of them are soon relaxing in the Krell laboratory, testing each other's brainpower while the Skipper looks on. Products of a therapeutic age, both men know their Intelligence Quotient down to the last integer while the Skipper, as Morbius points out, "doesn't need brains—just a good loud voice." Altaira, on the other hand, is simply dumb. "Nothing human would ever enter your head," the Skipper remarks of her promiscuous behavior before telling her to put some more clothes on.

Meanwhile Doc is down in the Krell lab again, subjecting himself to the same atomic-powered "brain booster" Morbius used to double his own IQ. "You ought to see my new mind," Ostrow moans afterward, a burn mark the size of a silver dollar in the center of his forehead. "Up there in lights. Bigger than his now." Looks like someone has been trying to leap ahead of the evolutionary curve.

This is a good time to be comparing minds. At Los Angeles cocktail parties writers and artists, philosophers and psychiatrists are all talking up the beneficial effects of LSD. Joining Aldous Huxley and Gerald Heard at such gatherings are philosopher and radio show host Alan Watts, professional deep-sea diver Perry Bivens, TV producer Ivan Tors, novelist Anaïs Nin, plus psychiatrists and researchers Oscar Janiger, Sidney Cohen, Keith Ditman, and Arthur Chandler. In many ways LSD has taken over from Dianetics as the talking point of the moment, offering yet another therapeutic imperative, another scientific model for the future progress of humankind. More than simply modish, this shift indicates a continued slippage from the empirical to the anecdotal in the study of LSD: something for which Dianetics has helped to prepare the way. Talk and therapy have, in any case, rarely been strangers to one another. Over cocktails and canapés, the hallucination introduces itself into polite conversation as personal narrative. Descriptions of the LSD experience abound with tales of individuals giving birth to themselves, rapid accelerations back along the personal time track to confront the causes of existing neuroses, plus dizzying expansions of the human sensorium. "Without being a mathematician, I understand the infinite," Anaïs Nin confides in Oscar Janiger after one session. A Beverly Hills psychiatrist, Janiger has persuaded Sandoz to send him a stock of LSD for research purposes, passing it on to artists and writers to see what they come up with. With no preconceived objective other than experimentation for its own sake—a slightly more serious term for creative play—Janiger approaches the hallucinogen as a "plastic educator," leaving his volunteers relatively free to explore its influence while documenting the results with paper, pencils, and tape recorders.

In contrast to "the 'scientific' LSD boys," as Huxley has dismissively described them, Janiger's approach takes into account the extent to which environment and means of documentation affect the subject, both directly and metaphorically. The problem with testing LSD under laboratory conditions is that, thanks to its influence, there is no laboratory anymore—only conditions, sensitivity to which is heightened to the point where little else remains. As individual consciousness and the environment merge into one, the need for a wide range of enriched stimuli, such as those supplied by the tactile surfaces and rich color schemes of the modern suburban home, becomes increasingly apparent. Similarly, the slow unwinding of magnetic tape from one reel to another would seem to offer a perfect metaphor for how consciousness exists in time, allowing therapeutic revisits and revisions to past traumas and inhibitions.

One individual capable of appreciating this distinction is Myron Stolaroff, head of long-range planning at Ampex, a San Francisco company manufacturing both magnetic tape and tape recorders. His curiosity awakened while attending a lecture by Gerald Heard extolling the effects of mind-altering drugs, Stolaroff is soon playing host to Al Hubbard, who helps him relive his birth in a traumatic LSD experience. Firmly convinced that the hallucinogen is "the greatest discovery that man has ever made," Stolaroff agrees to work with Hubbard, introducing it to the Ampex workforce, in order to foster individual creativity and improve productivity. Thanks to LSD, they believe, Ampex will be transformed into the perfect successful company.

Such thinking is taking place in an entirely different dimension from that of the laboratory madness boys. It constitutes an evolutionary shift in consciousness not entirely dissimilar to the one represented in the contactee experience. A moment of recognition occurs; a secret understanding has taken place. "When you made contact," remarks Oscar Janiger of the exchange that took place between two LSD researchers encountering each for the first time, "it was like two people looking at each other from across the room, and with a sort of nod of the head ... like 'Welcome brother, you have now entered the Mysteries.'"

Compare this description with Orpheo Angelucci's encounter with Gerald Heard and consider how easy it would be to replace the word "researcher" with "initiate." The complex exchanges involved in the notion of contact ensure that there is increasingly little difference between the two. "To tell the truth," Morbius observes on first meeting Doc Ostrow, "I sometimes still miss the conversation of such gentlemen as yourself, Doctor."

When Doc dies in the Skipper's arms, muttering something about "monsters from the Id," Morbius sounds considerably less indulgent. "The fool!" he rages. "The meddling idiot! As though his ape's brain could contain the secrets of the Krell!"

But apes' brains are precisely what this film is about.

Considerable technological progress may well have taken place over the next three or so centuries, according to *Forbidden Planet*, but the evolutionary trajectory has become perceptibly skewed. Inasmuch as Morbius, with his artificially expanded intellect, is now a representative of the Krell and an indicator of what humanity is destined to become, he must also share his monsters with them. The Krell, having evolved to a higher mental and spiritual level with the aid of their brain boosters, forgot about their own baser selves, which turned on them at the exact moment of their dematerialization.

"Morbius, what is the Id?" the Skipper demands, again favoring discipline over the therapeutic. "It's an obsolete term, I'm afraid," Morbius replies distractedly, "once used to describe the elementary basis of the subconscious mind."

There is little time, however, to absorb the news that Freudian analysis has been consigned to the intellectual scrap heap in the twenty-third century or to wonder why exactly Morbius should regret it. The invisible monster from the Id is now at the door, demanding to be let in. Like Morbius himself, this creature "runs counter to every known law of adaptive evolution," as Ostrow observed when examining a cast of the invisible creature's claw.

But isn't invisibility close to divinity? "We're all part monsters in our subconscious," the Skipper concludes, "so we have laws and religion." Therapy is not only useless against the Id: it is positively dangerous.

Morbius never considers using the "plastic educator" on his daughter, Altaira. The prospect isn't even mentioned. Beautiful and loving to the point of promiscuity, able to charm the wildest of beasts, Altaira is a female counterpart to the Space Brothers. A space goddess of the type often encountered by the contactees, Altaira corresponds in dress and manner to Angelucci's Lyra, Adamski's Kalna, Bethurum's Aura, and early incarnations of fellow contactee Howard Menger's Marla. In fact, when Angelucci describes to Long John Nebel live on air how Vega, another space goddess, was "barely concealed by a transparent silken robe," he might well be speaking of Altaira. Nebel is consequently obliged to follow the Skipper in insisting that Vega be quickly covered up, suggesting that her robe was actually "translucent," just in case there are any misunderstandings.

Like the Skipper, Nebel knows that the beast, the mindless primitive from which even the Krell must have evolved, still lies just beneath the surface. Seen in this light, America's new national motto represents a significant change of evolutionary momentum, replacing the elementary basis of the subconscious mind with the guiding prohibitions of the Superego. By trusting in God, the nation may spare itself from the "monsters of the Id" contained within the formula "*e pluribus unum*," a Latin tag meaning "the one out of the many."

Certainly that's where *Forbidden Planet* is heading in its closing moments. "Your father's name will shine again like a beacon in the galaxy," the Skipper reassures a decently attired Altaira. "It will remind us that we are, after all, not God."

As the world of the Krell is reduced to radioactive vapor, this is an irony that perhaps even the Space Brothers might fail to appreciate: the nearer we approach the status of gods, the more we have to worry about our former selves.

## Egomaniac Empires

*Santa Mira, California*—The abandoned vegetable stand at the roadside should have been a clue: the intellectual super carrot is back, and this time he is not alone. "At first glance, everything looked the same," remarks Dr. Bennell at the start of *Invasion of the Body Snatchers*. "It wasn't. Something evil had taken possession of the town." The town is gradually becoming overrun by giant seedpods from outer space, but so far no one seems to have noticed. Appreciating that in Suburbia appearances are what matter, the seedpods have been assuming the identities of every community member, right down to the smallest detail.

Originally run in that staple of suburban family reading, *Collier's* magazine, the movie adaptation of *Invasion of the Body Snatchers* makes great play of the story's domestic settings. Shot in stark black and white, its eerie noir lighting captures everything from the lawnmower and swing seat out front to the pool table and cocktail bar in the den. Dance music drifts from a jukebox in the local nightclub while moonlight plays over the whitewall tires and hood ornaments of the automobiles parked outside. Suburbia has never been so enticing. No wonder the pod people are moving in.

They aren't the only extraterrestrial visitors keen to relocate from the desert to Levittown. In *Earth vs. the Flying Saucers*, Dr. and Mrs. Marvin can't settle down to a barbeque in their own backyard, an idyllic expanse of lawn enclosed by a white picket fence, without having aliens spy on them. Even Ed Wood manages to stretch his meager budget for *Grave Robbers from Outer Space* to include a patio scene featuring garden furniture and a display pack of Coca-Cola. Regulating the relationship between the strange and the familiar, the suburbs represent the successful colonization of a hostile universe. Far away on Altair IV, Morbius and Altaira still enjoy all the comforts of 1950s Suburbia from the banquette sofas and picture windows in their open-plan living area to the curved breakfast bar in the kitchenette. Their home even boasts a paved terrace in the backyard and a smart green trapezoid of lawn out front.

The pod people's arrival in Santa Mira confirms just how great an evolutionary leap the migration to the suburbs has become by mid-decade. The outward pattern and display of daily life here are accepted without a murmur. There is clearly an invasion going on, but what are the invaders actually doing? Fighting off the armies of the world? Blowing up Washington? Waging intergalactic war on Neptune? No, they're out in front of their new homes calmly mowing the lawn. With over 1.5 million houses built by 1955, and 1.4 million power lawnmowers sold to trim the neat swaths of green outside them, tending your lawn is the perfect way of claiming new territory.

Thanks to the pod people, Suburbia is now in danger of colonizing itself: the only ones not happy about this arrangement are those suburbanites who have yet to be replaced by the space spores. Are they crazy, or is something weird going on in Santa Mira? "Even these days it isn't as easy to go crazy as you might think," Dr. Bennell soothingly advises, "but you don't need to be losing your mind to need psychiatric help." Reports in 1956 reveal that chlorpromazine, used in the treatment of schizophrenics and by Dr. Ewen Cameron in his psychic driving experiments, has been administered to French troops serving in Algiers. Designed to act upon the mind "like a cast for a broken leg," chlorpromazine has a deadening effect on the feelings. This can have deeply disturbing consequences. "Suddenly stupor turns to despair," Jean-Paul Sartre later comments on the military use of torture against Algerian rebels. "Why in fact do we go to so much trouble to become, or to remain, human?" Quite frankly, you'd be crazy even to try. Calm and incapable of emotions, the pod people adapt effortlessly to the suburban lifestyle. Quiet contentment is much easier to attain when you no longer feel anything.

Meanwhile James Mason is flying apart as high-school teacher Ed Avery in *Bigger Than Life*, Nicholas Ray's highly charged portrait of life in a modern American household. All the hallmarks of domestic bliss are there: a TV dominating the lounge with a young son kneeling on the floor before it, a pretty wife and a refrigerator in the kitchen, packets of Lux and Surf on the countertop, travel posters in the hall, and twin beds in the master bedroom. The pod people could move in tomorrow, but Ed Avery feels very differently about the whole arrangement. "Doesn't this stuff bore you?" he demands of his son, ostensibly referring to the cowboy show playing on the TV but also giving voice to a much broader discontent. It seems that for the past six months he has been suffering from tense nervous headaches brought on by overwork. Pretty soon, Ed is bouncing off the ceiling under the influence of cortisone, a new miracle drug that is seriously upsetting his emotional equilibrium. But is the man or the drug responsible for this increasingly erratic behavior? "The trouble is inside you," Dr. Benell assures a female patient who is convinced that it is no longer her Uncle Ira who is mowing the lawn.

Being human means having to deal with monsters from the Id, and when laws and religion no longer work, there are always pills and alcohol, divorce, or promiscuity to serve as mental splints. Without them, life in the suburbs would become unendurable. "I didn't know the real meaning of fear until I kissed Becky," Dr. Benell observes after his old flame is transformed into a pod person. Unlike the USAF's use of the same rationale to explain away UFO sightings, the psychiatrist who diagnoses that Santa Mira is gripped by an "epidemic of mass hysteria" is absolutely right. Unfortunately he has mistaken the symptom for the cause: the least hysterical beings in Disturbia are the pod people themselves.

The only other entity able to contemplate life in the suburbs with such equanimity is Robby the Robot. "Why, he's a housewife's dream," remarks the Skipper, echoing a view of alien technology first expressed by Cal Meacham in *This Island Earth*. Meanwhile Robby putters around the Morbius household, fixing lunch and serving coffee. He may have been "tinkered together" by Morbius, but Robby is also a product of the Krell mind. Like the Mutant bred to perform menial tasks on Metaluna, his brain is completely exposed, encased in clear plastic. While the Mutant threatens to kill Faith Domergue, Robby is incapable of harming humans: a clicking mass of switches and lights, his mind appears to be entirely Superego in the same way that the Mutant's brain is all Id. "You see?" Morbius remarks as Robby's mental workings start sparking like a toy ray gun. "He's helpless—locked in a sub-electronic dilemma between my express orders and his basic inhibitions against harming rational beings."

To understand more fully the precise nature of Robby's "sub-electronic dilemma," one need only consult a twenty-page essay that has just appeared in Volume 1 of the journal *Behavioural Science*. Predominantly the work of Gregory Bateson, a founding member of the now discontinued Josiah Macy Conferences on Cybernetics, "Toward a Theory of Schizophrenia" introduces the concept of the "double bind" to the psychiatric community for the first time. Divorced from anthropologist Margaret Mead and currently residing in San Francisco, Bateson has applied Norbert Wiener's theories of communication and control to the study of schizophrenia. Accordingly, he describes the double bind as a form of psychological feedback loop produced by illogical and contradictory messages, most usually generated within the same family unit. Unable to position himself within a normal communicational network, the victim of a double bind is liable to experience feelings of panic, rage, or confusion, hear hallucinatory voices inside his head, or lapse into catatonia.

Robby's own double bind, however, is in direct response to the "basic inhibitions" that determine his behavior, much as the monsters from the Id are driven by their most basic urges. A walking, talking Superego, Robby even replaces the sexually rapacious Lieutenant Farman as Astrogator on the C57-D, cheerily piloting the flying saucer on its return journey to Earth at movie's end. Ultimately in control of nothing but himself, Robby may appear to walk and talk like a man, constantly being referred to as a male by the humans around him, but it soon becomes clear that he is no such thing. "He looks after us like a mother," Ostrow remarks of a robot that also runs off dresses, arranges flowers, and reminds his passengers to wear their seatbelts. Robby is actually that most emotionally constrained of all creatures: the suburban housewife. All inhibitions and no urges, she's practically a pod person already. It is, after all, Mr. Avery who is climbing the walls at home in *Bigger Than Life*, not Mrs. Avery.

Built from plans provided by Robert Kinoshita, an engineer who designs domestic washing machines, Robby goes on to make a personal appearance at the opening of "This Is Tomorrow," an early experiment in mixing art and architecture at the Whitechapel Gallery in London. "Just What Is It That Makes Today's Homes So Different, So Appealing?" is the rhetorical question posed by Richard Hamilton's poster for the exhibition. One glance at Robby should answer that. Meanwhile Joseph Engelberger creates a trial model for what will be the first industrial robot. Despite fierce opposition, Engelberger insists he won't have "any fun" unless the final product is explicitly referred to as a robot.

Back inside the human sensorium, urges and inhibitions continue to push against each other. Following up on his article in *Weekend*, Dr. Cameron publishes his paper "Psychic Driving" in the *American Journal of Psychiatry*. His patients are being subjected to increasingly prolonged periods of chemical sleep, followed by electroshock and insulin shock sessions, higher doses of LSD mixed with amphetamines, then even more time in the Sleep Room listening to tape-recorded messages repeated over and over again. "Clearly, if this thing worked over thirty repetitions," Cameron reasons, "it was only common sense to see what would happen if the repetition was increased tenfold, a hundredfold or even more." Some of those in Cameron's care have now heard the same message over five hundred thousand times.

Unfortunately, it is only "common sense" to step things up if the process is actually working. Cameron discovers that his patients are building up subliminal resistance, just like prisoners subjected to brainwashing and interrogation techniques. This in turn has led him to the conclusion that there must be some kind of "switching mechanism" that prevents them from responding positively to the increased repetition of the tape-recorded message. The correspondence between the human mind and magnetic tape has been extended, through Cameron's analogy of the "switching mechanism," to the point where it has become a paradigm for mental behavior itself. By not performing exactly like a tape recorder, Cameron seems to be saying, the mind has to be "disorganized" into responding like one by using the kind of shock techniques the boys at MK-ULTRA find so interesting. Cameron's patients start to fear being sent to the Sleep Room.

A recording can contain anything except the machine upon which it is being made: in other words, the recording is unaware of its own status as a recording. "I'm not sure it will ever be able to figure itself out," the psychiatrist remarks of the human mind in *Invasion of the Body Snatchers*, "everything else, maybe, from the atom to the universe, everything ... except itself." Halfway between a mechanical device and an electronic one, the tape recorder has also become an intermediary model for human behavior in the Space Age. The "electronic tonalities" heard on the soundtrack to *Forbidden Planet* are the work of Bebe and Louis Barron, former collaborators with John Cage, whose compositional approach has been heavily influenced by Norbert Wiener's theories on feedback loops. By deliberately overloading electrical circuits in their own musical version of a double bind, they are effectively "torturing" them into producing noises that can then be manipulated on magnetic tape. "At some stage," Wiener observes in *The Human Use of Human Beings*, "a machine which was previously assembled in an all-over manner may find its connections divided into partial assemblies with a higher or lower degree of independence." Audiences are consequently unaware that they are listening to the sounds of their own nervous systems collapsing.

Such illusions depend upon an absence of information in order to work. The April issue of *Popular Electronics* reveals how tape recorders are being used at Disneyland to persuade visitors that they are now entering the jungle. "In the Adventureland control room," it explains, "trumpeting elephants, roaring lions and rhinos, chattering monkeys— as well as the beating of native drums—originate from a bank of tape players. These machines play continuously a tape of any desired sound, repeating it at 10-second intervals." Not unlike those in Dr. Cameron's Sleep Room, the invisible Disneyland tape recorders can "repeat their messages 4,320 times daily."

Adventureland's jungle ride marks the public transformation of location into environment, space into sphere of influence. To further enhance the effects of what *Popular Electronics* calls "electronic realism," Ampex publicly demonstrates the first commercial videotape system in Chicago that same month. Developed in close association with the RAND Corporation, this technological advance facilitates the simultaneous broadcast of television programs across different time zones, ensuring that more people will be watching the same thing at the same time. With Myron Stolaroff and Al Hubbard busily introducing the Ampex workforce to the benefits of LSD, it is hard not to see such an innovation being attributed to heightened consciousness, particularly since Los Angeles psychiatrist Sidney Cohen has also been bringing various RAND analysts, including Herman Kahn from the Physics Division, back to his office for sessions on the drug.

The Ampex videotape system actually has its origins in the aptly named Project FEEDBACK. Based on a report edited by James Lipp of RAND's Missile Division, offering the first comprehensive overview of possible military applications of space-based systems, FEEDBACK's aim is to develop a satellite surveillance program utilizing the electromagnetic data storage and transmission technology being devised at Ampex. Having quit RAND's H-Bomb advisory group, Lipp has been arguing for an orbiting satellite capable of recording what it sees on videotape as it crosses time zones around the globe, just like a delayed television broadcast. The project's schedule, cost, and staffing recommendations are all based on Bruno Augenstein's RM: 1191 memorandum on ICBM research; the task of building the space reconnaissance vehicle eventually goes to Lockheed, following the first successful high-altitude flight of the U2 spy plane over the Soviet Union in 1956. Meanwhile the domestic interior depicted in Richard Hamilton's "Just What Is It That Makes Today's Homes So Different, So Appealing?" features an inverted moonscape in place of a ceiling and a tape recorder dominating the immediate foreground.

Having recorded his first songs on an Ampex machine back in Memphis, teen singing sensation Elvis Presley enters the US charts for the first time with "Heartbreak Hotel." The following day Russian premier Nikita Khrushchev denounces Stalin's "cult of personality" in a secret speech that critics dismiss as only marginally better kept than the news of Grace Kelly's marriage to Prince Rainier that same year. The echo on Presley's voice is a representation in sound of how fame, the cult of personality, is amplified by the new electronic media and reverberated around the planet. Artificially created in the recording studio by delaying sound through the medium of magnetic tape, the echo is also a cipher for space itself: "electronic realism" played back as empty illusion.

This recorded delay also marks the reorganization of sound in time. A one-man Adventureland, Elvis is accused by his critics of purveying "jungle music" to the youth of America and of singing in some strange, incomprehensible tongue. It is only when the alien message is played back at the wrong speed on a malfunctioning tape machine in *Earth vs. the Flying Saucers* that Dr. Russell Marvin can understand it. Extracts from "Heartbreak Hotel" are featured on a novelty record "The Flying Saucer" by Bill Buchanan and Dicky Goodman, released on the Luniverse label.

The divide separating teenagers from their parents has started to widen perceptibly. "Childhood is a congenital disease," Ed Avery informs his high-school PTA as the national birth rate continues to grow, "and the purpose of education is to cure it."

Allowing Altaira's education to stop short of the Krell "plastic educator," Morbius lets his daughter run around barefoot until the Skipper comes along in his flying saucer. Then the trouble starts.

"Mom, isn't Dad acting a little foolish?" remarks Avery's son of his father's increasingly addled behavior. Next thing anyone knows, Ed is planning to sacrifice him to the Almighty while quoting from the Old Testament.

The previous release by *Bigger Than Life* director Nicholas Ray is last year's *Rebel without a Cause*, which featured teen idol James Dean watching the destruction of the entire universe from inside Griffith Park Observatory. Dean himself died in a high-speed auto collision before the movie even came out.

Meanwhile the monster on Altair IV starts killing again once Morbius discovers that the Skipper has fallen in love with Altaira, thereby threatening his "little egomaniac empire." The only time the nature-loving Altaira wears shoes is after she has made her decision to leave Dad and run away from home: a course of action that results in the entire planet being blown apart. But for whose benefit does the suburban home, this new egomaniac empire of the senses, finally exist? "It isn't easy choosing between having a baby and buying a vacuum cleaner," a neighbor confides in *Bigger Than Life*, more pod person than hysterical human. "At least it shouldn't be." Billed as "America's Atomic Powered Singer" Elvis appears at the New Frontier Casino in Las Vegas, where watching nuclear explosions has long been one of the attractions. His failure to pull in the crowds, however, sees him angrily pulling out of his Vegas shows, vowing never to play the place again. It seems there just aren't enough kids in the lounges.

# 1957: CONTACT WITH SPACE

## Sputnik I

*Brand Management*—At the start of October 1957, the American people are surprised to discover a strange new sound sweeping the planet:
a monotonous, heavily accentuated beat that disturbs the relative peace
and order of their daily lives. It seems to come out of nowhere, spreading alarm and hysteria among those who hear it, arousing the gravest
fears for the future safety of the nation. For once, Elvis Presley isn't
behind the panic. "America's Atomic Powered Singer" suddenly finds
himself drowned out by a single piece of technology beeping ominously overhead.

"Until two days ago that sound had never been heard on this
Earth," a television announcer informs his viewers with absolute cer-
tainty. "Suddenly it has become as much a part of twentieth-century life
as the whir of your vacuum cleaner."

Put like that, it sounds quite reassuring. Household appliances aren't
usually considered that much of a threat. All the same, the announcer
seems concerned. Pretty soon the entire nation has grown concerned.
"The important thing is that the Russians have left the earth and the
race for the control of the universe has started," writes George Reedy,
aide to Senator Lyndon Johnson, who has been called upon to head
an official inquiry into precisely what has just happened. Launched on
October 4, 1957, atop a Soviet R-7 rocket, Sputnik I is now orbiting
our world. Seen from America's still earthbound perspective, it appears
that the Russians haven't so much started the race into space as already
declared themselves the winner by several paces. "No matter what we
do now," states John Rinehart of the Smithsonian Astrophysical Observatory, "the Russians will beat us to the moon ... I would not be
surprised if the Russians reached the moon within a week."

That night anxious groups of people in Times Square are interviewed
on TV. Asked if he admires the Russians for putting the world's first
artificial satellite into orbit, one interviewee squares off aggressively in

ION-PROPELLED
SPACE VEHICLE

TRAIL OF ROCKET
WITH SPUTNIK

BALLOON-LAUNCHED
FARSIDE ROCKET
SOARS 4000 MILES

U. S. SATELLITE

FARSIDE ROCKET

MANNED SATELLITE
(U. S. DESIGN)

front of the camera. "No, definitely not," he replies. "I say we should have been the first ones to have it, if there are such things."

A man in a white slouch hat eases up to the front of the crowd. "If I was in military service and fell down on the job like that," he remarks, "I could stand a court martial. Somebody's falling down on the job. Badly."

"We fear this," a woman adds in a quiet voice. "We fear that they have something out there that the majority of people don't know about."

Sputnik has not just entered their airspace; it has invaded their living rooms too.

As Don Keyhoe first came to realize back in 1948, the stars will never be the same again for these people. The night sky has now become outer space: alien, mysterious, and threatening. Back in Washington, Governor "Soapy" Williams sums up the nation's mood with a simple rhyme:

> *Oh Little Sputnik flying high*
> *With made-in-Moscow beep*
> *You tell the world it's a Commie Sky*
> *And Uncle Sam's asleep*

With Clare Booth Luce standing up in Congress to pronounce Sputnik "an intercontinental outer-space raspberry" in the face of American technological progress, this is not how things were supposed to go in International Geophysics Year. Calculated by astronomers at the International Council of Scientific Unions to take place when the sun's activity is at its highest, the "year" actually starts on July 1, 1957, and is scheduled to continue until December 31, 1958. During this extended period every aspect of Earth's science is to be studied, from cosmic rays, geomagnetism, and the physics of the ionosphere to glaciology, submarine trenches, and the motion of tectonic plates. For the first time, our world is to be examined as a global entity separate from, but intimately related to, the depths of space. As early as 1954 the council approved a resolution calling for artificial satellites to be placed in orbit around the Earth in order to map its surface from above.

At the same time, it is hard to think in positive terms of this planet and its inhabitants as a unified entirety when the first Sputnik has just been nudged into space by a military rocket. The most powerful launch vehicle in existence, the R-7 has been designed by the Soviets to deliver an atomic payload anywhere they want on the geopolitical map. By sending Sputnik flashing across the skies of America, the Soviet Union is effectively claiming them as its own.

About the size and shape of a basketball and weighing only 183 pounds, Sputnik I takes approximately ninety-eight minutes to follow its elliptical path around the Earth. With four long antennae pointing straight out behind it, the Soviet satellite has a space-age dynamism never before seen in the West, while its constant beeping, conjuring up the lonely depths of the cosmos, has now become the sound of space itself. Even as Sputnik threatens to replace flying saucers on the nation's collective radar screen, Canadian academic Marshall McLuhan addresses a conference of US radio workers worried that television is about to take away their jobs. "You've nothing to fear at all," he declares. "Your medium is unique, and the medium is the message, and will relate to any new medium." By publicly equating the medium with the message for the first time, McLuhan has managed to address directly the fears expressed by that anonymous woman interviewed on television in Times Square.

It is precisely because the medium is the message that it can so readily become the content of any new medium. Accordingly, the soft-spoken director of the Navy's Vanguard rocketry program John P. Hagen is drowned out by the sound of television cameras while giving evidence at Lyndon Johnson's subcommittee investigation into why the Soviets have so successfully stolen a march on the United States in space. Chairman Johnson orders the cameramen to work more quietly or get out. Moments later a light bulb falls from one of the chandeliers in the room, prompting comments about "these strange flying objects" everyone is seeing these days. Sputnik, it turns out, relates to UFOs in the same way that any new medium relates to what has gone before. Its real message is clear, however, and remains the same from Times Square to Washington: the only thing we have to fear is television itself.

1957: Contact with Space   187

In December the US Navy's attempt to put a satellite aloft ends almost as soon as it begins when the Vanguard rocket disintegrates in flames on the launch pad four seconds into its mission. The fact that this all takes place on live television does nothing to reassure an already fretful public. "OK, clean up," orders a voice from Vanguard mission control immediately after the explosion. "Let's get the next rocket ready." The following morning, sell-orders for Glenn L. Martin, the company responsible for Vanguard's first-stage fuel tanks, reach such a volume that the New York Stock Exchange suspends trading in the stock. Bars around the United States start advertising a new "Sputnik" cocktail: one part vodka, two parts sour grapes.

Vanguard's spectacular demise takes place exactly as German rocket scientist Wernher von Braun predicted it would. On the night America first heard about Sputnik, von Braun was at the Redstone Armory in Huntsville, Alabama, hosting a cocktail party for President Eisenhower's new Secretary of Defense, Neil H. McElroy. "We knew they were going to do it," von Braun cried excitedly as the news came in. "Vanguard will never make it. We have the hardware on the shelf."

Scientists, as President Eisenhower once remarked, are "just another pressure group," and von Braun is nothing if not skillful in this regard. The man who once pitched space exploration to the American public on Sunday-night television, courtesy of *Disneyland*, knows to whom he is speaking: that reference to having the Jupiter C "on the shelf" is particularly telling. Eisenhower's choice for Secretary of Defense is neither a military man nor an academic nor a career politician. Neil McElroy is a former promotions manager at Procter & Gamble, where his job was putting soap on supermarket shelves. He is the chief executive responsible for establishing the soap opera as a specific form of radio and television entertainment, something for which McElroy remains outspokenly unapologetic. "Soap operas sell soap," he remarks in defense of the genre's generally acknowledged lack of literary merit.

The selling of soap, however, represents a process whereby the media brings together health experts and city cleansing departments, manufacturers and advertising agencies, writers, producers, and actors in the promotion of hygiene as a mark of good citizenship. In other words, the man Eisenhower has put in charge of the nation's defense is already familiar with the integration of disparate expertise and technologies for the sake of a single clear purpose. This is what marks him out as the man of the moment. With defense spending being stepped down from an unprecedented $52.8 billion in 1953, just as the Korean War drew to a close, to a projected $41.1 billion for 1958, one of McElroy's first tasks is to find a way to diminish the rivalry between the services and private contractors over funding. "For God's sake turn us loose and let us do something," pleads von Braun, having watched the US Army Ballistic Missile Agency being passed over in favor of the Navy's Vanguard program. "We can put up a satellite in sixty days, Mr. McElroy! Just give us a green light and sixty days!"

In predicting Vanguard's failure, von Braun is taking a definite risk but also a calculated one. If events prove him right, he'll have his green light; if they don't, he'll be no worse off than he already is— and besides, who remembers an inaccurate prediction for very long? Criswell once boasted in private to a friend that he couldn't even look out the window and tell you what the weather would be like that day. While still at Procter & Gamble, Neil McElroy was responsible for drafting the "brand management" memo, a key document outlining a commercial strategy for increasing a product's "perceived value" to the customer. Brand management, the memo argued, is all about reassurance; and von Braun already has that covered. Reassurance counterbalances prediction: as carrier signals for a consumer society they have become equivalent to each other. Both express a confidence that something *will* happen—or in the words of the marketing slogan for the '57 Motor Show: "Suddenly it's 1960!" With his starched white shirt and distinctive clipped accent, the German rocket scientist has spent enough time on television and in the pages of color magazines to appreciate just how reassuring he can be.

Prediction and reassurance also come together in 1957 at the tardily completed Tomorrowland sector of Disneyland, where Monsanto opens its "House of Tomorrow" to the public. This abode of the future features insulated glass walls, picture telephones, ultrasonic dishwashers, and atomic food preservation, all housed within a durable plastic shell. Like the latest model home in Levittown, the House of Tomorrow ends up attracting more than twenty million visitors. Considering the location, this is probably not too surprising. Disneyland is the shape of brand management to come: the futuristic home's picture windows even offer a spectacular view of Sleeping Beauty's Castle at the end of Main Street USA. "Nature ended with Sputnik," notes Marshall McLuhan as it becomes increasingly apparent that a new historical period has just begun. The global "post-Sputnik" view of the world transforms it into a gigantic theme park where image is now the brand management of reality.

The tape-recorded jungle sounds of Adventureland find their echo on *Exotica*: the debut album from pianist and arranger Martin Denny. Birdcalls, croaking frogs, bamboo chimes, and exotic percussion, harmoniously blended together as "the Ultimate in High Fidelity," form part of what the cover copy describes as "the Sounds of Martin Denny." Abstract and remote, *Exotica* is a design concept in itself: not music, not moods, just the tasteful arrangement of individual sounds. To further enhance this acoustically enriched environment, an armchair with stereophonic speakers built into its wings is brought onto the market in 1957. With the Earth isolated in space by the sound of Sputnik orbiting overhead, its jungles now reduced to a listening experience to be enjoyed in the comfort of your own home, the true nature of reality resides in the ear of the beholder. Just ask any Elvis fan.

**Ecstasy and Regression**

*There, He Said It*—"For the first time the word ecstasy took on real meaning. For the first time it did not mean someone else's state of mind." So writes New York banker R. Gordon Wasson in "Seeking the Magic Mushroom," Part III of *Life* magazine's "Great Adventures" series. Vice-president of the Morgan Guaranty Bank, Wasson has been sneaking off every summer for the past four years to a remote village in the Mazatec Mountains of Mexico in order to study, participate in, and document the sacred mushroom ceremonies of the local inhabitants. Accompanying him on these field trips are his pediatrician wife Valentina and "society photographer" Allen Richardson. They may have come in search of a timeless visionary experience, but there is no question of them ever going native. "My God, what will Mary say?" Richardson wonders aloud, about to ingest "God's flesh" for the first time, recalling his own wife's warnings against putting "strange growths" into his mouth.

A formal portrait accompanying the seventeen-page pictorial essay shows Wasson in his sumptuous New York home surveying several mycological photographs and a primitive "mushroom stone" but with a tape recorder, that conspicuous symbol of space-age modernity, in the foreground. He and Richardson are also depicted grimly holding up metallic flashlights during an all-night hallucinatory ritual. Perhaps this is what enables Wasson to make such free use of a word like "ecstasy" in the May 13 issue of *Life*, right between the editorial "U.S. Business—A Golden Mood" and a second pictorial essay, "Getting and Spending the Teen-Age allowance: Youth's Money Runs into Billions of Dollars."

Wasson, in any case, takes the question of ecstasy very seriously. Having studied the spiritual aspects of mushroom lore with his wife for over thirty years, their findings are now available in *Mushrooms, Russia and History*, a richly illustrated two-volume limited edition from Pantheon Books. Also available in 1957 on the Folkways label, *Mushroom Ceremony of the Mazatec Indians of Mexico* is an album of recordings made by Wasson during his 1956 visit to the region. Taking part in this particular expedition, according to Wasson's account in *Life*, is the eminent mycologist Professor Roger Heim, head of the Muséum national d'Histoire naturelle in Paris, plus an American chemist—one Professor James A. Moore of the University of Delaware. In his acknowledgments, Wasson also gives special thanks to the Geschickter Fund for Medical Research, which, at Professor Moore's suggestion, has generously provided $2,000 to cover expenses.

What Wasson does not know at this point, however, is that the Geschickter Fund—like the Society for the Study of Human Ecology and occasionally also the Josiah Macy Foundation—operates as a conduit or "cut-out" for CIA funding into experimental drug research. Nor is Wasson aware that Professor James Moore of the University of Delaware has a case officer back in Langley on whose behalf Moore is now busily analyzing the mushroom samples he brought with him from Mexico.

At one remove further still from the scholarly pursuit of ecstasy, Ewen Cameron's psychic driving experiments are now being officially funded as "sub-project 68" of MK-ULTRA, thereby transforming Montreal's Allan Memorial Institute of Psychiatry into yet another CIA cut-out. In his continuing efforts to isolate and disable the mind's "switching mechanism," Dr. Cameron has taken to subduing and immobilizing his patients with shots of curare, traditionally used by South American Indians as a paralyzing poison.

"Hugo, prepare the scopolamine!" commands Dr. Alfred Brandon in the 1957 drive-in hit *I Was a Teenage Werewolf*. Dr. Brandon is intent upon releasing the primal self of teenage delinquent Tony Rivers. "I'm going to transform him and unleash the savage instincts that lie hidden within," Brandon declares, "and then I'll be judged the benefactor. Mankind is on the verge of destroying itself. The only hope for the human race is to hurl it back into its primitive norm, to start all over again." Writing in *Mushrooms, Russia and History*, Gordon Wasson is equally certain that the mind-altering effects of the sacred mushroom have "played a vital part in shaking loose man's early imagination, in arousing his capacity for self perception, for awe, wonder and reverence." Seen from the verge of destruction, ecstasy suddenly appears a lot less like a bold new initiative in brain chemistry than a return to safer, less complicated times. Lying on a dirt floor, tape recorder at his side, surrounded by chanting Indians high on mushrooms, Wasson represents another take on the personal time track, one that is as much evolutionary as it is therapeutic.

We now have to go back in order to move forward. Over the past twelve months or so, the public has been sold on the benefits of hypnotic regression. *The Search for Bridey Murphy*, in which a Virginia housewife recounts to her therapist while under hypnosis episodes from a former life as a housewife in eighteenth-century Ireland, is both a best-selling book and the subject of a highly popular movie. In *The Three Faces of Eve*, also on the best seller lists and already a successful film property for Twentieth Century Fox, a psychiatrist uses hypnosis to make mousy Eve White relive the childhood trauma that caused her personality to fragment. Both movies are presented as being ostensibly based on true stories, the original "Eve White" even being warned by her psychiatrist not to attend the movie's premiere as the experience of seeing herself played onscreen by actress Joanne Woodward might be "extremely harmful" to her therapeutic progress. Meanwhile the drive-in continues to be stalked by *The She-Creature*: a low-budget shocker in which a mysterious sideshow hypnotist named Lombardi commands his beautiful assistant to revert to her primal form as a glowing prehistoric sea beast. "Hypnotized! Reincarnated as a monster from hell!" runs the poster copy. "It can and did happen! Based on the authentic FACTS you've been reading about!" As the Krell recently found to their cost on Altair IV, introducing the beast and the mindless primitive to therapy makes them kissing cousins with monsters from the Id. "Men like Lombardi have put hypnosis back twenty-five years," a doctor observes in *The She-Creature*. "They've taken a modern tool of science and made a plaything out of it—worse than that, a weapon." This is not the first variation we've heard on that particular speech. Not unnaturally, Dr. Brandon's therapeutic meddling with the unreconstructed Id turns Tony Rivers, already the terror of Rockdale High, into a slavering werewolf. To experience ecstasy, as Wasson has discovered, is to commune directly with your own state of mind. To submit to regression, however, is to be taken up with someone else's. It's all a matter of control.

In November 1957, *Time* carries a brief obituary for Dr. Wilhelm Reich, "once-famed psychoanalyst, associate, and follower of Sigmund Freud, founder of the Wilhelm Reich Foundation, lately better known for unorthodox sex and energy theories." As if to mark this loss, Superman's virile presence disappears from the nation's television screens after his series is dropped from the schedules in 1957, while "Queen of the Pinup" Bettie Page abandons her career as a New York glamour model and vanishes without a trace. Not surprisingly, the nation's soaring birth rate lapses into a steady decline.

The author of *The Function of the Orgasm* and *The Mass Psychology of Fascism* died in his sleep while serving a two-year sentence in Lewisburg Federal Penitentiary, having spent the last two decades of his life studying "orgone": a form of energy Reich claimed to have found in all living matter. According to his theories, there is little that orgone cannot do, from controlling the weather to curing cancer. He has even built boxes, known as "orgone accumulators," which allow patients to harness its power. The US Food and Drug Administration placed an injunction on the sale of such items; and it is for shipping them across state lines in defiance of this ban that Reich has been imprisoned. The FDA also seized large quantities of Dr. Reich's publications, which it consigns to the flames of a New York City Department of Sanitation incinerator. Included in the FDA haul is Reich's last book, *Contact with Space*, published in 1957 by Core Pilot Press, in which he describes how orgone can be used to "interfere" with the flight of UFOs.

The FDA is having a busy time of it in 1957, also raiding a Scientology distribution center in Washington and confiscating twenty-one thousand Dianazene tablets. A vitamin compound that "runs out radiation—or what appears to be radiation" from the human body, Dianazene "proofs a person against radiation to some degree." On the grounds that this is false labeling, the FDA destroys the entire consignment. As L. Ron Hubbard points out in his 1957 publication, *All about Radiation*, "the greatest danger of radiation is not small, invisible particles drifting through the air, but the hysteria which is occasioned by the propaganda, the misunderstanding and threat which accompanies it. That hysteria is the threat, not the particles." Radiation, he assures his readers, remains "more of a mental than a physical problem."

It is easy to find fault with a man for telling people what they want to hear. The same issue of *Life* that carries Wasson's account of the magic mushroom ceremony also runs the science feature: "Drug Promises Immunity to Radiation." Nevertheless, in July 1957 the CIA opens file number 156409 on Hubbard and the Church of Scientology, while the FBI continues to keep a close eye on their activities.

"The problem of the doctor and his nervously ill patient," writes Dr. William Sargant in his 1957 book *Battle for the Mind*, "and that of the religious leader who sets out to gain and hold new converts has now become the problem of whole groups of nations who wish not only to confirm certain political beliefs within their boundaries but to proselytize the outside world."

An old friend of Ewen Cameron, Sargant offers a behaviorist analysis of religious conversion and political indoctrination in *Battle for the*

*Mind*, suggesting that the mechanisms involved in both might be usefully applied to more therapeutic ends. In an age of increasing specialization and professional isolation, such an approach blurs and conflates any distinction between the three processes, effectively making them functional versions of each other. "Politicians, priests and psychiatrists often face the same problem," he remarks, "how to find the most rapid and permanent means of changing a man's beliefs."

Sargant's book joins a growing library of titles that tend to treat their readers as a constituency of unwitting social laboratory rats. Recent additions include William H. Whyte's *Organization Man*, C. Wright Mills's *White Collar: The American Middle Classes*, Sloan Wilson's *The Man in the Gray Flannel Suit*, and Vance Packard's *The Hidden Persuaders*, which turns out to be one of the surprise best sellers of 1957. In it, Packard restages Sargant's *Battle for the Mind* using the advertising executives of Madison Avenue as his shock troops.

According to Packard's behaviorist take on selling in America, the creation of a passive nation of consumers through media manipulation and motivational techniques such as "depth psychology" and "subliminal suggestion" may even extend to Curtiss R. Schafer's theories of "biocontrol" as outlined at the 1956 National Electronics Conference in Chicago. An electrical engineer at the Norden-Ketay Corporation, Schafer envisions a future in which human consciousness is guided by electronics in the same way as a plane, a missile, or a machine tool is today. "The ultimate achievement of biocontrol may be the control of man himself," *Time* quotes Schafer as enthusiastically predicting. "A few months after birth, a surgeon would equip each child with a socket mounted under the scalp and electrodes reaching selected areas of brain tissue ... The child's sensory perceptions and muscular activity could be either modified or completely controlled by bioelectric signals radiating from state-controlled transmitters." The procedure, Schafer claims, will "cause no discomfort." It looks as though Hugo had better prepare more scopolamine.

Having little to do with "someone else's state of mind," ecstasy is not meant for the masses. Gordon Wasson may have written those magic words in the pages of a widely circulated popular magazine, but he did so at the invitation of a *Life* editor who chanced to overhear him recounting his Mexican exploits while lunching one afternoon at the Century Club. In the meantime Sidney Cohen and Gerald Heard have started running LSD sessions with Henry Luce, founder and president of *Life*, who enjoys them enormously, at one point conversing happily with God on his local golf course. However, the man who so loudly proclaimed the American Century has no interest in sharing his experience with the American people. "We wouldn't want everyone doing too much of a good thing," remarks his cosmopolitan wife Clare Booth Luce, who spoke so recently in Congress about hearing Sputnik's "outer-space raspberry."

An elite circle of financiers and businessmen, socialites and intellectuals has formed itself around the idea of pleasuring the mind with serious intent. Like most elite circles, this one remains highly protective of its privileges. Wasson's article, for example, is strangely silent about the exact name and location of the mountain village where he first ingested the sacred mushroom.

The chemical pursuit of ecstasy is even developing a terminology of its own as Dr. Humphrey Osmond argues with Aldous Huxley over what word might best describe the new experience. The former favors "psychedelic" over the latter's "phanerothyme"; but as both make their case in rhyming couplets quite as bad as Soapy Williams's, and as the average citizen may well require the services of a good etymological dictionary to understand what they're talking about, it is hard to predict which of these two terms, if any, will make it into common usage. Meanwhile Osmond presents "psychedelic" to the psychiatric establishment, offering it as a possible alternative to "psychotomimetic" during an address to the New York Academy of Sciences.

Further ripples and eddies of disagreement develop during June 1957 after Al "Cappy" Hubbard brings Huxley along to meet Gordon Wasson in his private dining room at the Morgan Guaranty Bank in New York. "Wasson likes to think that his mushrooms are somehow unique and infinitely superior to everything else," Huxley writes to Osmond of the encounter. "I tried to disabuse him. But he likes to feel that he had got hold of the One and Only psychodelic—accept no substitutes, none genuine unless sold with the signature of the inventor." Al Hubbard also attracts some criticism from Huxley over his attempts to initiate the hierarchy of the Catholic Church into the mysteries of LSD. Such efforts, however, have not been without their successes. On December 8, 1957, for example, a priest at the Cathedral of the Holy Rosary in Vancouver issues a special letter to the faithful. "We humbly ask Our Heavenly Mother the Virgin," he writes, "help of all who call upon Her to know and understand the true qualities of these psychedelics, the full capacities of man's noblest faculties and according to God's laws to use them for the benefit of mankind, here and in eternity." No one, perhaps not even Hubbard himself, can be sure precisely what "in eternity" means in this context, but it sure sounds like fun.

**Sputnik II**

*Ultimate Survival*—By the time Sputnik II is launched on November 3, barely one month after the first manmade satellite enters Earth orbit, it is evident that the Soviet initiative has ruled off the sky like the last page of an account book. Sputnik is not so much the shape of things to come as a sign of what is already here. An irreversible shift in perception has taken place, affecting everything. Viewed from above as well as below, the sky appears to be falling. "You people who live near the Nevada Test Site," runs an AEC booklet distributed in 1957, "are in a very real sense active participants in the Nation's atomic test program. You have been close observers of tests which have contributed greatly to building the defenses of our country and of the free world." By linking observation with participation, the Atomic Energy Commission is reaffirming the electronic media's influence upon the home in slightly different terms. The narrowing distinction between the actual and the illusory within the domestic environment can also be seen as a widening disparity between what is happening and what is seen to be happening. Under Sputnik, the masses suddenly find themselves precisely nowhere. In their respective fashion, the sacred mushroom and the mushroom cloud both represent the displacement of popular experience from the edge of tomorrow.

Visiting Sidney Cohen's LA office for private LSD sessions, RAND analyst Herman Kahn finds their effects particularly illuminating. Like Gordon Wasson, Kahn spends most of his time lying on the floor, murmuring "wow" every so often. However, it is not "man's early imagination" but a full review of current bombing strategies against Red China that transfixes the tubby nuclear physicist. By applying game theory to the deployment of nuclear weapons, Kahn is among those who are beginning to see Armageddon as a winnable fixture. Deterrence is ultimately all about credibility: something every brand management expert from Neil McElroy to Vance Packard readily understands. "The weapons of the future may be a great deal closer upon us than we had thought," declares Secretary of Defense McElroy in response to the Soviets' aggressive Sputnik program, "and therefore the ultimate survival of the Nation depends more than ever before on the speed and skill with which we can pursue the development of advanced weapons." Recipients of the AEC's *Atomic Tests in Nevada* booklet may therefore be comforted to hear that the massive Pascal-A and Pascal-B blasts of 1957 are designed to ensure that a warhead will not detonate with a nuclear yield if its explosive components are accidentally burned or activated.

Just as Sputnik II settles itself into orbit, the Gaither Report on *Deterrence and Survival in the Nuclear Age* is presented to President Eisenhower. Aiming to "form a broadbrush opinion of the relative value of various active and passive measures to protect the civilian populations in case of nuclear attack and its aftermath," it argues that fallout shelters are of secondary importance to developing a stronger nuclear deterrence. "It finds," thunders Chambers Roberts in the *Washington Post* after copies of the report are leaked to the press, "America's long-term prospect one of cataclysmic peril in the face of rocketing Soviet military might and of a powerful growing Soviet economy and technology which will bring new political propaganda and psychological assaults on freedom all around the globe."

Under the nominal chairmanship of H. Rowan Gaither Jr., the prominent San Francisco attorney who helped establish RAND as an independent corporation back in 1948, the report's conclusions have been heavily influenced by Albert Wohlstetter's alarming analysis of SAC's inability to respond decisively to a Soviet preemptive strike. Civil defense, that ghostly subterranean housing project, counts for little without a swift and powerful second-strike response: what Nelson Rockefeller, chairman of Eisenhower's Psychological Warfare Panel, has recently described as "the will to resist." Both Wohlstetter and Herman Kahn have served as consultants on the Gaither Report, along with Paul Nitze, Truman's former director of policy planning, who is also responsible for the sensationalist gloss of the document's final draft. One of the more imaginative measures suggested by Nitze is the development of a "love gas" to be sprayed over the Kremlin, thereby rendering the Soviets more passive and amenable.

Following the Pascal-B explosion Eisenhower announces a two-year suspension of nuclear testing; and the International Atomic Energy Agency, to monitor all further tests, is finally established. With World War III already being waged in outer space, however, the planet doesn't appear to be getting any safer. "Another war would be double suicide," General Douglas MacArthur is quoted as saying in Reich's *Contact with Space*, "and there is enough sense on both sides of the Iron Curtain to avoid it. Because of the developments of science all countries on earth will have to unite to survive and make a common front against attack by people from other planets. The politics of the future will be cosmic or interplanetary."

Whether the Eisenhower administration has underestimated the American people's interest in space exploration or Truman never fully appreciated MacArthur, the Soviet Union's Sputnik program has created a public spectacle that even Disney and von Braun might envy. Aboard Sputnik II is a young female mongrel of no fixed name but commonly known as Laika, meaning "barker" in Russian. Fitted with a harness and electrodes to monitor her vital signs, Laika is the first terrestrial creature ever to venture into space. Also forming part of the payload are two photometers for measuring solar radiation and cosmic rays. At this time the Soviets have no way of returning either the dog or the instruments safely to Earth. The American press starts running stories in which young boys claim that aliens have tried to snatch their pet dogs: the only thing missing from their accounts is a rendering of the scene by Norman Rockwell. As it is, Laika dies within hours of takeoff due to overheating and stress.

Satellites focus the mind where flying saucers have so far only distracted it. Back at the start of 1957, keenly aware of how much the sky over

Times Square has already changed, Don Keyhoe forces T. Townsend Brown to resign as director of NICAP, then takes his place, appointing retired Rear Admiral Delmer S. Fahrney as board chairman. Hailed as "the foremost Navy pioneer for the development of guided missiles" Fahrney shares General MacArthur's concerns with outer space. "There are objects coming into our atmosphere at very high speeds," he informs the *New York Times* at a press conference held the day after being appointed NICAP chairman. "No agency in this country or Russia is able to duplicate at this time the speeds and accelerations which radars and observers indicate these flying objects are able to achieve."

Fahrney's comments to the *New York Times* do not so much anticipate official attitudes toward Sputnik as give direct voice to them. By the summer of 1957 NICAP is agitating for televised congressional hearings into UFOs, plus a closer working relationship with the USAF to "help prepare the public for any conclusions which might be released later." Also joining Fahrney on the committee's Board of Governors is former CIA director Vice Admiral Roscoe Hillenkoetter, last seen signing off on the agency's BLUEBIRD hypnosis project back at the start of the decade. Even as NICAP attempts to establish itself as a radical inversion of the Robertson Panel, the shift in public attention from Sputnik I to Sputnik II is shadowed by a sudden spike in UFO sightings throughout Texas and New Mexico. Motorists report an egg-shaped flying object whose presence causes the electric circuits in their vehicles to suddenly lose power. "Mystery Object Stalls Autos in West Texas" runs the main headline in the November 4 edition of *The El Paso Times*; but it is the front page of the *Fort Worth Star-Telegram* for the same day that really captures the mood of the moment with: "Whatnik Sidelines Sputnik, Woofnik."

The reports, however, tail off just as quickly as they begin, leaving the "Whatnik" as another statistical aberration to be investigated by an increasingly understaffed Project BLUE BOOK. The UFO's ability to exert an invisible influence over electrical systems, stalling engines and silencing radios, is a relatively new phenomenon: one that connects both to the new overheated world of electronic media, now exerting their unseen influence from space itself, as well as reaching back to much older thinking on the nature of power and its invisible presence.

Fantasy, after all, is nothing more than theory rendered unworkable. The advent of the OTC-X1 Circular Foil Space Craft is announced with a glossy brochure campaign in 1957. "We Have Won the Race into Outer Space" reads one promotional bulletin for this advanced scientific marvel. Let the Russians have their Sputniks, this cheery declaration seems to imply: we will very shortly have our very own flying saucer. "There is much talk," the bulletin continues, "of rockets and missiles and about the years and money it will take to get to the Moon and back or to make a platform where we can watch our 'enemies.' The total answer to space travel has long been contained in our pertinent summation of physical law that 'Any vehicle accelerated to an axis rotation relative to its attractive inertial mass immediately becomes activated by free space-energy and acts as an independent force.'"

The man responsible for this arcane formula is one Otis T. Carr, who claims to have known Nikola Tesla, having once worked as a night clerk at the New Yorker Hotel in Midtown Manhattan, where the great inventor kept an apartment. In return for delivering bags of peanuts to his door, so that Tesla might feed his beloved pigeons, Carr has learned many of the master scientist's secrets, especially those concerning how to derive free energy from the air itself. Nor is Carr the only one to follow this particular line of thinking: Al "Cappy" Hubbard, now happily contemplating a psychedelic eternity in heaven, also studied Tesla's ideas in his youth. Having died in penniless obscurity during the dark days of World War II, Tesla's name is now being honored once again; as preparations are made to ship his ashes to the Tesla Museum in Yugoslavia, it is becoming linked not only to electricity, magnetism, and radio waves but to an entire unseen order of energy, one that is free and all-pervasive. Demonstrating the fundamental generosity of the universe that surrounds us, this is the benign technology usually represented in sci-fi movies by a hand waving in empty space.

Try telling that to Morris Jessup, however. The Office of Naval Research in Washington has commissioned the Varo Manufacturing Company of Austin, Texas—a civilian electronics company employed upon Defense Department contracts—to transcribe the annotated pages from Jessup's *The Case for the UFO* and run off a limited number of cyclostyled copies, three of which are now in the author's possession. The ONR has also asked to see the letters Jessup received from Carlos Miguel Allende hinting at secret government experiments into anti-gravitational force fields that he claimed took place during World War II. The pursuit of limitless free power, unencumbered by the surly bonds of conventional engines and wiring, has often proved to be a dangerous one. Remember what happened to the Krell in their efforts to establish a civilization without instrumentality and how Wilhelm Reich's belief in the power of orgone led to his ignominious death in prison. Tesla himself died debt-ridden and alone. No wonder Jessup is beginning to view the future with increasing alarm. Free or not, there's always a cost. Appearing on the Long John Nebel show, Otis Carr reveals that the sticker price for the first ever manmade flying saucer will be somewhere in the region of $20 million.

"Commander," actor Hans Conried declares with great authority in *The Monster That Challenged the World*. "I have found people are always jumping to wild conclusions concerning atomic reactions. Science fact and science fiction are not the same. Not in the least." Considering Conried is appearing opposite an army of giant sea snails bent upon slowly invading California's canal system, it's a safe bet he knows what he's talking about. With space exploration becoming a staged spectacle for the masses and expanded consciousness an elitist pastime for the select few, brand management for the human evolutionary trajectory continues to maintain itself at the movies. "What was I?" muses the diminutive protagonist of *The Incredible Shrinking Man*. "A human being or the man of the future?"

He is but one part of a Cambrian Explosion taking place at drive-ins throughout this year, filling the screens with strange new threats and alien life forms. A full list of releases for 1957 would have to include *Attack of the Crab Monsters, The Monolith Monsters, Monster from the Green Hell, Attack of the Puppet People, The Amazing Colossal Man, The Giant Claw, Attack of the Giant Leeches, The Deadly Mantis, From Hell It Came, She Devil, Not of This Earth, Space Master X7*, and almost as an afterthought, *The Night the World Exploded*.

The men in rubber suits are working overtime just trying to keep ahead of the evolutionary curve—none more so than Paul Blaisdell, a former aviation illustrator for the Douglas Aircraft Company who now makes low-budget monsters for low-budget monster movies. His costume design helped transform Lombardi's female assistant into a prehistoric sea beast in *She-Creature*: a creation of latex and padding so reptilian in effect that it is being reused for *Voodoo Woman*, another monster flick released in 1957. Blaisdell's best work this year can be seen in *Invasion of the Saucer Men*: a sci-fi cheapie in which a bunch of beer-chugging teenagers in hot rods prevent the Earth from being taken over by a small army of extraterrestrial midgets.

"SEE teenagers vs. the saucer men!" runs the breathless poster copy. "SEE disembodied hand that crawls! SEE the night the world nearly ended! SEE earth attacked by flying saucers!" Originally intended as just another drive-in shocker, *Invasion of the Saucer Men* "sort of collapsed into comedy about three days into production because the whole thing was so ludicrous," according to Blaisdell. The result is an irreverent take on official attitudes toward flying saucers, parodying the perceived need for secrecy in the matter: "Just think of it," a junior officer marvels, "only this special unit and the President of the United States will know what happened here tonight."

As 1957 draws to its close, Reinhold O. Schmidt appears on the Long John Nebel show to describe his encounter with a group of middle-aged aliens who happened to set their spaceship down in Kearney, Nebraska. Dressed soberly in relatively conventional street clothes, their message is one that seems to suit these particularly troubled times: "Tell the people we mean no harm."

# 1958: MASS HYSTERIA

## Rocket Fever

*Douglas, Wyoming*–January 30. Following a hundred-mile-per-hour car chase, Nebraskan teenager Charles Starkweather, together with his underage girlfriend Caril Fugate, is arrested and charged with eleven counts of homicide. So ends a ten-day road trip that became a killing spree, many of the victims being murdered simply so nineteen-year-old Charlie and fourteen-year-old Caril could steal their cars and keep on moving. Over 1,200 state police and National Guardsmen are eventually mobilized to track them down. On January 31, the day immediately after their arrest, the couple are formally extradited from Nebraska to face trial in Wyoming, Starkweather preferring to die in the Cowboy State's gas chamber rather than the Cornhuskers' electric chair. At precisely 10:48 that night (EST), "Satellite 1958 Alpha," popularly known as Explorer-I, takes off from Cape Canaveral and successfully enters the stratosphere atop a reconfigured Jupiter-C intermediate range ballistic missile. Given ninety days by the Army Ballistic Missile Agency to put a satellite successfully into space, von Braun and his team require only eighty-four to fetch the Jupiter-C down from the shelf and rename it the "Juno I."

Still bleeping fixedly overhead, Sputnik I continues to remind everyone just how much things have changed.

Starkweather will inform his court-appointed psychiatrist how he liked to spend hours "gazing into the far miles of the sky ... like a cloud sailing away with an incredible slowness to bring intimate knowledge of myself." It is probably no accident that, having fled Nebraska, he does not wish to return to the state where Reinhold Schmidt has so recently reported his encounter with such sober-minded and drably dressed extraterrestrials. Charlie, after all, has always been proud of his close resemblance to James Dean. Schmidt's aliens represent a subtle retrenchment on the part of the contactees. Having preempted, perhaps even given a voice and presence to, the plethora of new electronic media, together with the intricate webs of information and detailed

revelations they have brought in their wake, the contactees are now being displaced from the outer edges of space.

The difference between alien spaceships and Soviet technology seems slight at the moment, related as they are in the eyes of the American public by the unmistakable shock of the inevitable. The truly unexpected—the genuine and incontrovertible bolt from the blue—tends to bring only resignation with it. The panic, shock, and indignation that have made the launch of Sputnik I into such a major incident are all the consequence of developments that have hitherto gone unnoticed or, more likely, been allowed to build up unacknowledged.

If the sky seems radically different to the American people all of a sudden, it is because the change has only just become apparent. Folded together into the same daily news cycle, von Braun and Charlie Starkweather both understand this in their respective fashions.

"Rocket Fever Grips Nation's Teenagers" cheers one enthusiastic newsreel, reflecting the nation's sudden reversal in attitude following the successful launch of Explorer-I into Earth orbit. Rather than being strange and threatening, outer space looks set to become the next big distraction after Elvis Presley and Davy Crockett hats. "More and more teenagers are passing up rock and roll for a rocket role," commentator Michael Fitzmaurice blithely remarks before very probably wishing he hadn't. It is never a good idea to indulge in feeble wordplay when so many eyes are upon you, especially since it has already become common knowledge that Elvis is about to be drafted into the US Army. Additional footage shows kids in dungarees and windbreakers firing homemade rockets into a cloudy sky, making bold attempts to send white mice aloft powered by what one teen scientist later describes as "little more than a pipe bomb with tailfins."

Throwing the Navy's choice of "Vanguard" as the title for its rocketry program back upon itself, Explorer-I also does Sputniks I and II one better by being the first satellite to carry an actual mission payload into space. Assembled by the Jet Propulsion Laboratory at Caltech and containing instrumentation designed by James Van Allen, Explorer-I is a missile-shaped extension to von Braun's Jupiter-C, designed to send back data on the radiation belts surrounding the planet. If, as prominent evangelist Billy Graham claims, the sight of President Eisenhower going to church even with the stark Soviet presence looming overhead has "sent a sigh of relief throughout the entire world," press photographs of JPL's William Pickering joining Van Allen and von Braun in triumphantly holding aloft a replica of Explorer-I is putting the smile back on more than a few faces in Washington. For all his strict observance, it is becoming clear that Eisenhower may have gravely misjudged the nation's mood. Assuming there was little public interest in outer space, he favored the Navy's Vanguard with its civilian involvement to the US Army's Jupiter-C, which has been on hold since 1954. Not surprisingly, Wernher von Braun holds an opposing view. "Just like the early states of aviation," he argues in a newsreel interview, "military funds will be necessary to start the show on the road."

But then von Braun has always understood space as public spectacle. By the time of his celebratory press conference following the launch of Explorer-I, von Braun has effectively transformed rocket science into popular entertainment, pulling out a slide-rule in front of delighted reporters to convert the satellite's current velocity from miles per second into miles per hour in a manner that even Charlie Starkweather can appreciate. Whereas Sputnik has maintained a strong auditory presence, being heard more effectively than it was ever seen, von Braun gives the distant satellite a visibility, if only by association. The press conference and the live television coverage from the mission control room become terrestrial ciphers for what is happening out in space.

Von Braun's critics say he behaves more like a salesman than a scientist: an accusation he is more than prepared to meet halfway. "I have to be a two-headed monster," he concedes in a major *Time* profile published on February 17, "scientist and public-relations man."

In PR terms, the difference between a missile and a rocket depends on whether it is the military or the public doing the listening. Von Braun may have transformed the Jupiter-C into the Juno I, the switch in gender making it sound like a more peaceful proposition, but *Time* still has him billed on its cover as "Missile Man Von Braun." As a two-headed monster, he is seen encouraging kids to join high-school rocket clubs while also taking every opportunity to assure Congress that "If we are to control this planet, we have to control the space around it." Significantly, *Time* reveals that von Braun does not own a TV.

Donald Keyhoe is enjoying an equally shaded relationship with both the media and Congress at this time. CBS has invited him, as the new director of NICAP, to appear in an episode of *Armstrong Circle Theatre* entitled "UFOs: Enigma of the Skies." Thinking he is to participate in a live televised debate with representatives of the scientific community and the United States Air Force, Keyhoe soon discovers to his dismay that the broadcast is to be tightly scripted beforehand with the Air Force closely vetting its content. By the time of transmission on the evening of January 22, Keyhoe is a less than willing participant in the program, having already accused CBS of caving in to editorial interference from the USAF.

"And now I'm going to reveal something that has never been disclosed before," he suddenly announces, departing from the approved lines of his script only to find himself joining a silence group of his own making.

With the feed from his microphone dramatically cut live on air, only those able to lip-read will learn that NICAP has been working with a congressional committee putting together evidence that "will absolutely prove that the UFOs are real machines under intelligent control."

Effectively silenced live on air only days before Explorer-I makes its carefully coordinated media presence known, Keyhoe's unheard statement indicates the extent to which not only communication but silence itself has been transformed. NICAP's involvement with Senator John McClellan's Senate Subcommittee on Investigations, testifying on how the Air Force has been withholding evidence of UFO sightings, is soon to yield some ambiguous results. On February 14 McClellan's chief investigator tells Keyhoe that the CIA was responsible for convening the Robertson Panel back in 1953. "Why did the CIA—and later the AF—evade any mention of the CIA link with UFO investigations?" the NICAP newsletter asks after receiving a heavily censored version of the Robertson Panel report. "It seems obvious from the CIA evasion that important facts about this long-hidden study are being kept from the public." In March, however, McClellan's subcommittee informs NICAP that it "does not intend to investigate the United States Air Force" with regard to UFOs. Meanwhile funding cuts at Project BLUE BOOK make the cataloging and study of any future sightings an increasingly difficult undertaking for its new director, Major Robert J. Friend. Under such circumstances, silence itself becomes an effective form of communication; among the "important facts" still being kept from the public is the CIA's concern that the Soviets may have intended to exploit the hysteria surrounding flying saucers to their own ends.

A further incident during the summer of 1958 reveals that Keyhoe's ability to read and interpret organizational behavior does not extend to NICAP itself. After George Adamski flashes a NICAP membership card on live television, Keyhoe learns that George Van Tassel, Orfeo Angelucci, Truman Bethurum, Howard Menger, Reinhold Schmidt, and hillbilly contactee Buck Nelson—who once said of his jaunt around the solar system aboard a flying saucer that he "couldn't see the sun because it was very dark in space"—have all been made honorary members. Keyhoe immediately revokes their cards, causing NICAP treasurer Rose Campbell, the woman responsible for issuing them in the first place, to resign in protest. The fantasy appears to be over before it has even started.

Radical change can often be read most clearly in terms of inclusion and exclusion. Following Wilhelm Reich's *Contact with Space*, another member of Freud's original circle, C. G. Jung, devotes what will be his last book to the subject of UFOs. As *Flying Saucers: A Modern Myth of Things Seen in the Skies* appears in print in the United States, the Bulletin of the Aerial Phenomena Research Organization of Alamogordo, New Mexico, lists the eminent psychologist as its "consultant in psychology." APRO also publishes a heavily edited version of an interview Jung originally gave to a Swiss news magazine back in 1954. "'Flying Saucers' Real, Psychologist Jung Says" runs a subsequent headline in the *New York Herald Tribune*. Somewhat embarrassed by such attention, Jung reveals that he had "good-humoredly" accepted the offer of an honorary membership from APRO director Coral Lorenzen but did not authorize the use of his name in such a fashion. As it is, *Flying Saucers: A Modern Myth of Things Seen in the Skies* devotes itself mostly to a close analysis of Orfeo Angelucci's encounters with flying saucers and their occupants.

Keyhoe's expulsion of the contactees from NICAP and his own edging out by the Air Force both occur just as outer space is being transformed into a tangible new line of demarcation. Taken together, the rocket's thrusting ascent and the satellite's orbital path constitute a translation of flying-saucer behavior into more practical terms. As a further sign of this change, the USAF ships off its experimental Avro-Car to a military museum in Virginia: the circular craft's performance in high winds has continued to disappoint, leading to the project being dropped by the Air Force. In fact, the only flying disc ever to perform successfully throughout the 1950s is the one invented by Fred Morrison. Known originally as "Morrison's Flyin' Saucer," his invention was originally picked up by the Wham-O toy company, which started marketing copies at fifty-nine cents a pop, first calling them "Pluto Platters" before changing the name yet again in 1957 to the more abstract, less obviously alien "Frisbee." Even so, the flying disc's sales are soon eclipsed in 1958 when Wham-O sparks a national craze for the hula-hoop: a brightly colored plastic ring designed to follow an eccentric orbit around its owner's gyrating hips.

Caught outside these lines of inclusion, Morris K. Jessup's actions have become increasingly erratic. In 1958 he leaves New York for Indiana, where he finds work editing an astrology magazine. Later in the year he returns to New York long enough to leave a copy of the annotated Varo edition of *The Case for the UFO* in the hands of friends for safekeeping. They can't help but note that Jessup seems more preoccupied than ever, convinced that something is about to happen to him. One in particular is shocked by the change in his vibrations. "They had taken on," she later remarks, "a sort of astral BO." Jessup then leaves New York again but, rather than returning to Indiana, goes missing instead. "Everything in space obeys the laws of physics," von Braun confidently observes in his *Time* profile. "If you know these laws, and obey them, space will treat you kindly."

Meanwhile, Secretary of Defense Neil McElroy, the man who helped establish brand management for personal hygiene at Procter & Gamble, sets up the Advance Research Projects Agency in an attempt to give America a technological lead over the Soviets. Created as a direct response to Sputnik, ARPA is to foster radically new approaches to scientific thinking by channeling funding through both military and civilian organizations. Soon the Army, the Navy, the Jet Propulsion Lab at Caltech, RAND, and the United States Air Force are all involved in space projects funded by ARPA. Thanks to McElroy, Big Science now has its first Big Organization. Not that this development does much to cheer Wernher von Braun. On September 11, 1958, ARPA rejects an initial funding application for Project ADAM, von Braun's plan to use a military rocket to send a man into space by the end of 1959.

Nor is this the only organizational shift with which he has to contend. In a further attempt to put smiles on a few faces in Washington, Congress has already passed the National Aeronautics and Space Act, bringing the National Aeronautics and Space Administration (NASA) into existence as of October 1. Von Braun and his team of scientists, many of whom have been with him since his earliest days at Peenemünde, threaten to quit when they learn of Eisenhower's plan to draft them in to what they perceive to be a predominantly civilian space agency. Eisenhower in turn threatens to yank their funding, and von Braun soon finds himself part of NASA's Mercury program, working toward putting the first man into space. The process of selecting suitable astronauts has, in fact, already begun. However, an early suggestion of sending prisoners up into orbit first is strongly reminiscent of the manner in which members of the prison population have been used in the past to test dangerous drugs and radioactive material, often without their knowledge or consent.

But then nobody really knows what any living creature, let alone a human being, can expect to find in outer space. As animal-lovers around the world gather to protest Laika's fate, it looks increasingly likely that Sputnik II will turn out to be the most expensive way of killing a stray dog yet devised by science. Still holding out hope for Laika's safe return, Dr. J. Allen Hynek, erstwhile secretary to the Robertson Panel, tells the *Daily Enterprise* that "it is possible to allow the dog to parachute to Earth still alive in a capsule by using radio devices in regular use in this country." This breezy confidence takes a further battering in December, when the nosecone from a US rocket containing Gordo, the first monkey to be sent into space, disappears without a trace in the South Atlantic after its parachute fails to open. "Missiles are really interim weapons," von Braun informs *Time* magazine. "This is because both nations have them. Man will always seek the ultimate weapon. And you know what this is? The ultimate weapon is what the other fellow doesn't have." Gordo is never heard from again.

## The Cult of Unthink

*The Colonial Theatre, Downingtown*—Up in the balcony the kids are settling in for a night of scary movies, unaware that the creaking old picture house is about to be overrun by a giant red mass of killer phlegm from outer space. We are somewhere on main street in a small town in America, and there is a lot of shouting and high spirits coming from the Spook Pit—as if everyone were actually looking forward to being scared. The only teenager not having any kind of fun is young Steve McQueen. He already knows about the red blob from another world and how dangerous it can be, but no one in authority will believe him. And why should they?

Consider how ideologically charged physical distance has become since Sputnik. In the wake of the Gaither Report's alarmist rhetoric, youthful Senator John Fitzgerald Kennedy speaks out for the first time against the "missile gap" he claims has opened up between the United States and the Soviet Union on the aging President's watch. The term is one much favored by the intelligence community and defense analysts to describe any advance the East has made over the West with regard to new covert weaponry and behavior modification techniques. As a direct consequence of what Senator Kennedy calls Russia's "Sputnik diplomacy," a "generation gap" as distinct as any technology or mind-control gap has also started to make itself apparent. How else to explain the 1,200 pictures filed by *Life* magazine alone of Elvis Presley's induction into the United States Army in March of this year?

Viewed in retrospect, as the success of Explorer-I heralds a "new generation" of ballistic missiles, and the mass media gather in force to capture every second of Private Elvis Presley's ritual haircut at the hands of an Army barber, there is something about nineteen-year-old Charlie Starkweather's flight into the wilderness that seems inevitable. "But Dad i'm not sorry for what i did," he writes from prison, "cause for the first time me and Caril had more fun … all we wanted is to get out of town." The young killer's faltering words frame a sentiment with which Steve McQueen—trapped between alien incursion and adult incomprehension in the aptly named confines of Downingtown—can to some extent sympathize.

Making a quick getaway, disappearing at high speed, defines one of the key dynamics of youth. Once the pastime of ex-servicemen looking for peacetime kicks, drag racing has become a major teenage obsession: what was once pursued on the dry lakebeds and abandoned airfields of Southern California has now taken to the streets and parkways as kids chop and channel old Mercs and '32 Fords in order to race them on quarter miles of public asphalt. The stripped-down, customized form of the hot rod, designed to be driven as fast as possible, connects the teenage racer to the futuristic technology and alien encounters of the desert tract. Drag racing is the teenage craze for rocketry turned inside out. Charlie Starkweather loved cars, after all: he enjoyed demolition derbies and games of chicken out on the prairie. By 1958 this passion for auto delinquency has made national heroes of Kenneth "Von Dutch" Howard and Ed "Big Daddy" Roth, both of whom customize cars and T-shirts with flamboyant designs featuring drooling monsters and flying eyeballs.

As outer space becomes increasingly institutionalized and administered, as gaps open up that can only be closed by an Act of Congress, it quickly becomes plain that there is no room for teenage misfits on this ride. Just look at the problems Steve McQueen is having. As a male adolescent, he is initially considered by the townspeople to be more of a threat than the steadily growing red mass that is currently devouring everything in its path. At this early stage a giant red blob from outer space can just as easily be read as the messy onset of pubescence as the threat of a worldwide communist conspiracy.

In fact, in a year when the *San Francisco Chronicle* uses the word "beatnik" for the first time, linking "beat" dropouts with the Soviet Sputnik, there is something about the nation's crazy mixed-up youth that seems fundamentally un-American. Even Allen Ginsberg's refutation of the term uses the language of incursion and takeover to make its point. "If beatniks and not illuminated Beat poets overrun this country," he

writes in a letter to the *New York Times*, "they will have been created
... by industries of mass communication which continue to brainwash
man." Ginsberg's choice of words would seem to indicate that the main
point of contention is not so much whether the nation will be overrun
but by whom.

To get an idea of what is actually at stake here, take a closer look at
some of the mindless fun the Blob is about to break up at the Colonial
Theatre. There is a marked discrepancy between what is being displayed outside the cinema and what goes on inside it. According to the
posters lining the sidewalk, tonight's Spook Pit screening is *The Robot
and the Vampire*, a feature presentation that appears to star Bela Lugosi and a mechanical creation closely resembling Robby from MGM's
*Forbidden Planet*. Unfortunately, Bela Lugosi is now dead; and the sets
and props from Altair IV, including Robby himself, have been cannibal-
ized for use in other, slightly less prestigious productions. Robby, for
example, has already appeared in *The Invisible Boy*, in which a scientist
uses a computer to understand his adolescent son, while costumes and
weapons left over from *Forbidden Planet* resurface in *Queen of Outer
Space*, a 1958 film production whose seriousness may be compromised
in some people's eyes by the presence of Zsa Zsa Gabor in the role of
a glamorous Venusian scientist. "Can't you see I'm *verking?*" she loudly
complains, flinging handfuls of dried grasses around her laboratory as if
conducting a class in flower arranging.

Such revising of established convention allows a lot of old material
to be readapted for a younger, apparently less discriminating audience.
Kids, after all, don't really know any better. The success of *I Was a
Teenage Werewolf* is immediately followed by the release of *I Was a
Teenage Frankenstein*, and history begins to repeat itself once more.
Universal Pictures has sold off its back catalog of old horror movies for
screening on late-night TV; and Columbia has struck a similar deal re-
packaging all its Three Stooges shorts for a new generation of viewers.
Monsters are, in any case, rarely allowed to come back as much more
than cartoon versions of their former selves. As Bela Lugosi learned to
his cost, your career is pretty much finished by the time you meet Abbott and Costello. He now lies, wrapped in one of his famous vampire
capes, in a Culver City cemetery, having succumbed to a heart attack in

the summer of 1956: a banal yet fitting way for a creature who feeds off blood to die. The past, reassuringly transformed into an eternal rerun, appears to be catching up with us.

What, however, are the kids watching in the Colonial Theatre as the Blob comes oozing in around their feet? It turns out to be a clip from *Daughter of Horror*, an art-house obscurity originally known to the few who have ever seen it as *Dementia*. Described by the *New York Times* as "a piece of film juvenilia," *Dementia* was shot cheaply in New York on black-and-white stock, and a voice-over soundtrack was added later. It tells a nightmarish tale of a teenage girl taking a murderous trip through a dark and mysterious city. Cops beat up drunks, Dad brutally murders Mom, the teenage girl stabs a lecherous playboy then finds his severed hand in a cupboard drawer. Fortunately, the Blob overruns the entire cinema before the kids get a chance to be corrupted by any of this.

The fractured narrative logic, the violent dream-like rapture within which *Dementia* takes place, suggests a pronounced change in perception. During the spring of 1958, in the same hotel in Paris where William Burroughs is busily lashing together the manuscript of *The Naked Lunch*, the artist Brion Gysin slices through a pile of newspapers with a Stanley blade and notices how the resultant fragments of newsprint form random arrangements from which new meanings emerge. The "cut-up technique," as Gysin calls it, throws meaning back on itself, aggressively exposing how time, memory, and consciousness no longer form a smooth continuity, especially in a culture mediated by the tape recorder and the television camera.

To the establishment, however, such a radical shift seems fundamentally regressive; the new, the experimental, and the disruptive are seen as further signs of *Forbidden Planet*'s "mindless primitive" at work. In "The Know Nothing Bohemians," published in the Spring issue of *Partisan Review*, Norman Podhoretz attacks the Beat movement for being "hostile to civilization," claiming "it worships primitivism," while Jack Kerouac's latest novel *On the Road* is dismissed by the CIA-funded journal *Encounter* as "a series of Neanderthal grunts." Robert Brustein goes even further in his *Horizon* article "The Cult of Unthink," condemning all of Kerouac's novels as "stupefying in their unreadability."

It is a little risky to be throwing around accusations of stupefaction in a society whose annual consumption of tranquilizers is now topping $150 million. Those with the greatest faith in progress tend to forget that evolution represents not only a break with the past but a rejection of the present as well. Viewed from the edge of nuclear annihilation, regression becomes a way of "unthinking the unthinkable." At the same time, to speak of a cult of "unthink" is to characterize the process itself as reversible: an assumption that starts once again with the premise that thought is somehow analogous to a recording transcribed onto magnetic tape, capable of being run backward and forward or even simply erased. Violent dream-like rapture may offer an escape from such straitened thinking, but it should also be noted that Charlie Starkweather silenced most of his victims by shooting them in the head.

Kids who just four years previously were in danger of having their minds rotted by comic books have other things to preoccupy them as the drive-ins and movie theaters continue to spawn strange new evolutionary hybrids. *The Brain Eaters*, directed by Bruno VeSota, who also appeared in *Dementia*, deals with a small town taken over by alien mind control at a time when 90 percent of all households in America own a TV set. Similarly, the cast of *Fiend without a Face* are menaced by flying brains brought into being by an atomic experiment, spinal cords still attached, capable of sucking the thoughts straight out of people's heads. Paul Blaisdell's *She-Creature* costume also makes one more public appearance in *How to Make a Monster*, the official follow-up to *I Was a Teenage Frankenstein*, while its creator is busy working on *It! The Terror from Beyond Space*. Set in 1973 aboard a rocket ship returning to the Earth from Mars, *It!* features another of Blaisdell's rubber monster suits, so tightly stretched over the sturdy frame of cowboy actor "Crash" Corrigan that its zipper occasionally appears on camera.

A savage predator driven to survive at all costs, this particular monster is given a little more onscreen presence through its feral snarls and rasping breath, produced by slowing down recordings of a normal human voice to about half their usual speed. Manipulating sound on magnetic tape in this way not only alters pitch and duration but also the listener's sense of scale. The slower the playback, the larger

216  *WELCOME TO MARS*

and more ponderous the effect becomes: civilized speech is quickly replaced by inarticulate "Neanderthal grunts." No wonder tape technology becomes associated with the aesthetically "primitive."

A similar trick is employed in *The War of the Colossal Beast* to convey the lumbering confusion of the giant mutant that was once Lieutenant Colonel Glenn Manning, unwitting victim of a "plutonium bomb" tested at Camp Desert Rock in 1957's *The Amazing Colossal Man*. Now over fifty feet tall, hideously disfigured, and completely insane, Manning is little more than an oversized consumer, picking up supply trucks and shaking out their contents like a child searching for the prize in a packet of breakfast cereal. The connection is not lost on Manning's sister, who happens to write copy for a San Francisco advertising agency.

"I can imagine myself going back to writing all those tired adjectives: 'tremendous,' 'gigantic,' 'colossal,'" she tearfully complains. "You know what they mean to me now, don't you? Glenn. A colossal freak."

Meanwhile, over at Dunston University the students are facing a slightly different form of regression in Jack Arnold's *Monster on Campus*. "Is this fish really one million years old?" asks clean-cut teen Troy Donahue, pointing to the latest acquisition in Professor Donald Blake's laboratory. In a plot twist unusual even for a movie of this type, the Professor unwittingly smokes a pipe containing the blood of a dragonfly that has come into contact with this prehistoric leftover. Transformed into a murderous Neanderthal type, he starts attacking pretty co-eds in a manner sure to displease the editorial staff at *Encounter*. A violent, drugged-up throwback to Gordon Wasson's enthusiastic vision of the sacred mushroom "shaking loose man's early imagination," Professor Blake's hallucinatory rampage comes just as the CIA is beginning to lose interest in LSD as an offensive weapon. The agency still manages to get twitchy, however, when it learns that Albert Hofmann, the man responsible for discovering LSD in the first place, has isolated the psychoactive elements in the mushroom samples brought back from Mexico by Gordon Wasson and Roger Heim. Working alone, Hofmann has synthesized two new substances: psilocybin and psilocin. "Nobody showed much eagerness to take on this problem," he later observes, "because it was known that LSD and everything connected with it were scarcely popular subjects to the top management." This does not prevent MK-ULTRA from attempting to buy up the entire supply so that Sandoz's latest hallucinogens might "remain an agency secret."

There are of course more advanced ways of creating monsters on campus than simply dosing them with drugs. Henry A. Murray, co-founder of the Department for Social Relations at Harvard and former advisor on officer training to CIA forerunner the OSS, is putting a group of twenty highly gifted male students through an elaborate series of tests. By exposing them to extensive psychological stress, Murray hopes to demonstrate that positive character patterns can be established, forming a kind of functioning Superego that will silence forever the mindless primitive grunting incoherently within. Participating in his experiments under the codename "Lawful" is a young Harvard mathematics student called Ted Kaczynski.

In such a manner is terror born. The colossal freak that was once Lieutenant Colonel Glenn Manning finally meets his end threatening a bunch of high-school students at the Griffith Observatory, where James Dean and Sal Mineo watched the universe explode back in 1955. However, these kids are here "looking for a Sputnik or something," meaning that they'd probably prefer to spend their time at the rocketry club than playing chicken out on some godless stretch of California highway.

**Masters of Infinity**

*Miraculous Forebodings*—The highway is what connects the Earth with space most closely at the moment. "It has been determined as a matter of Federal Policy that at least 70 million people would have to be evacuated from target areas in case of threatened or actual enemy attack," declares President Eisenhower's advisory committee on a National Highway Program. "No urban area in the country today has highway facilities equal to the task." By 1958, however, a forty-one-thousand-mile National System of Interstate and Defense Highways is under construction; heavy industry is encouraged to decentralize and relocate itself to the "wide countryside," taking its huge workforce with it. A third twelve-thousand-home Levittown opens in Willingboro, New Jersey.

To offer a new perspective on the suburban grid as seen from space, *I Married a Monster from Outer Space* shows aliens trying once again to fit into domestic life in the second half of the twentieth century. Obsessed with having babies while at the same time displaying clear signs of boredom and irritability, this particular group of extraterrestrials seem right at home in Suburbia. However, in a year when the Soviets allow the body of space dog Laika to return to earth in a shower of hot ashes, they also demonstrate a suspicious antipathy toward household pets. The aliens, it turns out, have chosen the wrong year to venture into the American suburbs to find unsuspecting partners with which to mate: the national birth rate continues its steady decline, despite forty-one thousand new motels having been opened. No wonder the moody visitors turn so readily to drink.

Not so much a final destination as a point of transition, the spread of the motel across the United States marks out a new geography for the Space Age, reflecting a common concern with speed and mobility. In 1958, the Ford Motor Company unveils its plans for the Nucleon: an atomic-powered family car. Instead of a conventional internal-combustion engine, the Nucleon will be able to travel over five thousand miles, thanks to the small nuclear reactor located in the vehicle's rear. The company's grasp of the future is somewhat compromised, however, when a Ford executive dismisses the Volkswagen as a ride for "gray-flannel nonconformists" just when NASA's parking lot is starting to fill up with VWs driven by members of von Braun's team of German rocket scientists. As car tailfins continue to grow, this is also the year chosen for the launch of the Ford Edsel, a car so carefully planned and exactingly designed for the driver of tomorrow that the company can barely give them away. Among the Edsel's many shortcomings is the distinctive vertical radiator that gives the vehicle's front assembly an unhappy, constricted look: "like an Oldsmobile sucking a lemon" some remark upon first seeing it.

Meanwhile Colonel Edward Hall of the Air Force Ballistic Missile Division combines points of transition with speed and mobility in his Minuteman concept: a revolutionary plan for the next generation of ICBMs. Extending the geography of the Space Age further still, Colonel Hall's plan calls for thousands of solid-fuel missiles to be based in unmanned, heavily reinforced, and widely dispersed underground silos linked electronically to a series of central launch control facilities. As such, Minuteman represents the suburban deployment of the missile. Inexpensive to build and maintain, scattered throughout the country in carefully arranged colonies safely outside the main population centers, these new artificial conurbations are a strategic refinement of the thinking behind Oak Ridge and Levittown. In February 1958 the Air Force Ballistic Missile Division sends Colonel Hall to Washington to brief the Secretary of Defense, the Secretary of the Air Force, and SAC's General Curtis LeMay. By July the AFBMD is selecting contractors while ARPA begins buying up circuit boards and other electronic components.

With nuclear tests taking place throughout the world at the giddy rate of one every three days, it pays to be this careful. Even SAC isn't immune from mistakes. In 1958 it accidentally carries out a preemptive nuclear strike on Mars Bluff, South Carolina, when the navigator aboard a B-47 grabs hold of the emergency release pin, sending an A-Bomb crashing through the bay doors to hit the ground fifteen thousand feet below. Although the device does not contain a fissionable core, it is still packed with enough conventional explosives to destroy property, level trees, and leave a crater thirty-five feet deep, injuring several people. Is it possible for the United States Air Force to hit a more appropriately named target? "Another name for Mars is death," runs the concluding message in *It! The Terror from Beyond Space*.

Things are now happening faster than ever. Roger Corman rushes out *War of the Satellites* within five months of Sputnik I's launch. Two months later US satellite Explorer-IV is launched as part of Project ARGUS. A joint venture involving the US Navy, ARPA, and Caltech, its aim is to investigate how artificial radiation belts created around the planet might be used as a possible weapon. Navy ships positioned at the equator fire missiles with nuclear payloads into the upper Earth atmosphere, where they are detonated. Launched on July 26, Explorer-IV will measure the resultant radiation levels. Their effects on radio and radar transmissions, as well as their ability to disable enemy ICBMs and endanger the crews of orbiting space vehicles, will be studied at the Air Force Special Weapons Center at Kirtland AFB.

These tests are carried out as quickly as possible before the international ban on atmospheric nuclear testing is enforced.

Events start to pile up as we draw closer to the future. During the same summer, USS *Nautilus* departs from Pearl Harbor under top-secret orders to conduct Operation SUNSHINE. Powered by its Westinghouse atomic engines, USS *Nautilus* will become the first ship ever to cross the North Pole, diving deep below the Arctic ice. "For the world, our country, and the Navy: the North Pole," announces the sub's commander, very much maintaining the spirit of International Geophysics Year even as it draws to its close. Meanwhile his crew pass their time underwater playing "Quiet Village," from Martin Denny's *Exotica* album, on the ship's jukebox.

That this should echo the opening of *It Came from Beneath the Sea*, where the crew of the atomic submarine listen to Hawaiian music, is no big surprise. Submersion has now become the new medium. Just as the naval conning tower is transformed into the suburban home through the introduction of high-fidelity "Living Stereo," so the recent shifts in perception brought about by the launch of the first artificial satellites—bringing outer space into the lounge via the TV set in the corner—connect the underwater voyage with the exploration of personal consciousness. Scuba diving has become a popular national pastime. Producer Ivan Tors and deep-sea diver Perry Bivens, two members of Oscar Janiger's circle who have experimented repeatedly with LSD, come up with *Sea Hunt*: a successful weekly television show that makes a big feature of its underwater action sequences.

What once seemed a natural environment is now as artificial as the compressed air breathed by Lloyd Bridges in the role of *Sea Hunt* hero Mike Nelson. This new medium can even grow opaque. The frozen white desolation of the polar ice cap, where the Thing first skidded to a halt back in 1951, still contains monsters. After Steve McQueen and his teenage pals defeat the Blob by freezing it with fire extinguishers, the resultant extraterrestrial snow cone is immediately airlifted to the top of the planet, rendering the world safe for "as long as the Arctic stays cold."

Satellites now come and go with the frequency of drive-in movie releases. After Explorer-I comes the first attempt to get Sputnik III off the ground on February 3, followed by Explorer-II on March 5, which also fails; a successful launch for Vanguard comes on March 17, with Explorer-III lifting off on March 26. What goes up may tend to stay there, however, particularly in the public imagination. This doesn't stop Sputnik I falling back to earth on January 4.

Sputnik II also comes down on April 14, just in time for King Baudouin of Belgium to open Expo '58 three days later. Also known as the Brussels World's Fair, this is the first international event of its kind to be held since World War II and is officially dedicated to World Peace and Economic Growth. The American Pavilion, in keeping with the fair's global theme, comprises a series of concentric circles, at the heart of which is a circular cinema showing the new Disney "Circarama" presentation: *America the Beautiful*, immersing its audience in the sights and sounds of the United States via a special 360° arrangement of cameras and screens. "We have yet to prove that democracy can produce a beautiful environment," Edward Durrell Stone, the pavilion's architect, will later remark in his essay "The Case against the Tailfin Age." Meanwhile over at the Philips Pavilion, Edgard Varèse's *Poème électronique*, the first full-length composition to be realized on three-track magnetic tape, is relayed to enthusiastic audiences over 425 loudspeakers. An accompanying array of colors and images are projected directly onto the walls of this lofty futuristic-looking space designed by the Greek mathematician and composer Iannis Xenakis at the behest of Albert Wohlstetter's old friend, French architect Le Corbusier.

"There are masks, skeletons, idols, girls clad and unclad, cities in normal appearance and then suddenly askew," the *New York Times* breathlessly reports of the resultant performance. "There are mushroom explosions so familiar to newspaper readers and moviegoers in an era of atomic bombs."

Somewhere between Disney's all-embracing *America the Beautiful* and the violently fragmented simultaneity of *Poème électronique* a new dimension has opened up that is as much aesthetic as it is political. "The United States is the abstraction of One World," observes Henry A. Murray of Harvard's Department for Social Relations. "The national citizen is obsolete and must be transformed into a world citizen." As critics prepare to dismiss music composed solely on magnetic tape as "primitive," Varèse's use of the word "poem" in the title for this revolutionary work is surely a gesture that Allen Ginsberg, the newly unacknowledged legislator of "unthink," may well appreciate.

The main attraction at the Brussels World's Fair, however, is the Atomium: a unit cell of an iron crystal magnified 165 billion times so that it towers 335 feet above the visiting crowds. A structure more appropriate to the age, however, is President Eisenhower's new atomic bunker, buried seventy-two feet into a hillside within the grounds of the Greenbrier Hotel in White Sulphur Springs, West Virginia. After three years of top-secret blasting and drilling, it boasts concrete walls several feet thick, plus twenty-five-ton steel doors. In the event of a nuclear war, this will be the new seat of government, able to generate its own power and shelter over 1,100 people during the ensuing apocalypse.

It is another sure sign that nuclear war is being treated as a winnable fixture. Like some Madison Avenue advertising campaign, it can now be fought entirely from behind a desk. Meanwhile the US Navy's development of the Polaris missile program alters the strategic positioning of nuclear force further still. Placing missiles aboard submarines no longer necessitates the use of reinforced silos or hangars to protect them, thereby making such weapons not only invisible but ubiquitous as well. The threat of thermonuclear reprisal can therefore come from everywhere and nowhere at the same time—as the recent voyage of the USS *Nautilus* beneath the polar ice cap has so clearly demonstrated.

Pretty soon a swivel chair will be all you need to dominate the entire globe. In association with IBM, Western Electric, Bell Telephones, and MIT's Lincoln Laboratories, the USAF has almost finished setting up SAGE, the Semi-Automatic Ground Environment. A gigantic air defense computer built into the basement of a windowless three-story blockhouse, SAGE can be accessed only through keyboards, screens, and light-guns, allowing its operators to call up and process information derived from the network of radar installations ringing the outer perimeter of the United States. SAGE is the first system to deploy digitized data over telephone lines and to present complex tides of information via graphic displays. It is also the first system in which man and machine are fully integrated together: every station comes equipped with an ashtray so the operator can still smoke while keeping watch over America.

Former Gestalt psychologist Joseph C. R. Licklider of MIT is in part responsible for structuring this new relationship between computer and human, which he broadly categorizes as "symbiotic." A friend of Norbert Wiener, Licklider has also taken part in the Macy Foundation Conference on Cybernetics. While at Harvard's Psycho-Acoustic Laboratory, he once attempted to put his own son in a "Skinner Box"— an early form of man-machine symbiosis operating in a controlled environment—to test some behaviorist theory, until the boy's mother intervened. SAGE's assembly language is the work of the System Development Corporation, a successful spin-off from RAND's Psychology Research Department, responsible for running simulated radar exercises on behalf of the USAF in an abandoned Santa Monica pool hall.

Bringing humans and computers further together in a simulated environment in 1958, the first computerized war game goes online at the Naval War College. The final version of NEWS, the Navy Electronic Warfare Simulator, is a two-sided, one-map game that takes conflict off the printed page, relocating it within computational space. ARPA starts to concentrate on data processing, communications, and artificial intelligence.

As if to emphasize how invisible human conflict is now becoming, the RAND Corporation gets together with the AEC during the summer of 1958 to propose that "clairvoyants should be employed in an attempt to foresee where Russian bombs would fall in the event of war." At the same time RAND starts work on a statistical study of the effectiveness of telepathic communication between land and sea in time of war. "Our submarines are useless to us now," reads part of RAND's report to President Eisenhower, "because it is impossible to communicate with them when they are submerged, especially when in Polar waters." Diving deep into this new medium, RAND analysts pursue underwater experiments to explore the possibilities of establishing telepathic contact during a nuclear war. They soon discover that coffee enhances the effect most. "Amplification of these phenomena," reports Ansel E. Talbert in the *New York Herald Tribune* for July 13, 1958, "may lead to new means of communication between submarines and the land and eventually perhaps between the Earth and interplanetary spaceships."

Earlier in the year Lyndon Johnson's subcommittee investigation into the space race between Russia and America publishes its findings, making clear the extent to which communication and control form a complex two-way process. "From space," Senator Johnson asserts, "the masters of infinity would have the power to control the Earth's weather, to cause drought and flood, to change the tides and raise the levels of the sea, to divert the Gulf Stream and change temperate climates to frigid."

The public's abiding fascination with flying saucers, C. G. Jung suggests, "may be a spontaneous reaction of the subconscious to fear of the apparently insoluble political situation in the world that may lead at any moment to catastrophe. At such times eyes turn heavenwards in search of help, and miraculous forebodings of a threatening or consoling nature appear from on high." It is a proposition that Wernher von Braun, the only man in history to have the undivided attention of Adolf Hitler, Walt Disney, and John F. Kennedy, can fully appreciate. "You know, some think of the earth as a safe and comfortable planet, and they say that space is a hostile environment," he tells *Time* magazine. "This is not really true. Earth is protected by its blanket of atmosphere, to be sure, but it is a disorderly place, and unpredictable. It is full of storms and winds, of fogs and ice, of earthquakes. It is also full of people—people with thermonuclear bombs."

With a war in space seemingly just around the corner, President Eisenhower records a Christmas message to be relayed from Earth orbit via the world's first telecommunications satellite as part of Project SCORE. "This is the President of the United States speaking," runs the fifty-six-word greeting. "Through the marvels of scientific advance, my voice is coming to you from a satellite traveling in outer space. My message is a simple one: Through this unique means I convey to you and all mankind, America's wish for peace on Earth and goodwill toward men everywhere."

As Chairman Mao announces the Great Leap Forward in China, presenting his economic reforms as an evolutionary break with the past, the John Birch Society is founded in the United States. Rigidly anti-communist and firmly opposed to anything even resembling Henry Murray's "One World" vision, the organization is named after an intelligence officer killed by Chinese communist forces in 1945: or as they put it, "the first victim of the Cold War." By the time the world gets to hear Eisenhower's Christmas message six attempts will already have been made by the USSR and USA to send a probe to the Moon, as if both nations were desperate to find somewhere as cold and as unwelcoming as the Earth currently appears to be.

# 1959: TEENAGERS FROM OUTER SPACE

## Progress and Its Discontents

*The Moon and Beyond*—"It is safe to state," the voice on the trailer confidently predicts, "that the grandchildren of some of the people in this theatre will not be born on Earth." After three years without a distributor, Ed Wood's *Grave Robbers from Outer Space* is back. The movie Criswell first narrated in 1956 is finally to be unleashed upon the American public as *Plan 9 from Outer Space*. However, even its coolly abstract new title, reminiscent of some classified RAND briefing paper, cannot hide the fact that the story still unfolds in the same obscure graveyard of possibilities.

Dead before the movie was even finished, Bela Lugosi is replaced in many scenes by Los Angeles chiropodist and hypnotherapist Tom Mason. Perceptibly younger and taller than the venerable horror star, Mason hides the deception behind a vampire's cape that permanently covers the lower part of his face. Meanwhile Gregory Walcott, *Plan 9*'s reluctant male lead, watches his career die for a second time following the 1958 release of *Jet Attack*: a jive-talking tale of armed combat in the Korean War dismissed by the *Motion Picture Exhibitor* as "badly written, poorly directed and acted." In the part of Lugosi's dead wife, Vampira shuffles wordlessly through the entire film. Having dated James Dean a number of times, she now claims to be in spiritual contact with the original "Rebel without a Pulse" following his death in a high-speed auto collision in 1955. "We share the same neuroses," she says of her links to the dead teen idol.

Eight prints of *Plan 9 from Outer Space* have been struck; and the film is scheduled to go out on the drive-in circuit in July, at the bottom of the bill. While Ed Wood busily readies himself for its final release, astronomer and UFO researcher Morris K. Jessup is preparing to take his own life. Having disappeared without a trace following his abrupt departure from New York late last year, Jessup has now reemerged in Florida, where his mood is becoming increasingly despondent. The notes and comments written by some unknown hand in the margins of his book, *The Case for the UFO*, including terms such as "dead ship," "measure markers," "force cutters," and "clear talk," continue to haunt him. The thought that he is being toyed with by minds far superior to his own sends Jessup sliding into an irreversible depression. The Navy, meanwhile, seems unconvinced—on the surface at least.

One month before Morris Jessup asphyxiates himself with the exhaust fumes from his car, the US government publishes details of Navy involvement in Project ARGUS, successfully launching three nuclear devices into space and detonating them three hundred miles above the Earth's surface. On the same day that this piece of news hits the wire services, ARPA representative W. L. Wilson addresses a conference at the California Institute of Technology, declaring that: "The US has put into operation a network for the detection of satellites in order to avoid surprise attacks launched from space."

Such revelations leave ghosts behind them. Seeping out from behind closed doors, secrecy communicates itself to the public through coincidences, strange connections, and hitherto undetected lines of influence. Conspiracy and paranoia start to haunt the institutionalized secret. "Can you prove it didn't happen?" challenges Criswell at the conclusion to *Plan 9 from Outer Space*.

It has all become a matter of interpretation.

Morris Jessup, for one, will soon be past caring. The future, or at least a version of it, dies behind the wheel of a station wagon in Dade County, Florida, on April 20, 1959. The verdict is suicide. "The National Safety Council keeps accurate records on highway fatalities," Criswell warns darkly from the soundtrack to *Night of the Ghouls*, another unreleased Ed Wood masterpiece sitting on the film laboratory shelves. "They can even predict how many deaths will come from a drunken holiday weekend. But what records are kept, what information is there, how many of you know the horror, the terror I will now reveal to you?"

Modern history is often the work of dead men in cars. Before killing himself, Jessup writes a long letter to late-night radio host Long John Nebel, "a straight suicide note" expressing its author's feelings of confusion, despair, and worthlessness. Jessup asks that a live séance be held on Nebel's show to contact his spirit.

Unfortunately, Nebel happens to be particularly busy at the moment. On April 19, the day before Jessup's death, he is visiting the Frontier City amusement park in Oklahoma, where Otis Carr's Circular Foil Space Craft is scheduled to take off on its maiden flight sometime over the Easter weekend. The OTC-X1 fails to launch, however, due to "technical difficulties." According to a subsequent press release, "a leak developed in the seam of the accumulator spraying mercury through the mechanism and making it necessary to disassemble and clean the parts." It is also claimed that the model of the OTC-X1 on display at Frontier City was never meant to be more than another fairground attraction: an "educational and recreational space ride" for public display only.

Later in the year Otis Carr invites Jack Benny, Art Linkletter, and Jack Parr to join him aboard the OTC-X1 on its first flight into deep space: a round trip to the Moon and back in under six hours due to take place on December 9. Despite having one of the most extensive private libraries on the subject of flying saucers, Jackie Gleason fails to be offered a seat—probably as a result of his publicly insulting a London taxi driver live on Long John Nebel's show. The taxi driver in question is one George King, recipient of telepathic transmissions from a Cosmic Master based on Venus by the name of Aetherius. "Prepare yourself," a disembodied voice commanded him in the kitchen of his London apartment back in 1954, "you are about to become the voice of the Interplanetary Parliament." Selected as the "Primary Terrestrial Channel" for messages from Cosmic Intelligences orbiting the Earth in spacecraft, King founded the Aetherius Society in 1956 and has now come to the United States in order to spread the word.

Gleason, however, doesn't seem to buy any of it. Instead he accuses King of being a fraud and a liar, openly challenging him to settle the matter in court.

"Now, George," Gleason cajoles, "look at the juicy opportunity you have. Here's a guy that you're talking to that's got a lot of dough. You can sue me for maybe a million dollars ... and maybe get it. And all you have to do to get it is bring one of your friends from Mars to OK this thing. And then you win."

His approach may have been influenced by NICAP's recent nine-point challenge to the self-professed contactees. "If the contactee had been called a fraud or hoaxer," point number eight impassively demands, "had the contactee filed a lawsuit for libel?"

George King demurs, however.

"I am a guest here, you see," he states in reply to Gleason's taunts and accusations. "Not in my house, you're not a guest," the entertainer retorts, causing the Primary Terrestrial Channel to hang up. "I think you're a phony!"

Can the future still be at issue once lawyers are involved? They always argue only from precedent. The live séance Morris Jessup asked to be held on Long John Nebel's show in order to contact his recently departed spirit is canceled at the last minute on the advice of Nebel's attorney, who feels that "the privacy of certain persons might be violated." In the words of the Great One himself: "Bang! Zoom! Straight to the Moon!"

A clearinghouse for just about anyone with an interesting theory or a bizarre experience to relate, Long John Nebel's talk show has played host to such prominent contactees as George Adamski, Orfeo Angelucci, Truman Bethurum, Daniel Fry, Howard Menger, and George Van Tassel. As the decade draws to a close, however, this may well prove to be their last great year. Adamski causes a storm of protest by appearing in public with Queen Juliana of the Netherlands; and eleven thousand people attend the 1959 Giant Rock Spacecraft Convention just as Van Tassel completes construction of his Integratron. It now stands alone in its own patch of desert: a stately enigmatic dome ringed with a single row of windows, looking like a cross between the Hale Observatory and a landed spaceship. Meanwhile, over in Los Angeles, at the first national convention of the Amalgamated Flying Saucer Clubs of America, George King dons a pair of dark goggles to relay messages from "Mars Sector 6."

It may never become clear quite how the Integratron is supposed to work, and Jackie Gleason's challenge goes uncontested by George King, but the Space Brothers continue to make considerable inroads on Earth. In December 1959, the Internal Revenue Service of the United States government rules that the Urantia Foundation be exempt from paying income tax. Based in Chicago, where the First Urantia Society was granted "Charter No. 1" in June 1956, the foundation has been

set up to distribute *The Urantia Book*: a vast 2,097-page cosmic rein-
terpretation of the Bible, comprising 196 "papers" revealing the future
history in store for the inhabitants of Urantia, otherwise known as the
planet Earth. The first thirty-one alone "depict the nature of Deity,
the reality of Paradise, the organization and working of the central
and superuniverses, the personalities of the grand universe, and the
high destiny of evolutionary mortals." As with George King's Interplanetary Parliament, which counts Jesus Christ, "Mars Sector 6," and
"Jupiter 92" among its Cosmic Masters, *The Urantia Book* presents
the universe as one huge interlocking spiritual hierarchy of mythic
personae, arcane wisdom, and cosmological enlightenment. Also included in the IRS exemption are the Urantia Brotherhood and the
Urantia Brotherhood Corporation.

Established as a nonprofit, educational, and scientific institution by
"electronics engineer" Ernest L. Norman and his wife Ruth, the Un-
arius Academy of Science is yet another organization that positions
itself on the fringes of tomorrow. The Earth, Norman and Ruth claim,
is still not advanced enough to join the other thirty-three planets of
the Galactic Federation. Taking its name from a technical-sounding
acronym that stands for the UNiversal ARticulate Interdisciplinary Understanding of Science, the academy is dedicated to "the connective
and higher spiritual understanding of consciousness as an evolutionary
mandate." Far from being displaced by Sputnik, the flying saucer has
simply moved further out instead. The measure of all superior technology, casting an even longer shadow over human expectations than
before, it has become the means by which progress is criticized not for
having gone too far but for not advancing enough.

All the same, reported sightings of UFOs are tailing off. With public interest declining and subscriptions dwindling, NICAP and APRO
start to compete with each other over membership. The open-minded
middle ground is stretched to the breaking point, caught between
the hardware of scientific detail and the extreme fantasies of contact.
Having scored a major publicity coup the previous year by claiming
C. G. Jung for her group, APRO director Coral Lorenzen begins
to suspect that Project BLUE BOOK is little more than a public-
relations exercise being run by the Air Force and that any actual

cover-up is taking place "at CIA level or higher." Meanwhile Donald Keyhoe learns to his dismay that Ed Ruppelt is planning to rewrite his *Report on Unidentified Flying Objects* with help from the USAF to reflect a more skeptical view. "Ruppelt must be under such severe pressure he feels no choice," Keyhoe writes in the June issue of *The UFO Investigator*, maintaining his close reading of USAF behavior. "He should be helped, if possible, not condemned."

After working at Holloman AFB in New Mexico over several years, APRO's Coral Lorenzen is coming to believe that NICAP may be wasting its time in attacking the Air Force. Under new director Major Robert Friend, BLUE BOOK no longer has the funding or the manpower to keep pace with the civilian saucer groups, often investigating sightings long after such organizations have already finished with them. In fact, its slow response in an age of missile gaps and computerized air defense systems becomes the object of much criticism in a major ATIC study commissioned in 1959. "The methods by which UFO reports are forwarded is by TWX or telephone from military installations, and by letter or phone from civilian organizations or private citizens," runs one of its observations. "This, when compared with the reaction time necessary for survival in event of an attack using modern weapons, is ridiculous." A recently renamed Aerospace Technical Intelligence Center considers any further association with BLUE BOOK as "extremely dangerous to prestige." In an effort to "strip this program of its aura of mystery" the ATIC consequently attempts to transform BLUE BOOK into an actual public-relations exercise by offloading it first onto the Office of Public Information and then the Air Research and Development Command, but neither body is interested.

Viewed from the outside, the planet is getting lonelier. Explorer-VI takes the first views of the Earth from space in early August 1959. The following month, after a couple of misfires, Russian probe Lunig 2 hits the Moon's surface, scattering hundreds of metal pennants bearing the insignia of the USSR around it. In early October, Lunig 3 completes an entire orbit of the Moon, taking pictures for the very first time of its far side. Back in Chicago, composer Sun Ra and his Galactic

Research Arkestra go into the studio to record "Rocket Number Nine Take Off for the Planet Venus" and "We Travel the Spaceways" for release on the El Saturn label. It was from Huntsville, Alabama, where the Juno I and the Jupiter-C were both created, that Sun Ra experienced his first "transmolecularization" to the planet Saturn and learned of his mission here on Earth. That took place back in 1936, long before the US Army Ballistic Missile Agency started linking gods and planets and rockets together.

"Perhaps on your way home," Criswell warns as *Plan 9 from Outer Space* comes to its close, "someone will pass you in the dark and you'll never know it, for they will be from outer space."

In June 1959, as *Plan 9* is about to open in a tiny theater on 41st Street in New York where it will continue to play for the next year and a half, US Postmaster Arthur E. Summerfield witnesses the first "Missile Mail" delivery to take place anywhere in the world. An SSM-N-8 Regulus cruise missile, its nuclear warhead replaced by two Post Office Department mail containers, is fired from the US Navy submarine *Barbero*: final destination the Naval Auxiliary Air Station in Mayport, Florida.

"This peacetime employment of a guided missile for the important and practical purpose of carrying mail," declares Summerfield upon witnessing the missile strike its intended target just twenty-two minutes later, "is the first known official use of missiles by any Post Office Department of any nation." He then goes on to predict that "before man reaches the moon, mail will be delivered within hours from New York to California, to Britain, to India or Australia by guided missiles. We stand on the threshold of rocket mail."

The postage charge on each item is just eight cents.

"We once laughed at the horseless carriage, the aeroplane, the telephone, the electric light, vitamins, radio, and even television," Criswell continues. "And now some of us laugh at outer space." He slowly rises to his feet, an elder statesman of the twenty-first century, ready to deliver his final message. "God help us in the future."

## The Naked Robot

*The Cheapest of Machines*—"Just now I was told I couldn't go to Disneyland," Nikita Khrushchev angrily announces during a state visit to the United States. "I ask, why not? Do you have rocket launching pads there? Is there an epidemic of cholera? Have gangsters taken over the place?" Too much of a security risk, the US government calmly explains, while President Eisenhower tries to ensure the Soviet premier spends his time visiting Levittown instead. Not that either world leader need worry too much. Both Disneyland and Levittown are on their way to Russia in the summer of 1959. Opening in Sokolniki Park outside Moscow on June 24, the American National Exhibition includes model homes and kitchens fitted with the latest in household technology, supermarket displays of convenience foods, rows of shining '59 automobiles, sewing machines, and hi-fi systems, plus Disney's Circarama presentation *America the Beautiful*, left over from the Brussels World's Fair and given a Russian soundtrack.

At the park's entrance stands a glittering two-hundred-foot geodesic dome designed by R. Buckminster Fuller and constructed from gold-anodized aluminum panels supplied by the Kaiser Aluminum Corp. Inside, color pictures of daily life in America flash across screens in an automated display devised by Charles and Ray Eames, while IBM's RAMAC 305 electronic brain "produces written answers in flawless Russian to any of 4,000 questions about the US." Combining the spectacular allure of Levittown with Disneyland's precise social engineering, Fuller's dome is perfectly placed to welcome Soviet visitors into an exhibition where fashion models are shown enacting such prime American rituals as barbeques, weddings, and honeymoons. "No man who owns his own house and lot can be a communist," according to William Levitt. "He has too much to do." The last time Buckminster Fuller collaborated with Henry J. Kaiser was back in 1957, raising an equally impressive geodesic structure outside the millionaire industrialist's Hawaiian Village hotel complex on Waikiki Beach. Acclaimed by Khrushchev, the Sokolniki Park dome is subsequently bought by the Soviet Union at cost price.

In Moscow to open the show, Vice-President Richard M. Nixon tells the Russian people about America's 44 million families, their 56 million cars, 50 million television sets, and 143 million radios. With free Pepsis being consumed at the staggering rate of nineteen thousand per hour by visitors to the exhibition, he knows that the magic is still in the big numbers. It is through them that the United States "comes closest to the ideal of prosperity for all in a classless society." After all, Nixon and his family were given a personal guided tour of Disneyland by Uncle Walt himself.

Which might help to explain the heated exchange between Premier Nikita Khrushchev and Vice-President Nixon that takes place inside the exhibition's suburban show home on June 25. Standing before the replica kitchen, complete with boxes of SOS detergent on its fitted countertops, the two men energetically debate the strengths and weaknesses of their respective economic systems. "Isn't it better to talk about the relative merits of washing machines than the relative strengths of rockets?" Nixon asks in front of what has become the center of modern pushbutton living. Considering how poorly American rockets have been performing recently, the Vice-President may have a valid rhetorical point. Even so, the "kitchen debate," as it comes to be known, is recorded for posterity using the color videotape system Ampex developed as part of RAND's Project FEEDBACK: something Nixon neglects to mention when praising this recent advance in US technology.

For his part, Khrushchev claims to be appalled by the kitchen exhibit, repeatedly stating that the Russian people prefer to focus on things that matter rather than the accumulation of luxuries. He even asks if there is also a machine that "puts food into the mouth and pushes it down." The question reveals once again that the differences separating communism from capitalism are pathological rather than ideological. It becomes a matter of psychological development. Khrushchev's remark hints at a degree of human passivity in the presence of machines. When Nixon shows off the US-made washing machine, the Soviet premier remarks that it "is probably always out of order," indicating once again the illusion of power and lack of actual control experienced by users of the modern pushbutton kitchen.

Increasingly machines are relocating to the suburban household in the form of TVs, stereophonic hi-fi units, radios, ovens, fridges, and floor polishers. At the same time, modern marketing and branding techniques have established a highly competitive Social Darwinism for things; the unprecedented variety, quantity, and cheapness of today's products mean that they must rely upon the free-market promise of fun and fantasy and a brighter tomorrow in order to sell themselves to a growing nation of passive consumers. Rising to the top of the US charts in 1959, Martin Denny's "Quiet Village" provides the ideal soundtrack for life in Suburbia, its title alone evoking the protracted materialist siesta that is unfolding. Such passivity is what finally allows the machine to force the food down people's throats.

While Aldous Huxley, Al Hubbard, and Humphrey Osmond continue their debate on how hallucinogens may best be used to shift human consciousness onto a higher plane, the commercial introduction of the Shockley Semiconductor marks the beginning of the Transistor Age: a point in the history of human development where the evolutionary agenda starts to be set by the machine. Recalling his last conversations with the mathematician John von Neumann before he died of cancer in 1957, Stanislaw Ulam describes how they "concentrated on the ever-accelerating progress of technology and changes in the mode of human life, which gives the appearance of approaching some essential singularity in the history of the race beyond which human affairs, as we know them, could not continue."

By redefining human beings as "the cheapest of machines," Curtiss Schafer's theories on biocontrol have helped create a new equivalence between the two; the economic laws of mass production and the social politics of the assembly line provide the ideal circumstances for human and machine to interact. General Motors now becomes the first American company to install Joseph Engelberger's industrial robots alongside regular factory workers at its die-casting plant in Turnstead.

As computer technology starts to advance from one generation to the next, however, the cost of "even a simple robot," as Schafer points out, remains "ten times that of bearing and raising a child to the age of sixteen." In a 1959 issue of the IBM journal *Think*, behavioral psychologist B. F. Skinner reveals how the principles behind his "Skinner Box" can be converted into a "teaching machine." According to the Harvard psychology professor, it is all a matter of programming. "The program,"

*Think* enthusiastically reveals, "is the medium through which the human being doing the actual teaching communicates with the student; and the machine, as we shall see, is only a device to help the student follow the program systematically."

Programming can only go so far in correcting the human computer. Although never doubting for one second the effectiveness of his psychic driving technique, Dr. Ewen Cameron is fast coming to the conclusion that an actual cure for schizophrenia is still beyond its present capabilities. Achieving some form of permanent change in his patients' condition is the best he can hope for at the moment, having decided that the repetition of verbal signals is "where direct controlled changes may be made" rather than in the use of drugs, ECT, or sensory deprivation alone. "Reorganization of the personality," Cameron declares, "may be brought about without the necessity of solving conflicts or abreaction or the reliving of past experiences." Running a tape of repeated commands effects "the direct building of new personality traits" after putting the old ones "out of circuit." The good doctor still has his doubts, however. "Why is it easier to listen to a tape than it is to listen to the patient?" he wonders out loud. "Could it be that listening to the live patient, the patient immediately evokes a negative response or better said, an inhibitory response?" The fact that this agonized question appears in a research paper under the heading "Playback" says more than enough.

Although acknowledging that it is "not absolutely—phonographically—exact," Sigmund Freud still firmly believed that a written transcription of his patients' words was preferable to any sound recording, allowing as it did all of their telltale slips and revealing errors to come through. The introduction of the tape recorder radically alters this process, however, transforming both the patient and the psychiatrist into a couple of machines exchanging data with each other.

Meanwhile, in the South 2 wing of The Allan Memorial Institute of Psychiatry, where Cameron's notorious Sleep Room is located, unconscious patients listen to hour upon hour of tape recordings emanating from loudspeakers located under their pillow or mounted on the walls of their room. Some even wander around the wards wearing football helmets wired up with headphones. Subjected to hearing the same taped message repeated thousands of times, many of them start regressing to the point where they can't even control their own bowels anymore.

"In the Sleep Room," a former head nurse later recalls, "we turned those patients every two hours, we got them up and fed them their meals. We had this table in the center of the room, if they were awake enough and we could get them up, lift them, sit them down and we would feed them and care for them. Nobody ever got any kind of bedsore or break in the skin. We were priding ourselves, if you can imagine, on how well we were caring for these people."

However well meant, such care must inevitably be seen as a thing of horror. It looks as though Khrushchev may well have been right: the capitalist West really does have a machine that "puts food into the mouth and pushes it down" after all.

Operating through the Society for the Investigation of Human Ecology, the CIA keeps the funds for Dr. Cameron's Sleep Room flowing. In April it busies itself establishing a new version of Margaret Mead's "evolutionary cluster" when the Josiah Macy Foundation convenes the first international conference on the therapeutic uses of LSD. Chairing the proceedings and more than ready "to make choices which set a direction" is long-time consultant to both the CIA and the Army Chemical Corps, Dr. Paul Hoch. Also in attendance are Gregory Bateson, responsible for the "double bind" model of schizophrenia, Dr. Sidney Cohen of Los Angeles, and Hollywood psychiatrist Mortimer A. Hartman, whose current client list includes actor Cary Grant.

The range of possibilities opening up before the participants "presenting on both anecdotal and empirical levels" now extends from the laboratory study of madness to personal growth. Under discussion are such issues as "psychological responses to psychotherapy by symbol representing" and the communication process under LSD.

"This meeting is most valuable," enthuses Dr. Charles Savage, formerly part of the US Navy's Project CHATTER, "because it allows us to see all at once results ranging from the nihilistic conclusions of some to the evangelical ones of others. Because the results are so much influenced by the personality, aims and expectations of the therapist, and by the setting, only such a meeting as this could provide us with such a wide variety of personalities and settings ... this is all of tremendous significance, for few drugs are so dependent on the milieu and require such careful attention to it as LSD does." All the same, "nihilistic conclusions" seem to predominate. "Actually, in my experience," Hoch asserts on the nature of the LSD experience, "no patient asks for it again." It is a statement that prompts instant agreement from some of the other psychiatrists present. Published as "The Use of LSD in Psychotherapy—Transactions of a Conference on d-Lysergic Acid, Diethylamide (LSD-25)," the minutes have been edited by Dr. Harold Abramson, another CIA consultant with close ties to the Army Chemical Corps. In fact, it was Abramson who treated Dr. Frank Olson during the psychotic episode that led to his suicide back in 1953 after Sid Gottlieb spiked his after-dinner drink with LSD.

By 1959, however, there are some even stranger new drugs to test. Trials begin in 1959 of quinuclidinyl benzilate, otherwise known as "BZ," at the Army's Edgewood Arsenal. Inhibiting the transfer of messages along the pathways of the nervous system, BZ renders the user "completely out of touch with his environment." Even more promising is the Parke-Davis animal tranquilizer PCP: a "nonlethal incapacitant" the CIA passes on to Dr. Ewen Cameron to test on his patients in the Sleep Room. "I do not contend that driving people crazy, even for a few hours, is a pleasant prospect," Major General William Creasey of the Army Chemical Corps argues from the pages of *This Week* magazine after proposing to the Senate that hallucinogenic gases be tested in crowded American subways. "But warfare is never pleasant."

Another tight little evolutionary cluster forms around Allen Ginsberg when he tries LSD for the first time at the Mental Research Institute in Palo Alto. Gregory Bateson, a former OSS operative, arranges for the session to take place, while Harold Abramson facilitates the supply of the hallucinogen and Charles Savage looks on. Wired up for EEG tests in a windowless room, the poet's responses are closely monitored. "Suddenly I got this uncanny sense that I was really no different than all this mechanical machinery around me," Ginsberg later remarks, recalling his fear at being "absorbed into the electrical network grid of the entire nation." In such a manner does the cheapest of machines transcend itself: an experience described as "electricity connected to itself" in Ginsberg's poem "Lysergic Acid," written while still coming down from the drug's effects. "Science, pure science," croons Dr. Benway, one of the main characters in William Burroughs's *The Naked Lunch*, published in Paris the same year.

To others, however, the reprogramming of the human computer often takes the form of vivid childhood scenes remembered with superhuman accuracy: a 3D tape of family conflicts acted out by Disney characters locked in some grand cosmic combat. More of this type of fun can be had in director William Castle's *The Tingler*. Released in 1959, this is the first movie ever made about LSD, and the kids in the Midnight Spook Pit are just going to love it. All the same, it must come as a bit of a surprise to Lucy, the demure and well-adjusted young girl in the movie, to discover that her legal guardian is married to creepy old Vincent Price. He is shown sitting in a pool of artificial light in the corner of a darkened living room, reading a book on LSD-25 and its effects upon the human nervous system. When her boyfriend Dave arrives to take her out to dinner, he slips Price a small package containing vials of a strange-looking liquid.

"You know, from the articles I've read, this is a very interesting drug," Price remarks.

"So is nitroglycerine," Dave snaps back, echoing a similar comment made about LSD by Richard Helms of the CIA back at the start of the decade.

"Dave," comes Price's mocking reply, "where is that 'all for science' attitude?"

With Lucy and Dave out on their date, Price is soon down in the lab, shooting up LSD. Rolling his eyes and gasping for air, he starts moaning into his Ampex tape recorder that the walls are closing in. They're suffocating him. He can hardly breathe. Ecstasy is turning to eye-rolling dangerous fun. Similarly, the Id has been transformed by William Castle into the Tingler, a lobster-like parasite living inside the spinal column of its human host. During the course of his experiments Price discovers that the only way to prevent the Tingler from feeding off the waves of raw fear that run through the body in moments of crisis is to scream as loudly as possible.

A deviser of inspired cinematic gimmicks, such as insuring his audience against dying of fright while watching one of his movies and "Emergo," in which skeletons fly out into the auditorium, William Castle is the favorite uncle of America's healthy, socialized youth. With the aid of rubber fright masks and bathtubs filled to the brim with fake blood, he is now introducing his kids to the Wonderful World of LSD. Shot in lurid color while the rest of the film remains in dreary black and white, the hallucination sequences look like a heart-stopping, grotesque, zonked-out parody of *The Wizard of Oz*. In total control of Downingtown's Colonial Theatre, William Castle takes teenage America for a ride through the chemically enhanced brain; and the boys and girls all seem to like what they see. Those big, bad monsters of the Id, it turns out, are nothing but cheap theatrical effects. Illusions. Entertainment. It won't be long before the kids are back, screaming for the real thing this time. Meanwhile Dr. Timothy Leary joins B. F. Skinner and Henry A. Murray as a lecturer in psychology at Harvard University.

**Scream for Your Lives!**

*Lobsters of the Stratosphere*—To promote his latest movie William Castle comes up with a great new gimmick: turning the monster loose on the audience. "Ladies and gentlemen, please do not panic!" Vincent Price warns as the shadow of the Tingler crawls along the bottom of the screen. "But scream! Scream for your lives! The Tingler is loose in this theater!" This is the cue for the projectionist to hit the "shock button," activating a number of small electric motors attached to selected seats dotted throughout the cinema. Thanks to "Percepto," as this ingenious promotional device is called, cinemagoers become part of the show: not only permitted to scream their heads off but actively encouraged as well. It becomes an immediate form of release in which everyone can participate. To enhance the effect, Castle plants shills in the auditorium to help start the screaming: by the director's own estimate, more than twenty million people experience Percepto.

Later the same year "What the Frog's Eye Tells the Frog's Brain," Jerome Lettvin's groundbreaking neurological study, is published for the first time in the *Proceedings of the Institute of Radio Engineers* number 11, volume 47. A former protégé of Norbert Wiener, Lettvin has been working with a team of MIT researchers, headed by Warren McCulloch, developing microelectrodes that can pick up the weakest signals generated by the brain and nervous system. Their findings reveal that the frog's eye is capable of performing far more complex tasks at a cellular level than hitherto supposed. "Our results show that for the most part within that area," runs part of the abstract, "it is not the light intensity itself but rather the pattern of local variation of intensity that is the exciting factor."

As Percepto demonstrates, the public immerses itself in the experience by becoming part of it. Having once scripted horror movies in Hollywood, Jerome Lettvin will probably appreciate better than anyone else what William Castle is up to. Whether out of fear, surprise, exhilaration, or despair, the screaming looks set to continue until the end of the century. In Boston, a bored projectionist tries pushing the shock button during a matinee screening of *The Nun's Story* just to see what will happen. An enraptured audience is watching Audrey Hepburn kneel in prayer with the other nuns at the time. As Castle has already expressed a concern that *The Tingler* will put people off eating lobster for life, one can only imagine what the effect might be.

"This work has been done on the frog," concludes the abstract to Lettvin's paper, "and our interpretation applies only to the frog." Even so, this is a great year for lobsters: they even appear in the movie *Teenagers from Outer Space* playing the part of a "Gargon herd" brought to California to be raised for food by Martians. "We are the supreme race," the spaceship captain declares. "We have the supreme weapons." A sensitive teenage crewmember named Derek runs off to warn the people of Earth about the impending invasion. He then spends most of the movie hanging out by the swimming pool in the backyard of a suburban home, chatting with the locals, while his zesty young colleagues zap anything that moves with their "supreme weapons," which turn out to be Hubley's "Atomic Disintegrator" cap guns on closer inspection. "Teenage hoodlums from another world on a horrendous rampage!"

screams the poster copy. "Thrill-crazed space kids blasting the flesh off humans!" Meanwhile, penned up in Bronson Canyon, the Gargons grow so fast they become mere shadows on a cave wall.

Further evolutionary delirium for teens to make out to this year includes *The Alligator People, Angry Red Planet, Invisible Invaders, The 4-D Man, The Hideous Sun Demon, The Giant Gila Monster, The Killer Shrews, Attack of the Giant Leeches, Missile to the Moon, Have Rocket Will Travel*, starring the Three Stooges stomping around Bronson Canyon pretending they are on Venus, and *First Man into Space*, in which a daring young test pilot is found to be horrifically transformed upon his return to Earth. "If he can drive a car," reasons an Air Force officer as the creature speeds off in a natty roadster, "he still retains some intelligence. He's not all monster."

Those Soviet pennants deposited on the lunar surface by Lunig 2 tell a different story, however. It looks as though the first man to walk on the Moon will be speaking Russian. NASA does little to alter expectations when presenting to the public its first selection of astronauts in April 1959. Known as the "Mercury 7," they are all US pilots with college degrees and slightly under average build. After rejecting the idea of sending prisoners into space, NASA considers using trapeze artists instead, until Eisenhower intervenes once again. Who, after all, has done more to extend United States airpower into the sky and beyond than the United States Air Force? Even Project BLUE BOOK increasingly appears as an attempt to organize behavior in outer space.

Unfortunately, NASA does not have enough equipment for all seven pilots to be photographed together in their spacesuits; for the official group portrait astronauts Donald Slayton and John Glenn both wear work boots painted silver instead of the standard issue footwear. "A man is a fabulous nuisance in space right now," James Van Allen comments in the May 4 issue of *Time*. "He's not worth all the cost of putting him up there and keeping him comfortable and working." At the end of the decade it looks as though NASA is finally making the right movie in the right location but on the wrong budget—just ask the makers of *Teenagers from Outer Space*.

Meanwhile CBS adds to its fall schedule a new type of drama series that successfully connects Suburbia with the Unknown. Sponsored by

General Foods and Kimberly-Clark, the manufacturer of Kleenex tissues, *The Twilight Zone* is positioned by its very title within the warped abstract terrain of the American suburbs: a place its creator Rod Serling refers to as "a fifth dimension ... as vast as space and as timeless as infinity ... the middle ground between light and shadow." Inspired by a walk across an empty sound stage, Serling's script for debut episode "Where Is Everybody?" features an apparent amnesiac wandering around a small abandoned town, desperately seeking clues to his identity. Only at the end of the show is he revealed to be an astronaut who has begun to hallucinate after spending four hundred hours in an isolation chamber. Never before has the modern domestic environment been linked so openly to experiments in sensory deprivation and the exploration of outer space. No wonder parents start to complain that their children are staying up late to catch further episodes.

"All America sits in front of television sets and those television sets exude, I am sorry to say, a considerable amount of radioactive material," L. Ron Hubbard observes in a lecture to Scientologists on November 29, 1959. "It's not huge, you know, but it's enough so that people who have made a habit of watching TV ... get the TV radiation."

Having relocated from America to England, Hubbard settles into a Georgian mansion in the heart of the Sussex countryside, where he spends his time experimenting in the greenhouse, irradiating plants with X-rays and hooking up tomatoes to E-meters to find out if they feel pain. "The production of plant mutations is one of his most important projects at the moment," the May 29 issue of the *East Grinstead Courier* informs its readers regarding the activities of "nuclear scientist" Hubbard. "By battering seeds with X-rays, Dr. Hubbard can either reduce a plant through its stages of evolution or advance it."

Hubbard is not the only one making extravagant claims about radiation at the moment. "Nuclear Miracles Will Make Us Rich," Edward Teller informs readers in an article for *This Week*. Putting a cheery public face on Project Plowshare, the Father of the H-Bomb reveals how nuclear explosions can be used "to engage in the great art of what I want to call geographical engineering—to reshape the land to your pleasure and indeed to break up the rocks and make them yield up their riches." Other proposed projects include generating electric power by pumping water through underground cavities heated by an atomic explosion, cracking rock open in order to extract natural gas, and building dams by collapsing canyon walls.

"Nikolai Tesla," Hubbard points out in his November 29 talk, "also did certain ground wave experiments that demonstrate that radio waves, FM waves, any other type of waves that he could isolate at that time, will travel just as easily along the surface of the ground as they will travel through the air."

In fact, there seems very little that radiation cannot do. Workers at the Fernald Feed Material Production Center, a uranium processing facility located in Ohio, become so contaminated while burying nuclear waste that doctors are unable to bring a Geiger counter anywhere near them without the needle jumping off the dial.

The newly elected governor of New York, Nelson Rockefeller, proposes an extensive program of fallout-shelter construction as the basis for "civil defense planning in our State and, in many respects, the Nation." As mathematicians at RAND refine their "Uniform Random Drops Model," used to chart the devastating relationship between blast and fallout in terms of radiuses covered and casualties amassed, the underground shelter replaces the hardened bunker as a last line of defense. This shift also indicates the extent to which defense strategy is being dispersed among the civilian population: hit the military installations first, the logicians propose, then threaten to do the same to the cities until your enemy climbs down. In Florida, newlyweds Melvin and Maria Mininson spend a two-week honeymoon sealed inside a fallout shelter, courtesy of a local radio station in association with Bomb Shelters Inc., a company whose business card features a picture of a mushroom cloud with the slogan: "It will save your life."

Located in the basements of schools and at the bottom of suburban backyards, the fallout shelter offers an updated take on the subterranean world of the Deros, the last surviving descendants of Lemuria, as described by Richard Shaver in the pages of *Amazing Stories*, back in 1947. As if to acknowledge this restatement of a modern myth, Ray Palmer declares that flying saucers are not from outer space at all but from secret bases hidden deep within a hollow Earth.

The conflation of military and civilian targets, whether sited above or below the ground, makes a bargaining chip of both in what is becoming an increasingly complex political game. At RAND, "Blue" and "Red" teams are encouraged to run thermonuclear exchanges as "diplomatic exercises": games of mathematical probability devoid of any political or historical background, based on a mere roll of the dice. By 1959 the logistics of deterrence has created an intellectual elite and placed them in charge. Who else is going to wage the technological war of the future? In the courtyards of their Santa Monica headquarters, RAND analysts challenge each other to Kriegspiel: a double-blind version of chess played on two boards in which neither opponent can see the other's moves.

Even among intellects as vast and cool and remote as these, Herman Kahn stands out. Able to devise strategies in which "only" two million people might die, the contemplation of thermonuclear war is, for him, all about the discovery of "more reasonable forms of using violence." In an age of fifty-megaton weapons capable of erasing entire populations, Kahn addresses the masses entirely in terms of their own inevitable disappearance; even if ninety million Americans die in some future conflict, he argues, that will still leave ninety million survivors ready to pick up the pieces afterward.

Extending Kahn's perception of thermonuclear war as a winnable fixture, fellow analyst Albert Wohlstetter publishes "The Delicate Balance of Terror" in the January 1959 issue of *Foreign Affairs*. In this seminal paper he issues a sharp warning against "confusing deterrence with matching or exceeding the enemy's ability to strike first." This is Governor Rockefeller's "will to resist" writ large. "To deter an attack means being able to strike back in spite of it," Wohlstetter contends. "It means, in other words, a capability to strike second."

The key munitions for such a "second strike" are the electronic components ARPA is now busily stockpiling: these will help to link the isolated suburban settlements of Minuteman ICBMs to the command and control centers dispersed across the country. Unlike the established balance of power between East and West, Wohlstetter's delicate balance of terror is neither ideological nor political but ultimately technological. "The world was probably destroyed by a bunch of vacuum tubes and transistors," laments Fred Astaire in the post-nuclear movie drama *On the Beach*. "Very likely a decision to initiate nuclear war cannot be made on the basis of strict calculation," concludes a top-secret RAND paper, "The Deterrence and Strategy of Total War 1959–61: A Method of Analysis." The threat of Massive Retaliation has been replaced by a nuclear standoff in which both parties try to convince the other that they have the capability to destroy the entire planet. In fact, they will have no choice. Like the bored projectionist at that Boston screening of *The Nun's Story*, they will be unable to prevent themselves from pushing the "shock button" when the time comes. Referred to officially as "Mutually Assured Destruction," this new strategy also goes by an acronym that perhaps only the "usual gang of idiots" working at *Mad* magazine can fully appreciate.

What the analysts at RAND are only just finding out, however, is that the "missile gap" thought to exist between the United States and the Soviet Union may not be as wide or as deep as originally feared. Since 1955 both SAC and the CIA have been revising their estimates, scaling them down from five hundred ICBMs to a possible fifty; high-altitude photographs, taken by the U2 spy plane or the CIA's new Corona reconnaissance satellite, will ultimately reduce the number of Russian missiles capable of reaching the USA to just four.

America's nuclear arsenal, in the meantime, continues its rapid expansion. In September the Air Force Ballistic Missile Division successfully launches a Minuteman first-stage motor directly from an underground silo, demonstrating that it can withstand a subsurface launch. Two months later a Polaris test missile is launched from the USNS *Observation Island* stationed just off Cape Canaveral. With the Arctic Circle presenting itself as the most direct line of attack between East and West, the chance to retaliate across a narrowing geographical divide offered by Polaris takes on increased significance. Very difficult to target accurately from a ship, however, Polaris may be of little use when it comes to bargaining with the Soviets over a possible second strike against civilian population centers. Even so, the USS *George Washington*, the first submarine to carry ballistic missiles, is commissioned in 1959.

"Adapt a complicated guidance system to a huge ballistic rocket? Convert it to a water-to-air intercept missile?" a narrator intones from the soundtrack of *The Atomic Submarine*, released the same year. "It was foolish, it was insane, it was fantastic, but it was their only hope … and the Earth's only hope!" Featuring violent low-budget encounters with an alien creature hidden deep beneath the polar ice cap and a nuclear submarine blowing a flying saucer from the desolate skies above it, the movie replays an increasingly familiar scenario. To complete the picture, Cary Grant uses a press conference on the deck of a pink World War II submarine to reveal details of his LSD therapy sessions with Mortimer Hartman. Speaking from the set of his latest feature, *Operation Petticoat*, Grant admits to taking the drug more than sixty times. "I have been born again," he declares. "I had to face things about myself which I had never admitted. I was an utter fake."

There is something about the image of a famous movie star sitting on the deck of a pink submarine, publicly praising LSD and scorning the fakery of his past life that suggests both a beginning and an end. Like William Castle's Percepto gimmick, it sets a monster loose among the audience, inviting them to participate in a new version of reality. Unable to find work since his show was dropped from the schedules in 1957, George Reeves, the actor who played Superman on television, is found sprawled naked on his bed, a bullet hole in his right temple. The police rule that the former Man of Steel took his own life after a heavy night partying, even though no fingerprints are found on the gun. Things take an even stranger evolutionary twist when the first Barbie doll goes on display at the American International Toy Fair in New York. A stiffly posed study of overdeveloped breasts and hips for little girls to play with, she is the first of a whole new race of Americans to be made entirely out of plastic. Available in shops from May 1959, Barbie comes with a miniature array of props and accessories, including a car, a fully equipped suburban home, and a boyfriend called Ken.

The cosseted well-being and luxury Barbie represents are the perfect correlative to what the nation's young consumers are experiencing as they cheerfully go about pumping $56 billion into the nation's economy by decade's end. "Employers will love this generation," remarks Clark Kerr, the University of California's newly appointed president. "They are going to be easy to handle." With white-collar office jobs outnumbering blue-collar ones for the first time by over two to one, the teenage passion for denim remains a little worrying, however. Linking the dungarees of early childhood with the utilitarian workwear of the manual laborer, it sets the wearer apart from the social compact made between production and consumption in the name of progress. To pull on a humble pair of Levi's is to declare that you have never outgrown them. Once photographed with his teenage girlfriend smiling for the camera in denim jacket and blue jeans, Charlie Starkweather will die in the electric chair on June 25, 1959.

If parents start to fear that monsters may have been let loose in their children's bedrooms, it may be because their children are the monsters. Consider what kind of world they are growing up in. It can all end tomorrow. Material progress no longer seems as closely meshed with human evolution as it once was; the anticipated leap into the future may not take place in a time or manner that can be so easily predicted. However, by now everyone from Richard Nixon to Chairman Mao knows that the only way to force the evolutionary curve to bend your way is by throwing large numbers at it. Market research reveals that there are already 196,500 beatniks in America alone.

While Edward Hunter, the man who coined the term "brainwashing" back at the start of the decade, becomes a prominent member of the John Birch Society and Elvis Presley ships out for West Germany after completing his basic training at Ford Hood in Texas, where debris thought to be from the crashed Roswell saucer was first examined, a nineteen-year-old former US Marine arrives in Moscow declaring that he wishes to defect. As a result, Lee Harvey Oswald's discharge from the Corps is officially reclassified from "hardship/honorable" to "undesirable." When the teenager attempts to slash his wrists after the Soviet authorities deny him permission to stay, Oswald is sent to a Russian psychiatric clinic for observation. Fearing that a further suicide attempt might spark an international incident, the Soviets allow Oswald to remain, finding work for him at the Goziront Electronics Factory in Minsk, turning out radios and televisions, along with technical components used by the military and in the space program. From this point on, there may be nothing left to look forward to but the sixties.

# CONCLUSION:
# THINKING THE UNTHINKABLE

> The power to build weakens; the courage to make plans
> extending to the distant future is discouraged; a lack of those
> with organisational genius begins to occur. Who still dares to
> undertake works where one would have to reckon with millennia
> for their completion?
> –Friedrich Nietzsche, *The Gay Science*

Mistrustful as ever of progress, Nietzsche seems unaware that he is
describing a future condition rather than a past one. Those who build
rockets do not necessarily leave the Earth in them. Daring requires
confidence: that is what prevents it from becoming a mere gesture of
despair. There is something inspirational and tragic about the image of
rocketry experts planning for a moment they themselves can never experience directly. It says something about progress, about history and
our relationship with future generations. First released in 1947, *Music
Out of the Moon* has remained in print ever since and is even said to
have been piped on board Apollo 11, at Neil Armstrong's request, during its long voyage to the Sea of Tranquility, where the first suburban
home was temporarily established in the summer of 1969.

By its very nature, confidence is also required when it comes to
"thinking the unthinkable," to use Herman Kahn's favorite phrase as he
contemplated global annihilation from the edge of the 1960s. It is, after
all, difficult to speak of "probability" in relation to an event that has
never actually happened. Or as one RAND analyst is said to have re-
torted during a particularly heated Pentagon briefing: "General, I have
fought just as many nuclear wars as you have."

We will never understand our world until we have come to terms
with its future: it is the age in which we live. The Cold War depended
upon internal division in order to maintain itself. Behind its various
feints, games, and strategies lay a perception of behavior as a form of
enforced conformity. People would only do what they were prompted
to do. This was the thinking that held the lonely crowd together, briefly connecting the forward thrust of material progress with the broader

evolutionary curve. To question the need for conformity, as a number of social scientists began to do at the start of the 1960s, was also to express a certain disappointment. The big shifts and changes anticipated between 1947 and 1959 had so far failed to materialize. Had it all been for nothing?

That depended on where you were looking. A second glance at the monsters running around in their children's bedrooms would have convinced a disappointed generation that something was still going on. What had begun as a consumerist trend was fast turning into an evolutionary tide that threatened to surge and break over existing society, transforming it forever. At home in the suburbs enough to contemplate leaving it behind forever, adept at existing in an electronic universe of recording and playback, the children born between 1947 and 1959 represented an unforeseen development in the internal divisions that characterized the Cold War. Not for nothing would they be referred to as "baby boomers": the rhetorical switch from "missile gap" to "generation gap" had done its work only too well.

Boasting the kind of numbers that turn all notions of confidence and conformity on their head, these were the kids who would take LSD for recreational purposes, who relied upon tape recorders to supply the weird studio effects their music required, and who could repeat the cosmic wisdom of the Space Brothers as if it were the Pledge of Allegiance. Brought up on space heroes and super beings, as revealed to them in comic books and TV shows, the whole galaxy was their birthright, just as *Mad* magazine and cheap B-movies had shown them how stupid and flimsy a construct daily life could be. To the subtle dismay of their parents, this was a generation capable of thinking the unthinkable as a matter of course. That their grand cosmological adventure should come to an end just as Neil Armstrong succeeded in bringing Suburbia to the Moon is another story, and it will have to wait for another time. History is the price we pay for progress. If the future should ever come to stay again, it will only be to haunt us.

# BIBLIOGRAPHY

George Adamski, *Inside the Space Ships*, Abelard-Schuman Inc., 1955

Francesco Adinolfi, *Mondo Exotica: Sounds, Visions, Obsessions of the Cocktail Generation*, Duke University Press, 2008

Isaac Asimov and Karen A. Frenkel, *Robots: Machines in Man's Image*, Harmony Books, 1985

Marina Benjamin, *Rocket Dreams*, Chatto and Windus, 2003

Margot Bennett, *The Intelligent Woman's Guide to Atomic Radiation*, Penguin Special, 1964

The Berkeley Pop Culture Project, *The Whole Pop Catalogue*, Plexus Publishing, 1992

Charles Berlitz and William Moore, *The Philadelphia Experiment: The True Story behind Project Invisibility*, Granada Publishing, 1980

Steven Biskind, *Seeing Is Believing: Or How I Learned to Stop Worrying and Love the Fifties*, Pantheon Books, 1983

David Black, *Acid: The Secret History of LSD*, Vision Paperbacks, 1998

Barry Blinderman (ed.), *The UFO Show*, University Galleries, Illinois State University, 2000

John Brosnan, *Future Tense: The Cinema of Science Fiction*, St. Martin's Press, 1978

John Carter, *Sex and Rockets: The Occult World of Jack Parsons*, Feral House, 1999

William Castle, *Step Right Up! Memoirs of a B-Movie Mogul*, Pharos Books, 1992

Carl von Clausewitz, *On War*, edited with an introduction by Anatol Rapaport, Penguin Classics, 1968

Alexander Cockburn and Jeffrey St. Clair, *Whiteout: The CIA, Drugs and the Press*, Verso, 1998

Anne Collins, *In The Sleep Room: the Story of the CIA Brainwashing Experiments in Canada*, Lester & Orpen Dennys, 1988

Beatriz Colomina, *Domesticity at War*, MIT Press, 2007

"Commander X," *Nikola Tesla: Free Energy and the White Dove*, Abelard Productions Inc., 1992

Flo Conway and Jim Siegelman, *Dark Hero of the Information Age: In Search of Norbert Wiener, the Father of Cybernetics*, Basic Books, 2005

Douglas Curran, *In Advance of the Landing: Folk Concepts of Outer Space*, updated and expanded edition, Abbeville Press Publishers, 2001

James Curtis, *James Whale: A New World of Gods and Monsters*, Faber & Faber, 1998

David Darlington, *The Dreamland Chronicles: The Legends of Area 51*, Henry Holt and Company, 1998

Mike Davis, *City of Quartz: Excavating the Future in Los Angeles*, new edition, Verso, 2006

Manuel De Landa, *War in the Age of Intelligent Machines*, Swerve Editions, 1991

Robert Elwall, *Building a Better Tomorrow*, Wiley-Academy, 2000

Karen Essex and James L. Swanson, *Bettie Page: The Life of a Pin-Up Legend*, W. Q. Hays, 1998

Christopher Evans, *Cults of Unreason*, Farrar Straus and Giroux, 1974

Hilary Evans and Dennis Stacy (eds.), *UFO 1947–1997: Fifty Years of Flying Saucers*, John Brown Publishing, 1997

Stuart Galbraith IV, *Japanese Science Fiction, Fantasy and Horror Films: A Critical Analysis of 103 Features Released in the United States, 1950–1992*, McFarland, 1994

Martin Gardner, *Fads and Fallacies in the Name of Science*, Dover Publications, 1957

Dee Garrson, *Bracing for Armageddon: Why Civil Defense Never Worked*, Oxford University Press, 2006

Jonathan Gathorne-Hardy, *Alfred Kinsey: Sex the Measure of All Things*, Pimlico, 1999

Grant Geissman, *MAD about the Fifties*, EC Publications, 1997

W. Terrence Gordon, *Marshall McLuhan: Escape into Understanding*, Basic Books, 1997

Rudolph Grey, *Nightmare of Ecstasy: The Life and Art of Edward D. Wood Jr.*, Feral House, 1992

Katie Hafner and Matthew Lyon, *Where Wizards Stay Up Late: The Origins of the Internet*, Touchstone Books, 1998

Oliver Harris (ed.), *The Letters of William S. Burroughs 1945–1959*, Viking, 1993

Richard Heffern, *Secrets of the Mind-Altering Plants of Mexico*, Pyramid Books, 1974

Jim Heimann (ed.), *All-American Ads of the 50s*, Taschen, 2001

Thomas Hine, *Populuxe*, Bloomsbury, London, 1987

Suellen Hoy, *Chasing Dirt: The American Pursuit of Cleanliness*, Oxford University Press, 1995

M. K. Jessup, *The Case for the UFO*, Bantam Books, 1955

Fred Kaplan, *The Wizards of Armageddon*, Stanford University Press, 1983

Donald E. Keyhoe, *The Flying Saucers Are Real*, Fawcett, 1950

Donald E. Keyhoe, *Flying Saucers from Outer Space*, Hutchinson, 1954

Friedrich A. Kittler, *Gramophone, Film, Typewriter*, translated with an introduction by Geoffrey Winthrop-Young and Michael Wutz, Stanford University Press, 1999

Donna Kossy, *Kooks: A Guide to the Outer Limits of Human Belief*, Feral House, 1994

Zbigniew Kotowicz, *R. D. Laing and the Paths of Anti-Psychiatry*, Routledge, 1997

R. D. Laing, *The Divided Self: An Existential Study in Sanity and Madness*, Penguin, 1964

Bill Landis, *Anger: The Unauthorized Biography of Kenneth Anger*, HarperCollins, 1995

Joseph Lanza, *Elevator Music: A Surreal History of Muzak, Easy-Listening and Other Moodsong*, Quartet Books, 1995

Martin A. Lee and Bruce Shlain, *Acid Dreams: The Complete Social History of LSD, the CIA, the Sixties and Beyond*, Grove/Atlantic, 1985

Desmond Leslie and George Adamski, *Flying Saucers Have Landed*, Werner Laurie, 1953

Arthur O. Lewis Jr. (ed.), *Of Men and Machines*, E. P. Dutton & Co., 1963

Marshall McLuhan, *Understanding Media: The Extensions of Man*, Routledge and Kegan Paul, 1964

Marshall McLuhan, *The Mechanical Bride: The Folklore of Industrial Man*, Gingko, 2002

Harry Medved and Randy Dreyfus, *The Fifty Worst Movies of All Time (And How They Got That Way)*, Angus and Robertson, 1978

Aimé Michel, *The Truth about Flying Saucers*, with a preface by Jean Cocteau, Corgi Books, 1958

Russell Miller, *Bare-Faced Messiah: The True Story of L. Ron Hubbard*, Michael Joseph, 1987

Jay Robert Nash, *Bloodletters and Badmen: A Narrative Encyclopedia of American Criminals from the Pilgrims to the Present*, Completely Revised, Updated and Expanded Edition, M. Evans and Co., Inc., 1995

Long John Nebel, *The Way Out World*, Prentice Hall, 1961

Eric Nesheim and Leif Nesheim, *Saucer Attack! Pop Culture in the Golden Age of Flying Saucers*, Kitchen Sink Press, 1997

Constance A. Newland, *Myself and I*, New American Library, 1962

Jackie Orr, *Panic Diaries: A Genealogy of Panic Disorder*, Duke University Press, 2005

Fernand Ouellette, *Edgard Varèse: A Musical Biography*, translated by Derek Coltman, Grossman Publishers, 1968

Vance Packard, *The Hidden Persuaders*, Pocket Editions, 1984

Raymond A. Palmer, *The Real UFO Invasion*, Green Leaf Classics, 1967

Louis Pauwels and Jacques Bergier, *The Morning of the Magicians*, translated from the French by Rollo Myers, Anthony Gibbs and Phillips Ltd., 1963

Curtis Peebles, *Watch the Skies! A Chronicle of the Flying Saucer Myth*, Smithsonian Institution Press, 1994

George Pendle, *Strange Angel: The Otherworldly Life of Rocket Scientist John Whiteside Parsons*, Harcourt, 2005

Sadie Plant, *Zeroes and Ones: Women, Cyberspace and the New Sexual Revolution*, Fourth Estate, 1997

RAND Corporation, *Project AIR FORCE 1946–1996, 50th Anniversary Report*, The RAND Corporation, Santa Monica, 1996

David Riesman, *The Lonely Crowd: A Study of the Changing American Character*, revised edition, Yale University Press, 2001

Theodore Rockwell, *The Rickover Effect*, Naval Institute Press, 1992

Paul Roen, *High Camp: A Gay Guide to Camp and Cult Films Vol. 1*, Leyland Publications, 1994

Franz Rottensteiner, *The Science Fiction Book: An Illustrated History*, Thames & Hudson, 1975

Edward J. Ruppelt, *The Report on Unidentified Flying Objects*, Ace Paperbacks, 1956

Gordon F. Sander, *Serling: The Rise and Twilight of Television's Last Angry Man*, Plume, 1994

Frances Stoner Saunders, *The Cultural Cold War: The CIA and the World of Arts and Letters*, The New Press, 2000

Jim Schnabel, *Dark White: Aliens, Abductions and the UFO Obsession*, Hamish Hamilton, 1994

Kerry Segrave, *Drive-In Theaters: A History from Their Inception in 1933*, McFarland & Company, 1992

Leslie Singer, *Zap! Ray Gun Classics*, Chronicle Books, 1991

Andrew Smith, *Moon Dust*, Bloomsbury, 2005

David Solomon (ed.), *LSD: The Consciousness-Expanding Drug*, G. P. Putnam's, 1966

Jay Stevens, *Storming Heaven, LSD and the American Dream*, William Heinemann, 1988

John F. Szwed, *Space Is the Place: The Lives and Times of Sun Ra*, Payback Press, 1997

V. Vale and Andrea Juno (eds.), *Incredibly Strange Films*, Re/Search Publications, 1986

V. Vale and Andrea Juno (eds.), *Incredibly Strange Music*, Re/Search Publications, 1993

V. Vale and Andrea Juno (eds.), *Incredibly Strange Music II*, Re/Search Publications, 1994

Jacques Vallée, *Anatomy of a Phenomenon: UFOs in Space*, Neville Spearman, 1966

Jacques Vallée, *Revelations: Alien Contact and Human Deception*, Ballantine Books, 1991

Eugen Weber, *Apocalypses: Prophecies, Cults, and Millennial Beliefs through the Ages*, Hutchinson, 1999

Michael J. Weldon, *The Psychotronic Encyclopaedia of Film*, Plexus Publishing, 1989

Michael J. Weldon, *The Psychotronic Video Guide*, Titan Books, 1996

George Hunt Williamson, *Other Voices*, Abelard, 1995

Edward D. Wood Jr., *Hollywood Rat Race*, Four Walls Eight Windows, 1998

John L. Wright, *Possible Dreams: Enthusiasm for Technology in America*, Henry Ford Museum and Greenwich Village, 1992

Nicky Wright, *The Classic Era of American Comics*, Prion Books, 2000

# INDEX

# LIST OF ILLUSTRATIONS

1947: "Glorious Vanu, Elder God, led us into battle against the fortress of Old Zeit" from "I Remember Lemuria," *Amazing Stories*, March 1945

1948: From "How the Flying Saucer Works" by Willy Ley; *Mechanix Illustrated*, March 1956 *

1949: Ester Gerston (crouching) and Gloria Ruth Gorden rewiring ENIAC (from the US Army Research Library)

1950: From "Life aboard a Space Ship" by Willy Ley; *Mechanix Illustrated*, January 1956 *

1951: Remington Rand UNIVAC advertisement; from *Scientific American*, March 1956 *

1952: "Moon Farms to Banish Starvation"; illustration by Frank Tinsley from *Mechanix Illustrated*, May 1954 *

1953: *Robot Monster*, original poster

1954: USS *Nautilus*

1955: Walt Disney (left) and Wernher von Braun (holding XR-1 space plane model) in 1954. Behind them is a model V2.

1956: Graphs representing effects of LSD; from "Experimental Psychoses," *Scientific American*, June 1955 *

1957: "A Sky Full of Satellites;" from *Popular Mechanics*, January 1958 *

1958: "Instrumenting an Earth Satellite;" from *Popular Electronics*, October 1958 *

1959: UNIVAC III at the OTTO group offices, 1961

* Images courtesy of blog.modernmechanix.com

## ABOUT THE AUTHOR

Ken Hollings is a freelance writer, lecturer, and broadcaster. His work has appeared in a wide range of journals and publications, including *The Wire, Sight and Sound, Strange Attractor Journal, Frieze,* and *Kritische Berichter,* and in the anthologies *The Last Sex* (Macmillan), *Digital Delirium* (St. Martin's Press), *Undercurrents* (Continuum), *London Noir* (Serpent's Tail), *Kraut Rock* (Black Dog Press), and *The Resistible Demise of Michael Jackson* (Zero Books). He has also written and presented critically acclaimed programs and series for BBC Radio 3, Radio 4, Resonance FM, NPS in Holland, and ABC on the evolving relationship between culture and technology. He is the author of the novel *Destroy All Monsters* (Marion Boyars, 2001) and the forthcoming book *The Bright Labyrinth: Sex, Death, and Design in the Digital Regime* (Strange Attractor Press).

# North Atlantic Books
# Berkeley, California

Personal, spiritual, and planetary transformation

North Atlantic Books, a nonprofit publisher established in 1974, is dedicated to fostering community, education, and constructive dialogue. NABCommunities.com is a meeting place for an ever-growing membership of readers and authors to engage in the discussion of books and topics from North Atlantic's core publishing categories.

NAB Communities offer interactive social networks in these genres:

NOURISH: Raw Foods, Healthy Eating and Nutrition, All-Natural Recipes

WELLNESS: Holistic Health, Bodywork, Healing Therapies

WISDOM: New Consciousness, Spirituality, Self-Improvement

CULTURE: Literary Arts, Social Sciences, Lifestyle

BLUE SNAKE: Martial Arts History, Fighting Philosophy, Technique

Your free membership gives you access to:

Advance notice about new titles and exclusive giveaways

Podcasts, webinars, and events

Discussion forums

Polls, quizzes, and more!

Go to www.NABCommunities.com and join today.